WOMEN AFTER TREATMENT

SOCIOLOGY SERIES

John F. Cuber, *Editor*
Alfred C. Clarke, *Associate Editor*

WOMEN AFTER TREATMENT
A Study of Former Mental Patients and Their Normal Neighbors

SHIRLEY S. ANGRIST, Ph.D.
Carnegie-Mellon University

MARK LEFTON, Ph.D.
Case Western Reserve University

SIMON DINITZ, Ph.D.
Ohio State University

BENJAMIN PASAMANICK, M.D.
New York State Department of Mental Hygiene

New York *APPLETON-CENTURY-CROFTS*
Division of Meredith Corporation

Copyright © 1968 by
MEREDITH CORPORATION

All rights reserved

This book, or parts thereof, must not be used or reproduced in any manner without written permission. For information address the publisher, Appleton-Century-Crofts, Division of Meredith Corporation, 440 Park Avenue South, New York, N. Y. 10016.

658-1

Library of Congress Card Number: 68-20043

PRINTED IN THE UNITED STATES OF AMERICA
E 03362

PREFACE

The study reported in this volume originated due to a concern about the usefulness of short-term psychiatric hospitalization for mentally ill women. While many studies of mental patients were conducted starting in the 1950's, nearly all centered on the hospital as an institution with its characteristic structure and the effects of that structure on patient and staff behavior. As the use of psychiatric drugs became widespread, and turnover in mental hospital populations increased rapidly, the focus of study began to shift from the effects of the hospital to the effects of the community upon the former patient. Clearly if hospitals now exerted only a brief, though intensive, influence on patients, the posthospital or between-hospitalizations periods took on increased importance. The true test of the effectiveness of short duration treatment for psychotic and psychoneurotic cases might lie in an analysis of the community and family settings to which released patients returned. For this reason we planned the study to include both social-environmental and psychiatric variables as possible factors influencing good or poor patient outcome. Indeed, this book may be viewed as a counterpoint composition moving between the psychiatric and the social elements which may affect patient outcome.

A central departure from the design of other patient outcome studies was the use of a sample of normal women against which to measure the role performance, expectations, and psychological functioning of the former patients. Patients have typically been contrasted with other patients but not with a sample of persons who have never received psychiatric treatment. Further, there is a paucity of research on what constitutes competent female functioning. The criteria for evaluating a man's functioning center on his breadwinning-jobholding reliability. It was assumed that most women cannot be assessed in this way but must be viewed and judged in their family and homemaking roles.

A second methodological feature of the research was the use of clinical evaluations of a sample of the former patients. These assessments were carried out by hospital psychiatrists in order to provide a basis for establishing the validity of home interviews conducted by psychiatric social workers. A third feature was the data collection procedure of interviewing both the former patient and a close relative, rather than relying on a single judgment of performance and expectations. Finally, the status of the initial cohort of patients who had been interviewed six months after release was ascertained seven years later in order to determine their long term ability to avoid readmission.

In this study three aspects of outcome after psychiatric hospitalization were evaluated. First, outcome was viewed as the former patient's ability to remain in the community, to avoid readmission. Second, outcome was viewed as the performance level achieved by the former patient. Good outcome in these first two senses would mean that the former patient was remaining in the community and was functioning at an adequate psychological and social level. The third aspect of outcome considered in this study was the adequacy of patient performance compared with the performance of neighboring healthy women.

The scope of the study, including the three separate criteria for evaluating outcome, and the specific measures of reliability and validity, led to a rather elaborate research design. Because of this, the book shows some redundancy in discussion and interpretation of results. Each chapter includes recapitulation of assumptions and findings when they are relevant to full understanding of the chapter. In this way, we have striven to present a book that may be read with ease and understanding.

We hope that the results and ideas presented in this volume will interest the many health professionals and social scientists dedicated to care, treatment, and research in the field of mental illness: medical sociologists, students of role theory and deviant behavior, specialists in social psychiatry, social psychologists, anthropologists, psychologists, psychiatrists, psychiatric and public health nurses, social workers, and administrators and planners of mental health facilities and services.

ACKNOWLEDGMENTS

There are innumerable people to whom we are indebted for the successful completion both of the research and of this book.

The staff of Columbus Psychiatric Institute and Hospital, including ward administrators, residents, nurses, and admitting office personnel, were all helpful in launching the study during 1958. Thanks are due to Ralph A. Patterson and James Craig, who were Hospital Superintendent and Clinical Director, respectively; they facilitated every phase of the research. Special thanks go to Irving Pine, who was a psychiatric ward administrator, for his willing assistance during the pretest stages of interviewing patients. Two senior hospital psychiatrists, Charles Cole and Leonard Ristine, carried out the psychiatric assessment interviews. The psychiatric social workers who conducted the home interviews with great dedication and thoroughness were: James F. Brumfield, Jane A. Gavin, Michael F. Houlihan, Carolyn Parker, Russell H. Richardson, Betty Sikking, Elizabeth K. Stern, John Tewart, and Benjamin E. Wheatley. Members of the Institute Study Center staff worked specifically on the outcome study. Among them, Patricia Karshner, as Study Administrator, supervised the collection and processing of data; she worked closely and cordially with both the interviewers and the study participants. Jon Simpson was responsible for computer data analysis; William McBroom and Judith Brown assisted in coding and statistical analysis. Lois Molholm collected data for the seven year check on the former patients. Joanne Friedman, Marcia Karlek, and Susan Haynes helped to organize the research results for chapter presentation and contributed some editorial assistance as did Clara Kline. Gloria Sterin took major responsibility for preparation of the index and also provided editorial assistance. Credit for typing and preparing the manuscript is due most particularly to Virginia Schenck who made possible its efficient completion. The senior author expresses particular gratitude to Erwin R. Steinberg, Dean of Margaret Morrison Carnegie College and of the Carnegie-Mellon University, College of Humanities and Social Sciences, for financial support and encouragement during the writing of this book. To Eva Lefton and Mimi Dinitz we extend thanks for their endurance and cooperation. The technical help and moral support of Stanley Angrist were indispensable vehicles by which this book could come to fruition. We acknowledge the support for the outcome investigation provided by Public Health Service Research Grant M-2953 from the National Institute of Mental Health. Finally, our heartfelt appreciation is extended to all study participants, the women and their husbands, other relatives or friends, who with willingness and hope provided the information to make the research possible.

We want to thank the following for permission to use tables from articles previously published by the authors: University of Chicago Press, *American Journal of Sociology,* Vol. 60 (July, 1962), pp. 79–87; American Sociological Association, *Journal of Health & Human Behavior,* Vol. 7 (Summer, 1966), pp. 106–113; American Medical Association, *Archives of General Psychiatry,* Vol. 4 (April, 1961), pp. 363–370; University of Toronto Press, *Proceedings of Third World Congress of Psychiatry* (June, 1962), pp. 237–241; University of North Carolina Press, *Social Forces,* Vol. 40 (March, 1962), pp. 248–254; National Association for Mental Health, *Mental Hygiene,* Vol. 45 (October, 1961), pp. 579–588.

S. A.
M. L.
S. D.
B. P.

CONTENTS

Preface	v
1 Posthospital Outcome: A Look at Patients and Their Neighbors	1
2 From Despair to Hope, Again	17
3 Ward, Posthospital Outcome, and Home Care Studies: A Review of Relevant Research	33
4 Study Design and Procedures	55
5 Rehospitalization: Illness or Rejection?	79
6 Factors Affecting Posthospital Performance	101
7 Former Patients and Their Neighbors	133
8 Summary, Issues, and Implications	159
Appendix A Instruments and Procedures	185
A Note on Instrument Reliability	185
A Note on Validity: The Psychiatric Assessment of Community Patients	187
Notice to All Residents	192
Letter to Patient's Family Doctor	193
Letter to Former Patient	194
Suggested Introduction for Interviewers	195
Hospital Record Data: Form I	196
Hospital Record Data: Form II	211
Interviewer Ratings	220
Patient Interview Schedule	225
Significant Other's Interview Schedule	234
Interview Schedule for Significant Other of Returnee	264
Letter to Neighbor	298
Interviewers' Procedure for Selecting Control Cases	299
Suggested Introduction for Interviewers	301
Appendix B Tables	303
Name Index	325
Subject Index	327

WOMEN AFTER TREATMENT

1

Posthospital Outcome: A Look at Patients and Their Neighbors

Despite the costliness and extensiveness of mental health services in money, manpower, and facilities, little is reliably known about the effectiveness of psychiatric care and treatment. Patients are released from mental hospitals and other psychiatric facilities daily, and it is a reasonable expectation that most will someday be rehospitalized and that many others, with only the forebearance of relatives, will remain at home even though they are quite incapable of all but minimal functioning.[1] This volume is concerned both with immediate posthospital success and failure and with the later performance of women mental patients. This concern is both longitudinal in the sense of comparing these women before and after treatment and comparative in the sense of comparing mental patients with their "normal" or at least never previously treated female neighbors. Not only is this work innovative in its findings but it also contributes to a perspective for the development of community psychiatry and community mental health programs.

[1] See Dorothy Miller, *Worlds That Fail: Part I, Retrospective Analysis of Mental Patients' Careers* (State of California, Department of Mental Hygiene, Research Monograph No. 6, 1965). See also Howard E. Freeman and Ozzie G. Simmons, *The Mental Patient Comes Home* (New York, Wiley, 1963).

THE MENTAL HEALTH INDUSTRY

Direct psychiatric care and treatment costs in the United States amount to some two billion dollars every year. The various states spend about half of this amount to support public mental hospitals. Only highways take a larger share of the state budgets. Millions more are spent by the federal government in its operation of the network of 41 Veterans Administration and other psychiatric hospitals, by the 46 counties which support local psychopathic hospitals, and by private individuals for psychiatric care in proprietary sanitariums and increasingly for care in psychiatric wings, pavilions, or wards of general hospitals. Additional and quite significant, though largely inestimable, amounts of money are expended for private psychiatric and other psychotherapeutic treatment, for outpatient care, and for other direct or quasi-psychiatric services subsumed under the generic heading of "counseling."[2]

Apart from money expenditures, mental health care and treatment facilities and services involve a considerable number of professional, semiprofessional, and nonprofessional personnel, many of whom are now in very scarce supply.[3] To be sure, the number so employed is not nearly enough to do much more than provide rudimentary and minimal care for many of the chronically ill patients. It will be at least another decade, and in all probability much longer, before the mental health manpower shortage can be reduced significantly. Still, and despite the glaring inadequacies in the provision of psychiatric care, perhaps as many as a quarter of a million people are employed full time in the mental health field. In addition to the 16,000 psychiatrists, there is also an impressive number of physicians, clinical psychologists, psychiatric nurses, psychiatric social workers, and occupational and recreational therapists who operate in psychiatric settings. Closer to patients than the professionals are the attendants, aides, and aide-clerks. Not only are these nonprofessional

---

[2] On the matter of the costs of mental health care, see Rashi Fein, *Economics of Mental Health* (Report to the Joint Commission on Mental Illness and Health, No. 2, New York, Basic Books, 1958). See also *Fact Sheet* (American Psychiatric Association and National Association for Mental Health, Nos. 1–17, 1957–1962).

[3] With regard to manpower problems, see George W. Albee, *Mental Health Manpower Trends* (Report to the Joint Commission on Mental Illness and Health, No. 3, New York, Basic Books, 1959). See also *Fact Sheet, op. cit.*

persons numerous and visible in psychiatric treatment settings, but there is growing evidence that they may also play a more important therapeutic or antitherapeutic role than the infrequently encountered professional staff.[4] To these thousands of operatives must also be added the many other employees and administrative personnel not directly involved in patient care or treatment. All of this manpower constitutes an important segment of the work force and something of an industry in itself. Communities vie with one another to be selected as sites for new institutions and protest vigorously any proposal to close, shift, or even reduce the size of an institution located in the area. As a matter of fact, institutions are being placed deliberately in pockets of poverty communities and in areas of high unemployment as a means of absorbing surplus manpower and stimulating the economy of the community. That few professional people can be attracted to such areas seems of far less importance to those who plan facilities than the prospects for employment of some professional or lay local people in these institutional settings.

These vast sums of money and people provide care and treatment ranging from the purely custodial, featuring few of the amenities, as in some of the state hospitals, to the most modern of therapeutic procedures and luxurious accommodations in a few voluntary hospitals and some private settings. While there are no exact figures of patients receiving any and all types of care, the best estimates indicate that as many as a million and a quarter patients are annually admitted to public or private hospitals or the psychiatric wards of general hospitals. By far the majority, about 80 percent of these patients are hospitalized in one of the nearly 300 public institutions, but an increasing number are annually being admitted to the psychiatric wards of general hospitals. Besides patients who require hospitalization, as many as 400,000 are seen as outpatients in mental hygiene clinics and similar treatment facilities.[5] This number is rapidly growing as more and more referrals are made to such agencies and as the stigma associated with psychiatric impairment gradually lessens. Finally, per-

---

[4] Nick J. Colarelli and Saul M. Siegel, *Ward H: An Adventure in Innovation* (New York, Van Nostrand, 1966).

[5] See *Action for Mental Health* (Final Report to the Joint Commission on Mental Illness and Health, New York, Basic Books, 1961), pp. 19–20. See also *The Comprehensive Community Health Center: Concept and Challenge* (Public Health Service Publication No. 1137, U.S. Department of Health, Education and Welfare, April 1964), pp. 8–9.

haps a half million patients are in treatment with private psychiatrists, clinical psychologists, and others.

Despite this tremendous outlay of human and monetary resources, extremely little is known about the effectiveness of the services rendered. In the absence of an inclusive and exhaustive reporting system, even the known recidivism and hospital readmission rates grossly understate the extent of treatment failure. This lamentable lack of a uniform reporting system involving all treatment facilities—public and private and in-patient and out-patient—is merely a symptom of a more general condition characteristic of the so-called problem solving and helping professions: the limited concern and limited responsibility for the recipients of care outside the immediate treatment context. Presumably as one consequence of the proliferation of knowledge, the specialization of services and the multiplicity of agencies, no one seems to be concerned with the "whole" patient in the treatment setting itself, to say nothing of the antecedent or subsequent life experiences of the patient. Treatment is typically seen in a very limited time dimension, and the patient's past, except when directly relevant in diagnostic or therapeutic decisions, and sometimes not even then, is largely overlooked. Taking the patient's history, a *sine qua non* of intelligent medical practice, is usually chaotic and disorderly, a chore often performed by social workers, or in large custodial settings even by clerks in a most perfunctory manner. It is hardly surprising that there is little interest in the outcome of care. As matters presently stand, mental patients tend to get "lost" as people, little different from students at multiversities, clients of social welfare agencies, or patients who receive medical attention in outpatient clinical centers.

The lack of concern with treatment outcome is thus partly a function of the complexity of the mental health industry, the diversity of service, the shortage of manpower, and all of the other usual and valid reasons. As in other problem-solving specialties, there is duplication of services, discontinuities in the provision of care and gaps in treatment facilities to the point that rational programming and "follow through" are rare exceptions to the more usual disorderly procedures. But the mental health field also suffers from more than these usual handicaps in measuring and evaluating treatment outcome. There exists the belief among many that evaluating treatment is a futile endeavor, since what passes for treatment is nonspecific and mostly palliative; patients do about as well without as with therapy. Others, especially those of a dynamic persuasion, conceive of treatment as a process of achieving growth, maturity, and insight. Under these circumstances, the objectification of outcome as a concept and as an event is viewed with suspicion. In this perspective "everybody" gains "something" from therapy. Then there are those who perceive of mental illness as a chronic condition of insidious onset and episodic character. Thus, the concept of outcome, particularly positive outcome, is considered unlikely except in a given and usually short time span; the longer the time period following treatment the greater the hospital readmission rate, *a priori.*

In more practical terms, and quite apart from theoretical considerations, most mental institutions are not equipped to do effective follow-up research or for that matter, research of any type. Finally, until the recent treatment revolution of the last decade or so, a very large proportion of patients were not returned to their communities for prolonged periods of time, if ever, so that determining the outcome of hospitalization was largely an academic concept.

For these and probably other reasons, outcome research has not been attempted until very recently. Most of the data on outcome, even now, are inadequate, being based on limited and restricted populations. There are still no adequate and reliable studies of the effectiveness of treatment in private institutions, in general hospital settings, in outpatient centers, and in private care. Nor are there definitive studies of the outcome of hospitalization in public institutions. There is, therefore, a long way yet to be traveled before the effectiveness of hospitalization and of any of the specific therapies can be assayed with much confidence. Given the varieties of settings—some extremely stressful—to which patients are returned, it is likely to be a very long time before accurate predictions about outcome are routine, or before enough is understood about the interactional setting to permit intelligent decisions about release, rehospitalization, the prediction of success after treatment, and the impact of different types of stress on patient functioning outside the mental hospital.

PREVIEW OF THE STUDY

This volume, therefore, presents a small but significant step in the direction of learning more about the *posthospital world and careers* of former mental patients to complement the increasing knowledge about the careers of patients *in* the hospital. More specifically the data concern the posthospital careers of women who have been mental patients. These female patients had all been consecutively discharged from a short term, intensive therapy institution—the Columbus Psychiatric Institute and Hospital—which was then a unit of the State of Ohio Department of Mental Hygiene and Corrections and a teaching and training hospital associated with the Department of Psychiatry of The Ohio State University. During the period December, 1958 through July, 1959, 376 female patients left the hospital and were returned to the community. Of this number 89 were omitted from the study because they failed to meet certain criteria: namely, return to an address within a 13 county catchment area served by the hospital, and successfully remaining out of a mental hospital for a minimum of 15 days following discharge. This left 287 former patients as study subjects. In general, these women, while probably reasonably representative of female patients in voluntary and intensive treatment centers, were different from committed patients in public mental hospitals. On the whole, our patients had shorter treatment histories and most had never been previously hospitalized. They also exhibited less severe impairment and far more frequently were given diagnoses of psychoneuroses, character trait disorders and other nonpsychotic designations as compared to state hospital patients. At the same time, they were of considerably higher socioeconomic status and seemingly from more cohesive and less destructive family constellations.

All patients were followed up and evaluated six months after discharge. This evaluation included a home visit by a psychiatric social worker and interviews with the former patient and a "significant other," most often a husband but sometimes a parent, other relative or even a friend serving as the informant. In addition to obtaining the usual background information, the interviews focused on the performance of the patients as women, wives, mothers, and housewives; on the quality of their interpersonal relationships; on the extent and content of their social and recreational patterns; on the expectations for performance of the patient by both the patient and the significant other; on the level of "tolerance of deviance" of the responsible relative; and on the "intrapsychic symptoms" by type and severity.

In addition to these interviews conducted by the psychiatric social workers, a sample of the former patients were also evaluated by two psychiatrists. This assessment of mental status, intrapsychic symptoms and the extent of psychiatric impairment served as an independent clinical measure for purposes of validity. Beyond the clinical assessments, some 52 schizophrenic patients and their relations were restudied one year after discharge. Finally, and importantly, a control group of 157 never previously treated or hospitalized women were selected solely on the basis of their propinquity to the residences of the 157 former patients. This process of selection tended to minimize socioeconomic, racial, and style of life differences between the patients and their controls. In each instance, the *same structured schedules* were used by the *same interviewers* to obtain precisely the *same data* from the female controls and their significant others. The emphasis, as with the patients, was placed on instrumental role performance, expectations for performance, social participation, tolerance of deviance, and intrapsychic signs and symptoms.

UNIQUE ASPECTS

This abbreviated preview provides the necessary background against which the unique and significant contributions of this work can be described and discussed. The most important departure from other outcome research, and of greatest theoretical significance, was the *use of a comparative population of normal subjects*. A second major attribute concerned the use of only female patients. A third departure, primarily methodological in character, was the use of clinical evaluations for independent corroboration or refutation of the judgments obtained by the psychiatric social workers in home interviews with patient and family. A fourth innovation involved the perceptions of the patients themselves about their own status and functioning and the comparison of these judgments with similar judgments by the relatives. Lastly, an attempt was made to ascertain the status of the former patients and of the controls *seven years or more after the initial interviews*.

THE NORMAL CONTROLS

Although mental illness has been a problem throughout all of recorded history and in every known culture regardless of social organization, its exact dimensions and specifications remain subject to serious dispute. Estimates of prevalence range from under 10 to over 90 percent of the population! Some even deny the existence of mental illness as an entity, while others profess to see it in guises and forms unseen by others equally competent. Obviously, then, the questions of definition, delimitation, and diagnosis require utmost attention. Debate on this subject has ranged from the profound to the ludicrous. Some would so broaden the definition as to include any psychic difficulties which prevent the achievement of one's potentialities; to others the manifestations of mental illness are almost as varied as the spectrum of human behavior; to a great many more, mental illness in all of its diverse forms is defined in organic terms or simply as a symptom of some sort of brain pathology or neurological impairment. On the other extreme are the proponents of the view that mental illness can be described as a "myth" and that mental symptoms are basically expressions of problems of living and not of pathology. This latter position as stated by Thomas S. Szasz argues that the function of the myth of mental illness is to "render more palatable the bitter pill of moral conflicts in human relations." Or, using Szasz's own colorful "gut-level" illustration, it is easier to fight the battle of stomach acid than to face up to marital or other conflict. To Szasz, much of mental illness is not "real" illness; the latter subsumes only symptoms which are reasonably independent of subjective judgment and of social and cultural norms.[6]

A body of sociological literature, too, most of it theoretically quite provocative, has developed out of attempts at definition and specification. Thomas J. Scheff, for example, has made a very strong case for the proposition that the symptoms described as mental illness represent a departure from "residual" social norms. When the norm violating behavior cannot be labeled as merely uncommon, ignoble, immoral, evil, criminal but is violative of norms which are taken for granted, then it is usually defined as "mental illness."[7] In this sense, mental illness is a cover term for severe psychosocial misbehaviors, inappropriate thinking, and feeling distortions. Erving Goffman, David Mechanic and many others of late have been reflect-

---

[6] Thomas S. Szasz, *The Myth of Mental Illness* (New York, Hoeber-Harper, 1961).

[7] Thomas J. Scheff, *Being Mentally Ill: A Sociological Theory* (Chicago Ill., Aldine, 1966), Chapter 2.

ing on the theme that mental illness is the result of social definitions which the patient accepts. Unlike more specific and acute diseases and disorders, mental illness becomes a role, much like any other role. Through interaction with others, a label—"crazy," "sick," "abnormal," "psychotic"—is imposed on the actor. The acceptance of this role, with its internal logic and consistency, compels the actor to assume the duties and obligations, the stigma, and everything else which is inherent in the role itself. Willingly or otherwise, expectations which derive from the sick role envelop the actor and compel him to conform to the expectations of others.[8] By implication, then, treatment must present a new role set to the patient. The mutual acceptance of this nonsick role and expectations for performance in thinking, feeling, perceiving, and communicating represents successful treatment.

Without attempting to evaluate critically the theoretical issues raised in the various models—the disease, dynamic, moral, and the sick role—some consensus does exist about the nature, quality and content, if not the specifics, of the psychiatric disorders. Few deny the existence of intrapsychic symptoms as such. It is in the meaning of this content, its etiology and its treatment that paths markedly diverge.

The foregoing contains the rationale for the use of a normal control group. There are two principal ways of logically evaluating the effectiveness of treatment. One is to compare the performance of the patient before and after treatment. It is possible in this way to indicate "movement," gain, improvement, and rejection of sick role following therapy. The chief drawback, however, is that the status and functioning of the person relative to normal persons both before and after treatment may still be grossly inferior, despite marked positive change. What is needed is some indication of the norm or standard against which the assessment of recovery is made. The second method, therefore, is to compare a treated (experimental) group with a normal (control) population. In this way it is possible to get a realistic estimate of the performance of former patients relative to that of a never treated population with essentially the same char-

[8] Erving Goffman, *Asylums* (New York, Doubleday-Anchor, 1961); and David Mechanic, "Some Factors in Identifying and Defining Mental Illness," *Mental Hygiene*, Vol. 46 (January 1962), pp. 66–74.

acteristics. This latter approach, when coupled with the former, provides the most valid basis for assessing posthospital outcome now feasible. It offers, moreover, the possibility of empirically evaluating the foregoing theoretical propositions concerning the definition and the nature of mental illness. The disease, dynamic, sick role, and other models thus become subject to test and comparison.

FEMALE PATIENTS AS SUBJECTS

Women, as a demographic category, are grossly underrepresented in nearly every type of deviancy. Their rates of crime, delinquency, alcoholism, narcotic addiction, suicide, and schizophrenia are persistently lower than the rates for males. A number of explanations for this phenomenon have been invoked ranging from the "natural superiority" of women, the greater liability of males to brain and other damage and to physiologic impairments from conception to earlier death, and to the social control system which restricts, controls, socializes, and rewards females more adequately than males. Of the various interpretations of the indisputably lower female deviancy rates, two deserve special mention. First, female roles tend to "mask" female aberrance. Female deviancy is less visible and consequently less likely to result in official recording and in community sanctions.[9] As mother, wife, and as woman, the female functions in settings which shield her misdeeds from public view. Female alcoholics drink at home and can be sheltered by family members in a protective conspiracy. There are no job firings, no revolving doors in jails and workhouses and only a very few driving-while-intoxicated charges. Female suicide attempts involve pills and poison more than guns and knives. The latter are more likely to come to public attention. In short, the culture of women not only shelters and protects them from contact and contamination with deviant norms and values, but it reduces the visibility of deviancy, offers greater protection to those who do become deviant, and results in treatment and rehabilitation rather than in punishment. By the same token, though, female deviants who do become known officially are

[9] On this matter of masked deviancy, see Otto Pollak, *The Criminality of Women* (Philadelphia, University of Pennsylvania Press, 1950); and Bertha J. Payak, "Understanding the Female Offender," *Federal Probation*, Vol. 27, No. 7 (1963), pp. 7–12.

probably, as a group, more extremely deviant than the average officially treated males.

Second, female deviancy and aberrance are more "tolerable." The fear, disgust, and annoyance displayed toward the male is noticeably less toward the female. One aspect of this greater tolerability is the lesser aggressiveness, actual or implied, in female aberrance. In the gamut from crime to mental illness, men tend to "act out" more than women. This acting out is more difficult to manage and therefore poses a greater threat. The tolerance of female aberrance is nowhere more evident than in the sex offenses. Those of women—homosexuality, prostitution, abortion—are devoid of the potential for physical harm. Those of men—rape, other assaults, molesting, exhibitionism—are explicitly or implicitly more "dangerous" and therefore less tolerable.

Another aspect of this greater ability and willingness to tolerate female aberrance is that in an industrial society productivity is the measure of man. The male who is unable to work and support himself and family is defined as either sick or lazy or a moral reprobate. His deviancy and dependency are evident to all. Men who cannot work and are dependent, even when only a consequence of automation or a downturn in the business cycle or after retirement, lose status. Adequate occupational performance is a critical criterion of mental health for the man but such a criterion is still largely absent for most females. In middle class America, at least, it is easier to tolerate and carry a poor housewife and mother and an inadequate wife than a sick breadwinner who cannot obtain or hold employment. In other words, inadequacy in the performance of sex-linked instrumental roles is a more serious disability in the male than in the female.[10]

The focus in this volume on the posthospital situation of women supplements the growing body of empirical information about the male after hospital treatment. Of special significance was our attempt to measure the outcome of hospitalization *in terms of the customary roles of women.* Since no employer or co-worker can provide objective details on the quality of the performance of these roles as mother, housewife, and neighbor, the need for comparison with the perform-

[10] When women are heads of households and act as breadwinners, this kind of masking cannot occur. See, for example, Lloyd Rogler and August B. Hollingshead, *Trapped: Families and Schizophrenia* (New York, Wiley, 1965).

ance of normal and/or never psychiatrically treated women should be evident.

PSYCHIATRIC ASSESSMENTS

Another important innovation in the work reported in this book was the psychiatric assessment of a sample of the women. The significance of this procedure was two-fold. In several European countries, and in at least one research study in the United States, a mental health team including a psychiatrist stands ready to make home visits and to treat acutely ill patients at home. In this arrangement, the psychiatrist and other team members can more realistically evaluate the mental status of the patient, the interpersonal situation in the home, and the adequacy of the patient's performance.[11] In the more typical situation, the patient is evaluated in an office by a psychiatrist who has little or no access to the pertinent elements and stresses in the life situation. He may not even take the case history himself. The pathology he finds in the mental status of the patient is thus divorced from the instrumental activities involved in daily life. As a rule, therefore, psychiatrists tend to overstress intrapsychic symptoms while relatives focus on role performance and on the burdensomeness of caring for and dealing with the patient. To achieve a more balanced picture, clinical judgment *and* daily experience with the patient are *equally necessary*. The psychiatric evaluations, then, were obtained both to complete the picture and to get some idea of the relation of the judgments of the relatives to those of a psychiatrist.

INTERVIEWS WITH RELATIVES AND PATIENTS

Most outcome studies which have sought to determine the posthospital adjustment of former patients have relied on the perceptions of the relatives alone. The judgments of the patients themselves and of other evaluators such as psychiatrists, employers, and co-workers have not been utilized. This is rather surprising since it is the improved adaptation of the patient which is, after all, the central focus of treatment. The reasons for this neglect in using patients as evaluators are simple enough to discover. Patients are not considered re-

[11] Joshua Carse, Nydia E. Panton and Alexander Watt, "A District Mental Health Service: The Worthing Experiment," *Lancet,* Vol. 4 (January 4, 1958), pp. 39–42.

liable informants about their own condition. Some are still sick, others are fearful of rehospitalization, and all can hardly be expected to provide objective self-reports. Nevertheless, there are some very compelling bases for including rather than excluding former patients as informants. Psychiatric social workers have pointed out that the former patient is often not the sickest one in the family. The relative may be as, or even more, disturbed than the patient after treatment. Patients' evaluations may thus be more accurate than those of the significant others. At least they ought to be sought as a means of completing the picture.

There is also a sociological purpose in seeking information both from patient and significant other. This concerns the possibility of testing the idea that expectations and behavior are related. Specifically, there is the question of whether expectations elicit behavior or whether actual behavior modifies expectations. For example, would the former patient be expected to see that meals are prepared, or is someone else in the household responsible for this? If the patient is unable to take care of meal preparation, is she still expected to do so, or is she excused while someone else takes over that responsibility? Equally pertinent is the question of whether patients see themselves in the same way as their relatives do. Unless both sets of definitions and expectations are obtained—of the patient and the significant other—tests of this aspect of symbolic interaction theory are not possible. If labeling and stigma are as important as some sociologists suggest, then the effect of such labeling should be reflected in the patient's feelings about the self, in his attitudes and relations with others, and in his projections for future conduct. None of these data can be obtained without including the former patient as a study subject rather than only as an object. The results of including the patient offset the problems involved in doing so. One of the most interesting findings of this study and an explanatory hypothesis have resulted from using the patients as judges of their own posthospital adjustment.

SEVEN YEARS LATER

Long term follow-up studies are only now beginning to appear, although the need for such longitudinal research has been undisputed. Such work is particularly vital for chronic conditions in which preventing episodic recurrence rather than effecting a cure is the more realistic goal. The hard fact of subsequent rehospitalization can be considered an index of failure to succeed in the community. Charting the ebb and flow of such readmissions over a substantial time period can be crucially important in two ways. First there is the chance to ascertain the posthospital time periods which yield the highest readmission rates. The second involves the differences and similarities of early and late readmissions. Although limited in scope, the data over seven years provide an interesting perspective on rehospitalization.

PLAN OF THE BOOK

This chapter has been a preview of a study of the outcome of treatment in a mental hospital for women patients. Chapter 2 traces the changing patterns of psychiatric care and treatment and describes the sudden transformation in these patterns since the Second World War. It is difficult to visualize the enormity of this psychiatric revolution and its consequences for returning the responsibility of patient care to the community. Without this revolution, the whole concept of posthospital adjustment would have been premature, if not absurd. In Chapter 3, the antecedent and parallel research, our own and that of others, is reported. This is treated in three areas: (1) studies of mental hospital ward organization and psychiatric policies and practices related to care outcome and to patient and staff behavior; (2) antecedent research on the posthospital adaptations of released patients; and (3) research on the functioning of patients who receive home care and other services in lieu of hospitalization. Chapter 4 contains a detailed description of the design, procedures, interviews, respondents, tests, and measures utilized to obtain the data on posthospital outcome in this study. Special sections are devoted to the format for achieving the psychiatric assessments and the second follow-up. In Chapter 5, the findings on rehospitalization are presented, contrasting the successful and readmission cases. Rehospitalization is related to social background characteristics, to previous psychiatric treatment history, to familial variables, to expectations, and to tolerance of deviance. In Chapter 6, some of the basic hypotheses are tested. These include propositions about social class, expectations, tolerance of deviance, and psychiatric variables as they relate to posthospital performance. Chapter 7 presents a description of the normal controls and compares these women with the former patients in all pertinent respects—background, psychiatric condition, and performance. The same hypotheses are tested with this normal population. Chapter 8 contains a recapitulation of the study and its findings and offers an interpretation of the results and the implications for theory and practice.

2

From Despair to Hope, Again

It sometimes seems that mental hospitals—like prisons, sanitoriums, and other "total institutions" which house people who pose an intended or unintended threat to the community—have always been with us. In truth, however, the mental hospital is a reasonably recent addition in the history of man's frequently faltering and usually unsuccessful attempts at coping with deviancy and creating a safer, more peaceful and tolerable social environment. That the mental hospital was not a felicitous innovation is all too apparent. Less apparent, however, has been the tremendous impetus for change in this long moribund establishment which may yet be transformed into the humane and therapeutic setting envisaged by its early proponents.

THE EMERGENCE OF DESPAIR

The mental hospital made its formal debut toward the close of the eighteenth century.[1] Although asylums date back considerably further than this, the real and pressing need for the asylum was a

[1] For historical perspective on the origins and development of the mental hospital, see Albert Deutsch, *The Mentally Ill in America* (New York, Columbia University Press, 1949); and *Action for Mental Health* (Final Report of the Joint Commission on Mental Illness and Health, Chapter 2, New York, Basic Books, 1961); and Shirley Angrist, "The Mental Hospital: Its History and Destiny," *Perspectives in Psychiatric Care* (December 1963), pp. 20–26.

consequence of industrialization and urbanization. The urban setting, built around a factory system, required the removal of dependent, disruptive, and deviant persons. The growing complexity of existence, the anonymity and impersonality, the stresses and tension, the inadequacies of housing and limitations imposed by space, and the decay of kinship relations and solidarity made it virtually impossible to tolerate the aberrant and nonproductive person in this setting. To many students of the subject, these same factors seem also to have a causative role in the etiology of mental illness.

Before the advent of the mental hospital, disturbed persons were differentiated on two levels: the private and public cases, and the dangerously and harmlessly insane. Families of substance tended to care for their own harmlessly sick members at home. The more aggressive and difficult were chained and locked from public view in cellars and attics. Less fortunate still were the impoverished and homeless "lunatics" who, when considered to be nonviolent and harmless, were treated as paupers. When the largesse of the town ran out, these paupers were sent on their way to beg and wander in other communities. They were aliens in the classic sense. Hopeless, helpless, everywhere demeaned, beaten, scorned and ridiculed, the lot of these insane was indescribably bad. Worse yet was the lot of the more violent, aggressive and regressed; they were burned, whipped, and pilloried. Some roamed the countryside as wild men creating fear and apprehension everywhere they went.

Early attempts were made to get the insane out of the community and the countryside. These attempts usually resulted in herding them into unsatisfactory almshouses and jails. Later, crusaders like Dorothea Dix devoted their time and energies to urging the state legislatures to assume the burden of establishing more modern and humane state hospital facilities. It is thus ironic that the state hospital system, in its day a revolutionary innovation of enlightened thought, should have fallen on such bad days so soon and for so long.

What the mental health crusaders had in mind were facilities and practices patterned after the religious and the privately sponsored institutions in France and England. In France, Phillippe Pinel in 1792 struck the chains from patients in the two asylums he superintended—an unheard-of act of courage considering the image of the mentally ill in the public mind. His introduction of "moral treatment" had a profound effect on mental hospital practice. Moral treatment involved not only the application of humanitarian ideas but the implementation of the principle that patients will respond to the examples set for them, that gentleness and mildness are superior to coercion as treatment models. William Tuke in England, also in 1792, built a retreat for his co-religionist Quakers. The York Retreat, as it was called, featured nonpunitive methods of handling the "guests."

A few of the public mental hospitals in the United States in the early decades of the nineteenth century incorporated these enlightened principles of treatment. The first superintendents of these hospitals viewed the role of the institution as a place wherein the sick could be sheltered and treated as human beings. The public mental hospital represented a giant stride in the care of and concern for the mentally ill, at least for the first quarter century of its existence. But the initial enthusiasm and reforming zeal which motivated the early superintendents and their staffs were soon dissipated. Most professionals wanted no part of the institutions. Manned largely by nonmedical, indeed nonprofessional staffs, these hospitals found it hard to provide even some of the minimal amenities of life. Once hospitalized, a patient's chances of ever being discharged as improved were slim. Inside the locked wards guarded by burly attendants, patients were usually left to wander the corridors, to stare vacantly into space, to retreat even further from reality. Separated from family and friends and the realities of daily existence, without activities and stimulation, patients frequently regressed into the back wards from which there was almost no hope of return. This dehumanization, the mechanical restraints, desperate overcrowding, periodic epidemics, and wholesale despair came to characterize these hospitals. Facilities aged and deteriorated, staffing remained geared to custody and not to treatment, resources were diverted to other state activities, legislatures and politicians sometimes made playthings of the hospitals, and the public remained apathetic and uncaring. Moral treatment and the concept of cure had little place in this setting.

Under these circumstances, the public mental hospital was soon diverted from the mainstream of American medical practice. Still, there were occasional innovations. Most of these changes had no long range importance and a few simply reflected the more fashionable medical and pseudo-medical practices of the time. The list ranged from homeopathy through electrotherapy and included the use of counter irritants, venesection, the use of surgery to eradicate focal infections, hydrotherapy, and most recently, prefrontal lobotomy. In almost every instance, the introduction of these techniques was hailed as a major breakthrough, or at least as a milestone in the evolution of treatment. In nearly each case, the new practice was soon found wanting and was replaced by a newer technique.

A few important discoveries did alter some of the mental hospital practices in a positive way. Improved health practices and better sanitation reduced the frequency of epidemics and the spread of communicable diseases. Much later the introduction of the sulfas and antibiotics practically eliminated the scourge of some of the diseases which had claimed the lives of many of the patients in the past. Between these developments, there were a few specific discoveries which brought renewed hope. There was initially the treatment of cretinism with thyroid and its prevention by iodides. There was also the use of the arsenicals in the treatment of syphilis and the later addition of fever therapy for neurosyphilis resulting in a significant reduction of resident hospital patients. More recently, there was the introduction of the shock therapies and finally the psychoactive drugs. Suddenly after many years of inertia, lag, and futility, change is occurring so rapidly that there is once again reason to think and hope that care and treatment will be significantly improved in the years ahead.

THE WINDS OF CHANGE

The introduction of the psychotropic drugs—the single most important development in psychiatric treatment this century—and other converging trends resulted in a series of changes which have irrevocably altered the mental health treatment picture. In the last decade, therapy has begun to replace custody even in prolonged care institutions; small, intensive therapy institutions are beginning to replace the massive, deteriorating hospitals of the past; more professionals than ever before are being recruited into the various mental health specialties; patients admitted to institutions have an excellent chance of being discharged, usually within a year of confinement; the Bedlams, burly attendants, physical restraints, and pervasive atmosphere of futility are going or gone; and the public is no longer as terrified of the problem of psychiatric disorder. The stigma associated with psychological disturbance is lessening as the winds of change and the process of education gain momentum. Several aspects of this change have been more or less paramount. These include the changing hospital with shifts in the institutional population in prolonged care hospitals, the emergence of the tranquilized ward, and the development of the open door and the therapeutic milieu. There has also been the emergence of alternate facilities and recently the growth of the community mental health center approach.

THE CHANGING HOSPITAL

PATIENT POPULATION SHIFTS

One of the first results of the still ongoing revolution in the mental hospital has been the reversal of long term population trends. In the ten year period 1946–1955 the year-end resident patient population increased an average of 2.1 percent per annum. The peak population occurred at the end of 1955 at which time the 238 state hospitals contained nearly 559,000 patients. But beginning in 1956—the first year of the widespread utilization of the psychoactive drugs—the population has decreased steadily by an average of over 1.1 percent per year. At the end of 1962, for example, the resident population had declined to about 516,000 patients.[2] This welcome downtrend has taken place despite the fact that hospital admissions had been increasing at the rate of 7.4 percent per year during this same time period! The reduction in hospital population has been wholly attributable to the higher discharge rates rather than to any decrease in the numbers admitted. Further, although more patients than ever are being discharged after a shorter period of stay, the readmission rate has been steadily climbing. Thus, unless more is understood about the dynamics of posthospital adjustment, the gains in the discharge rate will be partially, and perhaps even wholly, offset by the increased rate of readmission.

Based on the best available estimates, 300,000 of the 770,000 persons admitted to public and private mental hospitals in 1965 and to the psychiatric services of general hospitals had been previously hospitalized. More definitively, a study in Maryland indicated that of the psychotic patients released within a year from three state hospitals, 17 percent were rehospitalized within 3 months, 37 percent

[2] Mental hospital trend data were obtained from the Biometrics Branch, National Institute of Mental Health.

within the year after release, and 45 percent within 18 months. The readmission rates of the psychoneurotic patients and those diagnosed as having personality disorders were 15, 28, and 32 percent respectively for the 3, 12, and 18 month posthospital periods.[3] In a California study, the incidence of rehospitalization among leave-of-absence patients within five years after release was over 70 percent.[4] In a carefully controlled study of schizophrenic patients admitted to Central State Hospital in Kentucky, every patient was released from the hospital after an average of only 83 days of hospitalization. However, fully half of these cases were rehospitalized within 30 months.[5] The experience in other studies has been comparable. The upshot of all of this is that the state hospital, once an institution of almost no return, has developed into a revolving door—at least for the younger psychotic patients. In view of this revolving door aspect, it is all the more urgent that the dynamics of success and failure following hospital release be understood and that posthospital services be inaugurated to improve the chances of successful adjustment after release.

The situation in the State of Ohio, in which the study reported in this monograph was done, more or less typifies the national situation. At the end of 1955, there were 28,663 patients in the various state institutions. This number declined substantially to 23,946 in 1961 and to 22,365 in 1964. Despite a sizeable increase in the general population, the number of hospitalized patients is projected to increase to only 25,901 by 1970. This decrease in the actual average number of patients in mental hospitals every year since 1960 has occurred in the face of an increase of 30 percent in admissions from 1960 through 1964.[6] Although there were some special factors involved in these changes which are of a nonrecurrent nature, nevertheless the situation is clear. While both admissions and readmissions are rising, the even greater rate of discharges is presently offsetting what

[3] See "Patterns of Retention, Release and Rehospitalization," (Statistics Newsletter, State of Maryland, Department of Mental Hygiene, December 10, 1965).

[4] See Dorothy Miller, *Worlds That Fail: Part I, Retrospective Analysis of Mental Patients' Careers* (State of California, Department of Mental Hygiene, Research Monograph No. 6, 1965), p. 24.

[5] See Benjamin Pasamanick, Frank Scarpitti and Simon Dinitz, *Schizophrenics in the Community: An Experiment in the Prevention of Hospitalization* (New York, Appleton-Century-Crofts, 1967).

[6] See Comprehensive Mental Health Planning Project, Executive Task Force on Treatment and Research, State of Ohio, pp. 88–96.

might otherwise have been a most dismal condition of overcrowding. It is for this reason that in both Ohio and in the nation the late President Kennedy's call for a reduction in the number of patients in prolonged care hospitals by 50 percent in 1970 seems within reach.

THE TRANQUILIZED HOSPITAL

Not only has there been this favorable downturn in in-patient numbers but the hospital itself has undergone an amazing transformation in its "climate." Bedlam is no more. Hospital ward noise level has been reduced to the point that outsiders can hardly distinguish these from wards in other medical settings. Gone is the hyperactive, unmanageable, disturbed patient. The restraints, the bars, the locked doors, and the huge keys carried by ever present attendants have also begun to vanish. Vanishing too, are the prefrontal lobotomy as a management technique and the seclusion rooms for making patients more tractable. Even the use of the shock therapies has been drastically curtailed.

This improvement in ward climate is all the more important because now and in the forseeable future the public mental hospital will continue to serve as the major, and in some instances as the only, mental health facility for the poor, the senile, and the chronically mentally ill. While custodial care is undesirable and obsolete for most patients, the need for such care may be indispensable for long term patients hospitalized for 5, 10, 20 or more years. The improvement of the environment for these patients through drugs and the creation of the tranquilized ward has been a major achievement.

It remains true, of course, that the gulf between patient and staff is unbridgeable.[7] The patient still suffers the deprivation of his freedom, the loss of decision-making power, the endless rules, many needless, which reduce him to dependency status and enforce his subordination. The certified mental patient is deemed to have lost all capacity for managing his affairs. He is ordered to arise in the morning, told what clothing to wear, when to eat, when to go to occupational or recreational therapy, when he can have visitors, how long they can stay, and where he can see them. He may be forced to wander the corridor because the rooms are closed after a certain hour in the morning. He is told when and where he can smoke, when to shower,

[7] See Erving Goffman, *Asylums* (New York, Anchor, 1961).

and sometimes must get permission to shave with a razor blade. There is a time for everything and usually an aide to observe and watch over him in the most intimate of daily activities.

With all of these handicaps which serve institutional structural requirements better than they do patient needs, the tranquilized ward is still like the addition of a window in an airless room. Some of the outside world is coming through and breaking down the isolation of the world of patients from the world of reality. The psychoactive drugs have introduced moral treatment in pill form. Robert Felix, former Director of the National Institute of Mental Health says:

> In the whole of *materia medica,* I suspect that the tranquilizers are the only substances whose responses have been measured or observed not only on the persons who receive the drugs but also on those who live and work in the same surroundings. We have known for some time that if mental hospital patients can be made aware of the staff's sympathetic perception and high expectations, the patients will tend to fit the roles which are set for them. It has also been evident that every improvement in the patient's behavior tends to enhance the staff's attitudes toward him. In the tranquilizers we have found a valuable means by which both staff and patients have been able to help each other to perform at a higher and more constructive level.[8]

THE OPEN DOOR AND THE THERAPEUTIC COMMUNITY

In addition to the clinical deficits such as hallucinations, delusions, shallowness of affect, disordered speech, and the disorientation of many patients at admission to prolonged care hospitals, life on mental hospital wards tends to result in further symptoms which in clinical terminology are typically referred to as "deterioration." Deterioration is observed most often in schizophrenics but other long term patients are also likely to evidence many of the same symptoms and problems. Deterioration usually involves a slowing down in test reactions, memory lapses, confusion, and disorientation as to time, place and person, a further flattening in affect, a state of apathy, institutional dependence, generalized incompetence, and a lack of interest in the environment. These symptoms of institutionalization have been referred to as the *social breakdown syndrome,* as institu-

[8] As quoted in *Action for Mental Health, op. cit.,* p. 39.

tional neurosis, and as deindividualization, disculturation, psychological estrangement, isolation, and stimulus deprivation.[9]

No matter how tranquil the ward, deterioration and regression involving these and other deficits are likely prospects for most patients. One alternative, of course, is to create a therapeutic environment on the ward. Another is to treat and release patients from the hospital as soon as possible, relying on community agencies and facilities to provide outpatient services for those who require continued help. Best of all alternatives is the development of community programs to prevent hospitalization entirely. Clearly, these are not either-or choices but rather concurrent goals to be pursued in the general betterment of mental health care.

The therapeutic community concept developed in the 1940's, before the discovery of the tranquilizing drugs, as an extension of analytic psychodynamic principles.[10] Mainly, it reflected the revolt against the impersonal, custodial, antitherapeutic, and dehumanizing aspects of the traditional state hospital ward. The therapeutic community theme is that all interaction within a hospital setting—between patients, patients and staff, and staff with staff—must and can be so ordered as to redound to the benefit of the patients. The goal of this structuring is to create a warm, encouraging, conflict-free, reassuring setting, with a minimum of stress for the patient. In this more normal environment, and with few rules and restrictions and many ongoing activities, the processes of disculturation, stimulus deprivation, and isolation are reversed. Patients can be motivated to participate in healthy interactional patterns and to regain interest in the world of people and events rather than in their own privatized existence.

Therapeutic communities are built around the elimination of the traditional physical and psychological concomitants of security and custody. Every vestige of the custodial mentality is anathema. In practice this means that the institution or at least the ward is open so that patients can move freely from one place to another as they see

---

[9] See, for example, *Mental Disorders: A Guide to Control Methods* (American Public Health Association, Inc., Chapter 1, 1962).

[10] See Maxwell H. Jones, *The Therapeutic Community* (New York, Basic Books, 1953); and Alfred H. Stanton and Morris S. Schwartz, *The Mental Hospital* (New York, Basic Books, 1954); and Robert N. Rapoport, *Community as Doctor: New Perspectives on a Therapeutic Community* (Springfield, Ill., Charles C Thomas, 1960).

fit and without the restrictions and stigma imposed by bars, locked corridors, attendants with keys, and routine head counts. As on the outside, the sexes are free to interact, to visit with one another, and to plan social events. Instead of the typical institutional approach to the feeding of patients, therapeutic communities focus on a restaurant type of service featuring small tables, table service, and associated amenities. Frequently a snack bar and a small kitchen are part of the facility, and these are heavily patronized particularly in the evening. The contrast with traditional units is quite marked in this respect.

In other areas, therapeutic communities attempt to eliminate, or at least to modify, the distinctions between staff and patients. Both staff and patients wear civilian clothes and address each other as might persons of comparable rather than of superior-inferior status. Indignities customarily associated with patient status, such as lack of privacy and supervision in intimate matters, are deemed unnecessary and undesirable. In addition, patient organization and participation in deciding ward policies and practices are encouraged. Group therapy is a highly valued technique. This type of therapy may vary from simple "gripe sessions" to the most involved role playing activities and guided group interaction procedures.

The therapeutic community, still largely confined to private and short term treatment centers and only rarely found in public prolonged care institutions, is surely a welcome innovation. Not only does it tend to humanize the ward but it also represents a break with the traditional custodial orientation. The open ward has been a vital force in altering the patients' conceptions of themselves as crazy and unworthy and beyond redemption. In the process the public conception has also been altered. As the mental hospital ward comes to feel and look like any other ward, the stigma of mental illness decreases. In turn, this helps attract more and better trained staff. Patients who dread hospitalization can now be prevailed upon to seek treatment, including institutionalization, much sooner than before. If early treatment prevents the "hardening" of the disease and improves the chances for recovery and rapid return to the community, then the therapeutic community has surely been important in encouraging this outcome.

Together, the shifts in the patient population, the tranquilized ward, and the therapeutic community, have represented the revolution which has and is still taking place inside the state hospital. These profound changes have improved the entire climate and made it possible to foresee an end to the "total institution" characteristics of the state hospital.[11] Most important of all has been the return home of growing numbers of patients who heretofore might have remained hospitalized to the end of their lives. This internal hospital revolution compels increasing attention to the family and community setting where, after all, most patients will return.

NEW FACILITIES AND CONCEPTS

Very much the same factors which resulted in the disaffection with the mental hospital and the changes enumerated above, plus other compelling reasons as well, have led to the emergence of a whole spectrum of new services and facilities. Many of these services originated in the last twenty years; a few are even more recent. These agencies and facilities have emerged as additions to and substitutes for hospitalization. Their emergence, together with the trends in the hospital itself, have reinforced each other. The net effect has been that more patients are in the larger community than ever before. And while still very little is known about hospital adaptation, even less interest has been shown in the daily coping behavior and functioning of the nonhospitalized patient and those formerly institutionalized. The continued expansion of community treatment facilities in lieu of hospitalization, or consequent to it, makes it imperative that research be directed to the posthospital and nonhospitalized psychotics in the community.

While it is probably true that the patient load usually expands to the maximum of any facility, the converse, that facilities expand to embrace the demand for service, is by no means true. The picture of mental health facilities stands as testimony to both of these propositions. Since the conclusion of World War II, the demand for psychiatric services has far exceeded the resources; in existing settings, the long waiting list is the rule and not the exception. There are several major reasons for the phenomenal yet not nearly adequate growth of these psychiatric facilities. The first is that the drug revolution which affected the mental hospital so dramatically also made it possible to maintain many patients outside the hospital setting. The

[11] See Erving Goffman, *op. cit.,* Chapter 1.

changes in public attitude toward the mentally ill had much to do with the utilization of other than prolonged care facilities. The increase in the number of psychiatrists from 4,000 to 16,000 in less than 20 years, most of them in private practice, favored the development of new community facilities. Similarly, the acute nature of many types of psychiatric disorder made it possible to utilize short term treatment and to establish psychiatric wards in general hospitals. Once this occurred, and medical insurance plans began to incorporate room and treatment benefits in their schedules, added impetus was given to the establishment of short term institutional care facilities. Finally, federal government involvement in the mental health field, through construction monies, research, and training grants, and through the National Institute of Mental Health, provided the final push necessary to make community facilities and action programs a reality.[12]

To document this progress, there were at least 2,000 out-patient psychiatric clinics in the United States in 1965, an increase of nearly one third from the number in existence in 1955. Many of these are part time and nearly all have long waiting lists. These mental hygiene facilities are particularly important in the treatment of adolescents—precisely the age group in which the discrepancy between treatment demand and supply is greatest.[13] Additionally, there had been the growth of short term institutions specializing in the treatment of the acutely ill. These facilities sometimes serve as teaching and research centers as well. An especially important recently added facility has been the establishment of wards in general community hospitals for psychiatric care. In 1965, more than 495 general hospitals—one in every nine—had separate units or wards for treating psychiatric cases. At least as many more general hospitals now admit psychiatric patients to their regular facilities. Recently, community mental health centers featuring a variety of services have moved from plans and blueprints to reality. In 1964, there were some 234 psychiatric programs in existence implementing some or most elements of a community mental health program.[14]

[12] See Benjamin Pasamanick, Frank Scarpitti and Simon Dinitz, *op. cit.,* pp. 12–18.
[13] See *Planning Psychiatric Services for Children in the Community Mental Health Program* (American Psychiatric Association, December 1964), pp. 3–4.
[14] See *Comprehensive Psychiatric Programs: A Survey of 234 Facilities* (Joint Information Service of the American Psychiatric Association and the National Association for Mental Health, 1964).

These developments are ample evidence that the prolonged care hospital is no longer solely responsible for mental health services. Other agencies are sharing the burden to an increasing degree. Nevertheless, the selectivity of patients in these new public facilities is such that the poor, chronic, psychotic patient remains largely the continued responsibility of the state hospital.

THE COMMUNITY MENTAL HEALTH CENTER

Change itself is probably the greatest stimulant for more change. The cumulative impact of the various changes in the last 25 years—the drug revolution, the development of a wide range of new facilities such as receiving hospitals, psychiatric institutes, outpatient clinics, treatment facilities in general hospitals as well as concomitant attitudinal change—signaled the end of an era in psychiatry and in the entire mental health field. Most urgently needed, now that psychiatry had rejoined the mainstream of both medicine and behavioral sciences and that mental patients were being increasingly treated in a rehabilitative framework, was the integration of services as well as the expansion and addition of new ones. Assuming treatment needs to be arranged along a spectrum ranging from supportive care and counseling on the one extreme to prolonged care on the other, the gaps all along the line needed to be eliminated. The focus, too, had to be changed. Clearly, the first and best line of attack on the problem of mental disorder was to deal with it in the community itself. The only way to achieve sufficient manpower for treatment was to place greater reliance on professionals already in the community such as physicians, nurses, psychologists, social workers, and teachers. Thus, in helping patients in the local community, manpower resources could be used which would be unavailable in a prolonged care setting. The orientation also began to shift to embrace ideas which had been heresies not long before. For example, there was no special reason why patients could not be at least evaluated at home by a team of specialists before being hospitalized; nor why such home visiting care could not be more or less continuous over a short time period in lieu of hospitalization; nor why partial hospitalization such as day or night care would not be sufficient and indeed superior to other kinds of service; nor why more emphasis should not be placed on reaching the untreated, coordinating present facilities, establishing a central statewide reporting system with which hopefully even private hospitals would cooperate, retooling the archaic training techniques in psychiatry and the other mental health specialties, and supporting basic clinical and program research. Inevitably, many of the older heresies have been incorporated in the new community mental health center program model.

It is probably unnecessary to trace each step in the evolution of this model, such as the creation by Congress of the National Institute of Mental Health in 1949, the report of the Expert Committee on Mental Health of the World Health Organization, and the work of the Joint Commission on Mental Illness and Health. The report of this Joint Commission and its recommendations became the basis of the message to the Congress by the late President Kennedy in February, 1963 urging a new orientation to mental health problems. The message in part follows:

> I propose a national mental health program to assist in the inauguration of a wholly new emphasis and approach to care for the mentally ill. This approach relies primarily upon the new knowledge and new drugs acquired in recent years which make it possible for most of the mentally ill to be successfully and quickly treated in their own communities and returned to a useful place in society.
>
> Central to a new mental health program is comprehensive community care. Merely pouring Federal funds into a continuation of the outmoded type of institutional care which now prevails would make little difference. We need a new type of health facility, one which would return mental health care to the mainstream of American medicine, and at the same time upgrade mental health services.[15]

Eight months after the presentation of this message the Congress enacted Public Law 88–164. This act authorized federal expenditures of $150 million for the construction of community mental health centers in the fiscal years 1965–1967. This allocation amounts to only a part of the construction funds to be spent. The remainder will come from the states or local agencies on a matching basis. This is the first time that all states became simultaneously involved in planning, constructing, and implementing mental health programs—in itself an achievement.

[15] John F. Kennedy, "Mental Illness and Mental Retardation," Special Message to the 88th Congress, February 5, 1963.

In May 1964, specific regulations governing the nature of the services to be covered in the comprehensive community mental health center were issued.[16] In order to qualify for federal construction funds, a proposed comprehensive community mental health center must provide a minimum of five *essential* services: in-patient, out-patient, partial hospitalization (with day care as the minimum), emergency 24 hour services in at least one of the three preceding areas, and consultation and education services to community agencies and professional persons. In addition to these essential activities an *adequate* community mental health center should also include five other constituents: diagnostic services, rehabilitative therapies such as vocational and recreational, pre- and after-care activities, training services and research, and evaluation programs.

More generally, these community mental health centers must conform to the three principles underlying the entire program: comprehensiveness, coordination, and continuity of treatment. For comprehensiveness, a full range of mental health services is available across age groups and diagnostic categories. This guideline is an attempt to remedy one of the most significant defects in community services—the absence of a full spectrum of services. The principal gaps, of course, are in the partial hospitalization facilities, in out-patient activities, in pre- and after-care services, and in training, education, and research. The second principle, coordination, is predicated on the common sense idea that mental health treatment agencies ought to cooperate with one another and with other health and welfare agencies. Not only will this avoid needless duplication but it will save the patient from becoming lost among the agencies. The function of the center will be to make sure that the necessary services are available to the patient and his family regardless of which special agencies must be called upon to provide them. Finally, the objective of continuity of treatment simply means that the center will be responsible for seeing that a patient receiving service in any one element of the total program will also be eligible for treatment in any other element. In this way patients will be able to move easily and freely through all the possible services from emergency to after-care and even vocational training without getting lost in the confusion of referrals and waiting lists.

[16] See Community Mental Health Centers Act of 1963, Title II, Public Law 88–164, Regulations, *Federal Register,* (May 6, 1964).

UNRESOLVED PROBLEMS

There are as yet extremely few programs and facilities which qualify as comprehensive community mental health centers. But the principles underlying this approach seem to have been accepted by the mental health professionals with a degree of unanimity rarely exhibited about any previous development.[17] With this consensus and with federal monies available for implementing these concepts, there is little doubt that many such centers will be fully operative in the very near future. It is to be hoped that the faith placed in this approach will not be as badly dashed as were the investments and hopes in previous "breakthroughs" in treatment like the creation of the mental hospital itself.

Whether the millenium has arrived or not is debatable. In any event the concept of the institutional "career" of the person as a patient, which concerned medical people and behavioral scientists for so long, is fast losing relevance. The new and real problems now concern the adjustment of former patients and of the persons whose hospitalization has been either delayed or prevented entirely. One very relevant issue now is how to prevent the increasing readmission of former patients to mental hospitals. Is the revolution in the mental health area merely to be symbolized by the substitution of a revolving for a locked door?

As even more patients are returned to their homes and communities and as others are intercepted before being hospitalized, research must be undertaken to answer vexing and unresolved questions about the processes of adaptation, coping, and adjustive behavior; on family processes and interaction; on the meaning and effects of stress; on the whole gamut of measuring and assessing former patient functioning; on the feasibility of drug regimens; on the effects on children of keeping patients at home; on the relative merits of different types of living arrangements for the pre- and posthospital patients; and to many other puzzling issues. This volume addresses itself to some of these many problems.

[17] There are, of course, some discordant notes. See H. G. Whittington, "The Third Psychiatric Revolution—Really?" *Community Mental Health Journal*, Vol. 1 (Spring, 1965), pp. 73–80.

3

Ward, Posthospital Outcome, and Home Care Studies: A Review of Relevant Research

Our work on the posthospital adjustment of former mental patients in a short term intensive treatment hospital was a function of the "state of the art" of psychiatry. It would have bordered on the absurd to mount such a study much before the introduction of the psychoactive drugs, the tranquilized hospital, the therapeutic ward, the shifting mental hospital population, the cumulative impact of psychodynamic theorizing on public attitudes, and all of the other dramatic changes profiled in the preceding chapter. These innovations resulted in renewed interest in the adjustment problems of the mentally ill after hospital treatment or home treatment, and our study reflects this concern.

Three streams of empirical research have followed in the wake of these changes: research on ward climate, patient and staff behavior and interaction; research on the outcome of treatment in mental hospitals; and research on the efficacy of treatment modes other than hospitalization. Since all three of these streams are highly relevant for our hospital outcome study, representative investigations in each group will be presented. In this manner, it will be possible to chart studies, both antecedent and parallel to our own, which provide the framework and background for this undertaking.

WARD STUDIES

One principal aftermath of the psychiatric revolution is the changing character and function of the mental hospital. Most aptly described now as a "revolving door" or warm bed setting, its major function, for new admissions at least, is no longer mere custody. The chief concern has become the rehabilitation of acute and even of chronic patients so that they may remain in the community after release reasonably free of psychiatric symptoms and able to passably perform their instrumental roles.

In the ongoing changeover from a custodial to a therapeutic structure, the model most commonly embraced has been the "therapeutic community" pattern. Maxwell Jones' view, of course, was to reject as fallacious the customary and traditional presumption that a patient's life required regulation and supervision for his own welfare.[1] Instead, he urged that patients be allowed to function as adults. Because of this, and his other major concerns about the reorientation of professional conceptions of the mental patient, wards were opened and the other changes related previously were introduced. In the name of therapy and democracy, patient councils and government were frequently organized so that the recipients of care could learn to participate in decisions involving their own welfare. Ward reorganization, which was surely central to the therapeutic community conception, sometimes also occurred. Most often, however, the ward meetings, conferences, and gripe sessions were the sole elements in the initial conception to be implemented. The therapeutic community movement resulted in a considerable interest in the varying types of ward organization and their consequences for patient behavior in the hospital, for staff behavior, for the relations of patients and staff vis-à-vis one another, for social distance between the various role incumbents (psychiatrist, nurse, attendant, patient) as well as for other aspects of hospital function.[2] In addition, legitimate questions were raised about the relevancy of differential ward practices on case

[1] Maxwell Jones, *The Therapeutic Community* (New York, Basic Books, 1953).
[2] Alfred H. Stanton and Morris S. Schwartz, *The Mental Hospital* (New York, Basic Books, 1954); and Milton Greenblatt, Richard H. York and Esther L. Brown, *From Custodial to Therapeutic Patient Care in Mental Hospitals* (New York, Russell Sage Foundation, 1955).

outcome and the functioning of former patients. Two empirical studies will be reported which reflect, even if they do not necessarily typify, the considerable number of investigations spawned by the psychiatric revolution.

THE COLUMBUS PSYCHIATRIC INSTITUTE
AND HOSPITAL WARD STUDIES

In a ten year period beginning in 1956, a series of studies[3] was undertaken by a social research group at the Columbus Psychiatric Institute and Hospital.[4] This programmatic research followed three major lines of development. First, a number of specific investigations attempted to determine the influence of ward organization and psychiatric orientation on patient behavior and staff functioning. Second, a posthospital study was begun to see whether, among other variables tested, differential ward organization and procedures had any bearing on case outcome. Third, a complicated and difficult experimental investigation was started to determine the relative merit of home care under drug therapy and nursing care as a substitute for hospitalization. This latter work will be described later in this chapter.

The Columbus Psychiatric Institute and Hospital, a short term intensive treatment, training, and research institution, contained five wards—three female and two male. These wards could accommodate 126 patients. It was hospital policy that both male and female patients be assigned to a ward solely on the basis of available bed space.

[3] A series of papers by Simon Dinitz, Mark Lefton, Benjamin Pasamanick and others have reported the results of these ward studies. See, for example, "The Ward Behavior of Psychiatrically Ill Patients," *Social Problems*, Vol. 6 (Fall 1958), pp. 107–115; "Correlates and Consequences of Patient Interaction and Isolation in a Mental Hospital," *Journal of Nervous and Mental Diseases*, Vol. 127 (November 1958), pp. 437–442; "Psychiatric Orientation and Its Relation to Diagnosis and Treatment," *American Journal of Psychiatry*, Vol. 116 (August 1959), pp. 127–132; "Status Perceptions in a Mental Hospital," *Social Forces*, Vol. 38 (December 1959), pp. 124–128; "Decision-Making in a Mental Hospital: Real, Perceived and Ideal," *American Sociological Review*, Vol. 24 (December 1959), pp. 822–829; and "Mental Hospital Organization and Staff Evaluation of Patients," *A.M.A. Archives of General Psychiatry*, Vol. 2 (April 1960), pp. 462–467.

[4] The description of the Columbus Psychiatric Institute and Hospital which follows is of the time the studies were begun. In recent years, the character of the hospital has changed. It is, for example, no longer a facility of the State of Ohio Department of Mental Hygiene and Corrections but rather a unit of the Ohio State University Hospitals of the College of Medicine.

Each ward was a relatively self-contained unit consisting of all the necessary facilities for patient care and treatment.

Each of the five wards was headed by a psychiatrist. The staff complement included three or four psychiatric residents, four graduate psychiatric nurses, an aide-clerk, aides, and service personnel. The psychology, social work, and occupational therapy departments assigned a clinical psychologist, psychiatric social worker, and occupational and recreational therapist to each ward. Each ward team was responsible for the psychiatric treatment of a daily census of 25 to 27 patients—about as fine a patient-staff ratio as one could hope for in a state supported facility.

One especially interesting aspect of hospital organization concerned the tremendous latitude granted the ward chief in organizing and operating his service. As a result, and apart from the formal organizational blueprint to which all wards conformed, the five services were readily distinguishable from one another in several very important respects. These included the extent to which different forms of treatment were utilized, the manner in which the varying specialists were defined and functioned on the ward, the conduct of staff and case meetings, the diagnosis given patients, the mean and differential length of hospitalization of the patients by ward, the use of trial visits, and many other ways.

These interward differences were an outgrowth of the psychiatric orientation and perspective of the ward administrator. One chief was largely psychodynamic in persuasion, another milieu oriented, the third mostly organic, the fourth reasonably eclectic, and the fifth mostly interested in the character disorders. These perspectives were translated into the differential practices mentioned before. For example, the average length of hospitalization varied from 37 to 60 days in the three female wards; on the dynamic wards, 74 percent of the females were receiving individual psychotherapy, only a few were on tranquilizers, and not one was subjected to electroshock therapy (EST); on the organic ward, fewer were on psychotherapy, many more on drugs, and quite a few were getting EST. On these three female wards, the percentage of patients diagnosed as schizophrenic seemed to be mostly dependent on the orientation of the ward administrator. At different times, the range of patients diagnosed as schizophrenic varied from 20 to 67 percent on the same ward. Similarly, ward meetings were conducted so differently that on one ward the session rarely lasted a half hour. During this conference each patient was discussed briefly and decisions made about her status. On another ward, these conferences consumed most of the morning and were conducted along the lines of a grand case presentation. The more instructive, illustrative cases, few in number, were presented and each specialist was asked to share his evaluation and insight. Rarely were specific decisions—about remaining or leaving the hospital, campus privileges, changes in medication—taken at these conferences.

Such "natural" differences in ward practices—as opposed to experimentally induced differences in procedure—occurred because the various administrators were convinced that some practices were more functional and therapeutic than others. These widely differing conceptions of the most efficacious manner of structuring a ward were apparent. Not so obvious was (1) the effect of this variation for overt patient functioning in the hospital, (2) more extended effects, if any, on the posthospital functioning of the patients, and (3) the consequences for staff interaction and operation on the wards.

In order to determine the consequences of interward organizational variations on overt patient behavior, the five wards were charted alternately on a predetermined schedule. Recordings of patient behavior were taken every half hour during the working day and over a three week period. In all, about 110 observations were made of each of the 147 patients involved. These observations were designed to provide a three part description of patient activity centering on whether and with whom the patient was interacting, the precise location of the patient on the ward, and the nature of the activity observed.

In general, the results failed to substantiate the hypothesis that the specific psychiatric and organizational policies of the ward decision makers critically affected the overt ward behavior of the patients. The observed patterns of the patients seemed to be hardly distinguishable by ward. Patient activities, in time, space, and type, varied little by unit. Such differences as were observed could be attributed to the social characteristics of the cases and their diagnostic classifications. The most impressive differences in ward conduct were associated with sex, age, length of hospitalization, and diagnosis. It appeared that the special organizational features of any given ward were less relevant for patient behavior than the fact of the all encompassing nature of the hospital itself, the process of institutionalization, and the special characteristics of the patient including the nature of his illness and impairment.

The female patients were followed up after discharge in the study reported in this monograph. The results, by ward at least, were disappointing. No differences in outcome were found in relation to hospital ward assignment. As in other research as well, outcome was associated more with diagnosis, family variables, and socioeconomic status than with most other variables. Thus, the climate of the ward failed to result in the expected consequences for patient behavior during and after hospitalization. Far more disturbing were the findings concerning staff relations as a function of ward organization and structure. On the traditional bureaucratically organized ward, there appeared to be far less staff dissatisfaction than on the more equalitarian ward emphasizing psychotherapy. The logic seemed to be that on the ward featuring a medical model of organization, all operatives understood their prerogatives in the hierarchy. They expected little in the way of decision-making power and had little. As a result there was minimal dissatisfaction with the ward, if not with the system. On the more therapeutic ward each operative—resident, psychologist, nurse, social worker, and occupational therapist—was deeply enmeshed in ward discussions, plans, and activities. Status distinctions tended to blur and the usual hierarchical assumptions were disavowed. This equality was largely surface; the real decisions were still made by those empowered by the system to do so. Consequently, ward operatives tended to become disenchanted with their lot precisely because their expectations for power and status were higher than those of their counterparts on the traditional medical ward. On the latter, at least, the structure was quite clear and there was no deluding oneself as to role or status.

THE PALO ALTO STUDY

Fairweather and his associates in the Veterans' Administration Hospital at Palo Alto conducted an interesting experimental study[5] which sought to determine whether small problem-solving groups of patients constituted a superior method of ward organization than the traditional form. The study design, the very model of systematic experimental research, involved setting up a small-group ward with

[5] George Fairweather, *Social Psychology in Treating Mental Patients: An Experimental Approach* (New York, John Wiley and Sons, 1964).

all the changes this implied in the interactional patterns, rules and regulations, and in the traditional procedures on a hospital ward. The daily schedule on the experimental ward was altered by the introduction of task groups. These groups engaged in a ward housekeeping task for one hour and held meetings during which decisions about group members were discussed during a second hour. Only in this respect did the experimental and traditional ward chosen as the control situation differ.

The patients on the two wards—experimental and traditional— were alike in all important respects such as background characteristics and previous psychiatric experience. These patients were classified into four groups based on diagnosis and length of hospitalization: nonpsychotic, psychotic with less than two years previous hospitalization, psychotic with two to four years prior institutionalization, and psychotic with over four years hospitalization. On the experimental ward there were 111 patients during the 27 week course of the study. There were only 84 patients on the traditional ward during this time. This discrepancy in numbers resulted from the significantly shorter average hospitalization of the experimentals.

The patients in the two treatment and four diagnostic groups were followed up exactly six months after discharge. This was done through the use of a questionnaire sent to the significant other with whom he lived. The questionnaire items, multiple choice in character, dealt with patient rehospitalization, employment, friendships, communication with others, degree of illness, drinking behavior, nature of residence, membership in community groups, and involvement in leisure time activities.

The results indicated that while there were few differences in these nine areas of evaluation of posthospital functioning, more of the experimental subjects remained out of the hospital (46 versus 36 percent). This difference, however, was not significant statistically. Statistically acceptable differences were obtained with regard to employment, friendships, and verbal communications with others. More small-group ward patients were employed, maintained friendship relationships, and were able to communicate with others than patients from the traditional ward.

A factor analysis based on 120 by 120 correlation matrix of within hospital and posthospital measures revealed something more substantial: only two variables were importantly associated with successfully remaining at home, the sheer amount of previous hospitalization, and the situation to which the patient returns in the community. The less the amount of previous institutionalization, the more likely the patient was to remain home at least six months after release. Patients returning to supportive living arrangements also did better. These variables were clearly more relevant than the traditional or small-group ward structure. In short, the carryover of the effect of differing ward practices to the posthospital setting was by no means the critical difference in posthospital adjustment.

MENTAL HOSPITAL TREATMENT OUTCOME INVESTIGATIONS

Wholly germane to our enterprise are a series of studies which have involved the assessment of posthospital adaptation. All of these investigations are similar in some respects to each other and to the work in this volume. None, however, included a control population of "normal" women, independent psychiatric assessments of mental status and impairment, and cross-checks of former patients' perceptions of their own functioning with those of their significant others. These earlier and concurrent investigations are widely distributed geographically and in the types of patients studied. Their chief similarity concerns the finding that successful outcome is a function of the interplay of psychiatric, interpersonal (familial), and structural variables and that no one aspect of this configuration accounts for very much of either the total success or failure rate. By implication only, these studies seem to indicate that rehospitalization is perhaps more dependent on the psychiatric variables while the level of performance is perhaps more closely associated with structural components in the posthospital setting.

THE ARKANSAS STUDY

One of the earliest and most provocative of the mental hospital outcome studies was reported by Leta Adler.[6] The investigation con-

---

[6] Leta McKinney Adler, "Patients of a State Mental Hospital: The Outcome of Their Hospitalization" in Arnold Rose, Ed., *Mental Health and Mental Disorder* (New York, W. W. Norton Company, 1955), pp. 501–523; Leta McKinney Adler, James W. Coddington and Donald D. Stewart, *Mental Illness in Washington County, Arkansas: Incidence, Recovery and Posthospital Adjust-

cerned the hospital and posthospital careers of 1054 patients—white and nonwhite, male and female, and rural and urban admitted from two dissimilar Arkansas counties to a state hospital during the years 1930–1948. Comparative data on the general population in the two counties was utilized.

Two principal sources of information were relied upon in charting the hospital and posthospital careers of the patients. These included hospital record data and interviews with close relatives of patients in the community. These interviews, conducted by sociologists, psychologists, and social workers, were completed in one county in 1949 and in the other in 1950. The structured interview schedule emphasized the following areas of functioning: occupational adjustment, social participation, marital, and family adjustment, a composite of these called total adjustment, and a rating of the personality adjustment of the former patient.

Not unexpectedly, the patients represented the lower socioeconomic segment of the two counties from which they were drawn. Their educational attainment was lower and proportionately more were unskilled. The admission rates were higher for men than women, for older than younger persons, and for the nonmarried as compared to the married. Diagnostically, most mental disabilities were represented among the patients. Nevertheless, as elsewhere, the chief diagnostic categories were the various subclassifications of schizophrenia, psychosis with arteriosclerosis, and the senile psychoses. General paresis was also high in the rank order—a diagnostic category now almost wholly eliminated among new admissions.

The 1054 patients were hospitalized an average of 27 months (including all admissions of each patient). During their hospitalization, 34 percent died compared to an expectancy of 3 percent in a general population. Another 13 percent died after hospital release, 31 percent were living at home, 1 percent were in another mental hospital, and the location and outcome in nearly 7 percent were unknown. Thus, the posthospital adjustment of 326 patients, 31 percent of the total cohort, was studied. These patients, living at home, were not typical of the original group: they were younger at

---

ment (Fayetteville, Arkansas, University of Arkansas, Research Series No. 23, July 1952); and Leta McKinney Adler, "The Relationship of Marital Status to Incidence of and Recovery from Mental Illness," *Social Forces,* Vol. 32 (December 1953), pp. 185–194.

initial admission; fewer were senile; and the functional psychoses as opposed to the brain syndromes were overrepresented.

The results, based on the patients living at home at the time of the interview were as follows:

1. In terms of the number and percentage of patients who were working and on their Work Regularity Scale scores, the patients were doing no better and sometimes worse than just prior to hospitalization.

2. In a second area of functioning, social participation, the former patients were involved in organized groups to about the same extent characteristic of general populations. Their informal participation was considerably more extensive than their organized group involvement.

3. In general, patients were not as successful in getting married or in staying married. Nevertheless, in the area of marriage and family life, about two thirds were reported getting along reasonably well with their families.

4. Putting the separate scales and assessments together, the total evaluation of recovery and adjustment indicated that 26 percent of the patients were doing as well or better than they had been prior to the onset of the illness; some 51 percent were less adequate than in their pre-illness status; 17 percent showed no substantial improvement and were inferior to their pre-illness level of adjustment in about every respect; and 6 percent were grossly inadequate to the point that they required help in even such basic activities as eating or dressing.

5. The only major background variable which differentiated the well from the poorly adjusted was marital status. Married patients were superior functioners to those who were single, divorced, widowed, and separated.

6. Favorable outcome was also positively associated with promptness of treatment following onset. The more prompt the hospitalization, the better the outcome record.

As important and pioneering as this study was, it failed to do more than touch this very complex problem of posthospital outcome briefly. No hypotheses as such were tested. Most regretfully, no information was obtained from the relatives about the patients at the time of the interviews. This precluded comparisons of the successes and failures. In summary, this pioneering investigation paved the way for the more systematic studies which followed.

THE LONDON STUDY

The work of the Maudsley group in London, England[7] on case outcome after hospitalization not only provided a cross cultural comparison but raised some very exciting questions about the role of familial stress for the functioning of schizophrenics. The study group consisted of male patients, born in England, aged 20 to 65, and discharged to an address in the Greater London Area from seven mental hospitals in or near London between July, 1949 and June, 1956. In all, 240 patients qualified for study inclusion; 229 or 95 percent were followed. Of these, over two thirds were schizophrenics whose average age was 39 and more than three fourths of whom were unmarried at time of admission. Their minimum length of hospital stay was two years and the mean 6.5 years. At release 14 percent were rated as recovered, 65 percent as relieved, and 21 percent as not improved.

One year after discharge, 31.6 percent of these long term former schizophrenic patients had relapsed (failed), 25.8 percent had made a poor adjustment, 17.4 percent a partial adjustment, and 25.2 percent, a full adjustment. These outcomes bore little relationship to age, recorded diagnosis, or length of hospitalization. On the other hand, successful outcome was associated with clinical status at time of hospital discharge, subsequent employment status, and the settings in which patients lived. Discharged patients who accepted residence with siblings or in lodgings did better than those who went to live with parents, wives, or in large hostels. Residence was significant for outcome even after allowing for the fact that sicker patients were sometimes released to parents but rarely ever to lodgings. The obvious implication of these findings is that schizophrenics do better when family pressures are minimal and poorly when subjected to the usual pattern and stresses of family life. Since hospitals are often unwilling or unable to discharge patients except to near and responsi-

[7] George W. Brown, G. Morris Carstairs and Gillian T. Topping, "Posthospital Adjustment of Chronic Mental Patients," *Lancet* (September 28, 1958), pp. 685–689; and George W. Brown, "Experiences of Discharged Chronic Schizophrenic Patients in Various Types of Living Groups," *Milbank Memorial Fund Quarterly,* Vol. 37 (1959), pp. 105–131.

ble relatives, this very policy may in itself be jeopardizing successful hospital outcome by returning patients to pathological family interactional patterns and pressures.

THE MASSACHUSETTS STUDIES

The work of the Maudsley Hospital group in England found its counterpart in the research of Simmons and Freeman in the United States.[8] This research was conducted in two phases. The earlier pilot studies were organized around the concept of tolerance of deviant behavior as the critical variable in hospital outcome. Tolerance of deviant behavior was operationally defined as "the continued acceptance of the former patient by his family members, even when he fails to perform in instrumental roles." Further, structural, interactional, and attitudinal variations in family settings were postulated as affecting the tolerance of deviance level which, in turn, was associated with posthospital success or failure.

The initial empirical results seemed to confirm the general thesis. Patients returned to a parental situation were rehospitalized less frequently but performed more poorly than patients returned to a conjugal setting. In the latter, the patient either performed adequately or his spouse would be more apt to return him to the hospital. Mothers were more tolerant of poor performance than were wives. The results of a second study of 182 male, white, native born, discharged hospital patients, aged 20 to 60, tended to expand and confirm the earlier findings. Specifically, Simmons and Freeman found that low level posthospital performance was associated with (1) the presence of other males in the household who could play the roles and perform the duties of the patients, (2) lower class status, and (3) low expectations on the part of their families. Conversely, high level performance was related to being the sole role incumbent, middle class status, and high expectations for performance. At this point, the tolerance of deviant behavior hypothesis seemed to be a most significant variable in case outcome.

Two later investigations, however, cast serious doubt about the meaning of these relationships. In a much larger study involving 649 of 714 male and female patients released during a six month period

---

[8] Howard E. Freeman and Ozzie G. Simmons, *The Mental Patient Comes Home* (New York, John Wiley and Sons, 1963).

in 1959 from nine state and three Veteran's Administration hospitals in eastern Massachusetts, Simmons and Freeman found that 63.9 percent of the male and 60.2 percent of the female patients succeeded in remaining home for at least one year. They also found that symptomatic or bizarre behavior and florid signs and symptoms, not inadequate instrumental role performance, were the most probable bases for rehospitalization. As important as the structural, interpersonal, and cultural variations in family life are, these in themselves do not appreciably alter the reaction to bizarre or extreme behavior.

THE OAKLAND, CALIFORNIA PROJECT

The Oakland study[9] was a retrospective investigation of the posthospital careers of 1,045 patients released *on leaves of absence* from several mental hospitals in northern California. These patients were referred to the Oakland Bureau of Social Work which functions as an after-care facility. The 1,045 cases constituted the entire group of patients released to that office during 1956. The Oakland Bureau saw most of the former patients and other family members in the central office; some 20 percent of the cases were also seen at home by one of the dozen psychiatric social workers who manned the after-care agency. In some 10 percent of the cases, patients were given intensive casework services; 70 percent were seen three or four times a year, and the remainder were seen only if they needed some kind of service. These patients were generally carried for about a year before being discharged.

Data were obtained on the patients from hospital files and case records. An attempt was made to read and code these records in such a manner as to be reasonably confident of their reliability. In view of the subjective variables sought and the differences in the quantity and quality of the case folder contents, high reliability was not an easy matter to achieve. The coders estimated, for example, that 74 percent of the case records were "generally adequate." Because of the nature of the data, the limitations imposed by the case record approach were not particularly critical.

The patients were retrospectively followed for five years, 1956–

[9] Dorothy Miller, *Worlds That Fail, Part I: Retrospective Analysis of Mental Patients' Careers* (State of California, Department of Mental Hygiene, Research Monograph No. 6, 1965).

1961. Of the total number of cases, whose average length of mental illness was seven years per patient, nearly 72 percent of these *leave patients* required rehospitalization. The distribution of outcome was as follows: about 29 percent remained successfully in the community, 26 percent were rehospitalized once, 18 percent twice, 25 percent from three to ten times, and 2 percent more than ten times.

Rehospitalization was associated, as one might well expect, with the extent of the history of mental illness. The longer the history, the greater the probability was of rehospitalization. However, other normally important variables—diagnosis, sex, race, residence (rural or urban), occupation, education, and "gross" social class—were not very significantly associated with rehospitalization. Heads of households, married patients, and patients in cohesive family situations succeeded in remaining home more often than their opposite numbers. On this level, then, there were two principal findings: Patients with lesser histories and more integrated family situations were more likely to remain home.

Two other results were interesting. The first of these indicated that less than half of the former patients held any type of remunerative employment, and of those who found jobs, only a few were successfully competing in the labor market. The second presented significant evidence for the downward social mobility of the patients.

Beyond these "hard" data, the study descended into a morass of hypotheses drawn from legitimate theoretical concerns but largely untestable in terms of the restrospective data. In essence it appears that husbands and wives do better than sons and daughters or those living with other relatives or with persons other than relatives. High status in the family situation is associated with positive outcome. Failure in role performance, on the other hand, is likely to lead to rehospitalization.

From the some 36 hypotheses specified and based on the subjective data, most were accepted. The general problem in these hypotheses, as in those of Simmons and Freeman, is the difficulty in determining whether patients remain at home because they function better and live in more cohesive family settings, or whether they function better and indicate healthier family interaction patterns because they are improved and their pathology is in remission or at least, not as disrupting as before.

THE STOCKTON REHOSPITALIZATION STUDY

In an unusual companion piece, the authors of the Oakland study[10] attempted to get a three dimensional appraisal of the reasons for the rehospitalization of former mental patients. Leave of absence patients from the Oakland area who require rehospitalization are sent to the Stockton State Hospital. In this investigation, 249 consecutive returnees were interviewed between the middle of October, 1963 and the first of April, 1964. The purpose of the interview, conducted by a psychiatric social worker from the admitting office, was to determine the patient's assessment of his rehospitalization. Although conducted very shortly after readmission, 89 percent of the returning patients were able to respond in a relevant manner to the structured interview questions. To counterbalance the perceptions of the patients, a significant other of each patient was also studied. Some of the significant others were interviewed; most returned a mailed questionnaire. To complete the assessment, the psychiatric social workers at the Bureau of Social Work were sent questionnaires pertaining to the reasons for failure of their respective cases.

The reasons for hospital readmission were roughly classified into four groups: psychiatric problems, physical problems, family or environmental stress, and drinking difficulties. When the explanations for readmission given by patient, immediate other, and psychiatric social worker were correlated with each other, the findings were most disconcerting. Patients', relatives', and social workers' conceptions differed markedly. There was agreement on psychiatric problems as being the basis for rehospitalization in only 19 of 66 cases or 29 percent; on family stresses in only 7 percent of 83 cases. Overall, the three sets of evaluators failed to concur in 84 percent of the cases. As the patients viewed their rehospitalization, about 31 percent attributed this failure to psychiatric difficulties, 15 percent to family problems, and 14 percent to physical illness. Nineteen percent indicated they were tricked into returning by scheming others. To the significant others, the rehospitalization was necessitated mostly by psychiatric symptoms. Family and other problems were far less often stated as the basis for rehospitalization. The social workers at the bureau responsi-

[10] Dorothy Miller and William Dawson, *Worlds That Fail, Part II: Disbanded Worlds: A Study of Returns to the Mental Hospital* (State of California, Department of Mental Hygiene, Research Monograph No. 7, 1965).

ble for the after-care of the leave patients indicated that 40 percent of the 249 patients were rehospitalized because they evidenced psychiatric symptoms. In 10 percent of the cases financial and environmental (family) problems were thought to have been the cause of the return to the hospital.

Ironically, while all three groups rated psychiatric symptoms as primarily responsible for the failures while on hospital leave, they disagreed too frequently on the precipitants in the individual case. Whose judgment then is the most reliable in instances of failure? For that matter, whose evaluation is to be accepted in the face of conflicting reports? One way of avoiding the necessity for choosing among the conflicting views and reports is to utilize more specific criteria of posthospital outcome such as role performance. In this study, for example, only 37 percent of the patients had been able to find any kind of employment; of these two thirds earned less than subsistence amounts. There was also the matter of a drinking problem on which there was almost complete agreement. Many relatives also indicated that the presence of the patient caused too much hardship and anxiety and that he or she required "too much care." Apart from the grossly deviant behavior of seemingly very few patients, it appeared that the rehospitalization of many, whatever the stated reason, resulted from this general patient inadequacy and incompetency which is most effectively illustrated by these specific role and functioning items.

HOME TREATMENT OUTCOME STUDIES

The 1950's were witness to a drastic reduction in the average length of hospitalization and the highly increased rates of release from all types of mental hospitals. Concurrently many new and interesting experimental home treatment ventures were introduced as substitutes for institutionalization. These innovations and the interest in the posthospital adjustment of former patients provide strong evidence that research was finally catching up with the reality of psychiatric practices. The reality was that most patients could and would be at home for much of their career as patients and that little was known about them prior to or subsequent to their institutionalization. As patients spend less time in hospitals and more at home, it seems only too apparent that more attention should be directed to their functioning outside of the hospital ward. Thus, outcome studies are merely another facet of the more generalized concern in the adaptation of patients to features of everyday life in the community. This section will present and consider two studies which attempted to treat patients at home and to evaluate the results achieved. The major emphasis is not, however, on the programs per se but rather on the evaluation of the adjustment and performance of patients who remained at home.

THE MASSACHUSETTS MENTAL HEALTH CENTER—CES PROJECT

The Massachusetts Mental Health Center is a small intensive therapy, training and research hospital run under the aegis of both the state system and Harvard Medical School. While it is a relatively simple matter to obtain immediate admission to the local state hospital, the famous and heavily staffed MMHC normally maintains a waiting list of patients. Experience, plus some fact finding, indicated that 20 percent of the patients on the waiting list were not hospitalized, 60 percent eventually entered the MMHC facility, and the remainder were admitted to other hospitals. The obvious need to offer professional supervision to waiting list patients brought the Community Extension Service (CES) into the picture.[11] CES entered with the conviction that "treatment outside the hospital, when feasible, would nearly always be in the best interests of both patient and the community, and when outpatient and inpatient treatment might both be expected to yield a satisfactory outcome, the former was preferred."

The procedure involved reviewing the additions to the MMHC waiting list each day beginning in October, 1957 and ending in December, 1959. Persons meeting the following criteria became potential subjects: resident of Greater Boston, age 18 or older, and not currently hospitalized anywhere or in the MMHC in the preceding four years. The patient's referring physician was then contacted, the program explained to him, and his cooperation sought. If he agreed, CES found and then interviewed the prospective patient and family either at the clinic or in a diagnostic home visit. Assuming patient acceptance into the project, treatment then followed. The therapy was broad and inclusive and involved individual psychother-

[11] Milton Greenblatt, Robert F. Moore, Robert S. Albert and Maida H. Solomon, *The Prevention of Hospitalization: Treatment Without Admission for Psychiatric Patients* (New York, Grune and Stratton, 1963).

apy, drugs, electroconvulsive therapy, casework with patients and relatives, vocational and more general counseling, and day hospital care when required.

Psychotherapy was the method most frequently used. A staff psychiatrist saw patients as often as three times weekly at the outset and at a reduced frequency later. Sessions continued for an average of six months but in some cases lasted up to two years. Drugs were used with more than half the patients. Psychiatrists made a considerable number of home visits. Five of them averaged over 110 such visits yearly. Seven others paid an average of 19 home visits. Project social workers and nurses were also extensively involved in the home visiting program. The rest of this excellent program was obviously quite large in terms of funds and personnel. Given present funding, such a comprehensive program would be beyond the means of most communities.

In order to evaluate the effectiveness of this program, CES conducted a follow-up interview with patients and relatives a year after referral to the MMHC waiting list. In the 27 months of the program, 128 patients were served by CES. Their average age was 35.7 years, 71.9 percent were females, only 39 percent were married, nearly half were Catholic, and nearly two thirds were at least high school graduates.

Of great importance in assessing the results achieved by CES was the diagnosis and severity of illness of the 128 patients. Psychotics accounted for only 56 percent of the patients; the remainder were diagnosed as psychoneurotic or personality disturbance, or given some other nonpsychotic classification. Most importantly, only 37 percent were diagnosed as schizophrenic or paranoid reaction. Again, of the 128 patients, 30.5 percent had been both hospitalized and on outpatient treatment previously; 11.7 percent had been hospitalized only; 25.8 percent had been in out-patient treatment only; the remainder, 32.0 percent, had experienced no previous psychiatric contact.

The results were good but not as convincing as they appear to be at first glance. To begin with, almost half of the patients failed and were hospitalized (49.4 percent). These exclude, however, the 10.2 percent who were treated by CES in the day care program. Of those who had to be hospitalized, failure occurred within six months in all cases. In assessing these findings two considerations should be remembered. First, 20 percent of the patients on the MMHC waiting list were not hospitalized even without intervention. Second, and by far the most critical consideration, was the differential success rate by diagnosis. Of the 24 involutional and manic-depressive patients treated, three quarters were hospitalized. Similarly, a majority (59.5 percent) of the schizophrenics failed. The greatest success occurred with nonpsychotic patients, nearly three quarters of whom remained in the community.

THE LOUISVILLE EXPERIMENTAL HOME CARE STUDY

The Louisville, Kentucky experimental research study[12] was designed to determine whether home care for prolonged care hospital schizophrenic patients was feasible, whether a combination of drug medication and public health nursing care was effective in preventing their hospitalization, and finally, whether home care was, in fact, a superior approach to hospitalization. To obtain answers to these and related questions, the Institute Treatment Center was established in downtown Louisville in the latter part of 1961.

The staff of this clinic included a director, a part time psychiatrist, a psychologist, a social worker, and five nurses with public health nursing experience. Only one of the nurses had any prior training or experience in psychiatric nursing. Since the Institute Treatment Center was located about 20 miles from the state hospital, a psychiatrist was employed at the hospital to do the initial screening of patients to determine their eligibility for inclusion in the program. Newly admitted state hospital patients had to meet the following criteria to be admitted to the project: a diagnosis of schizophrenia, nonsuicidal or homicidal, between 18 and 60 years of age, residence in Louisville or surrounding counties, and having a family or relative willing to provide supervision of the patient at home. State hospital admissions who met these criteria were sent to the Institute Treatment Center for further evaluation. If the ITC staff psychiatrist confirmed the diagnosis and deemed the patient suitable for the program and the family agreed to cooperate, the patient was accepted into the program. The study director randomly assigned the patient to one of three groups as follows: home on drugs (40 percent), home on placebo (30 percent), or hospital control (30 percent). The ran-

[12] Benjamin Pasamanick, Frank R. Scarpitti and Simon Dinitz, *Schizophrenics in the Community: An Experimental Study in the Prevention of Hospitalization* (New York, Appleton-Century-Crofts, 1967).

domly assigned hospital control patients were returned to the state hospital. The home care patients were sent home to their families.

State hospital schizophrenic patients do not, of course, include all schizophrenics. Many schizophrenic patients, because their symptoms are not especially florid and can therefore be tolerated more readily, typically remain in the community and may never be hospitalized. To tap this population as well, particularly for the purpose of determining the effectiveness of drug medication, referrals from community sources other than the state hospital and from private physicians were welcomed. In order to qualify for inclusion in the study, these referrals also had to meet the same diagnosis, age, residence, family, and other requirements. The only difference, because of their ambulatory status, was that their random assignment, once accepted, included just two categories: home on drug or home on placebo.

Shortly after return home, the public health nurse assigned to the case visited the patient and family. The same nurse made weekly calls the first three months, bi-monthly visits during the second three months, and monthly visits thereafter. On every visit she left the medication prescribed by the staff psychiatrist. She also completed a written report on the status of the patient which was reviewed by the psychiatrist. Patients and families experiencing difficulties could also call the treatment center and speak to or make appointments to see the social worker and psychiatrist. Usually, however, it was the nurse who arranged for such consultation.

In order to obtain the data necessary to answer the questions about the feasibility of home care and the efficacy of drug therapy, various instruments, tests, and measures were used. These included:

Psychiatric evaluation. Two instruments (a psychiatric inventory and the Lorr IMPS) were used by the staff psychiatrist to evaluate the mental status of all patients on a regular basis. Home care patients were examined at intake and at six month intervals thereafter. Hospital control patients were evaluated at intake and again after 6 and 18 months whether or not they still were hospitalized.

Psychological tests. All groups were studied by the staff psychologist who administered the Wechsler Adult Intelligence Scale, a reaction time test series, and the Bender Gestalt and Porteus Maze tests. Testing periods were the same as for the psychiatric evaluations.

Social history. A complete social history was taken by the social worker at the time of admission of the patient to the project.

Nurses reports and ratings. The public health nurse completed a mental status rating form on each visit to the home care patient. This form was the Lorr IMPS. She also completed a behavior chart checklist, a physical status rating sheet, and a nursing report. All were submitted to the staff psychiatrist after each visit. The nurse also obtained a monthly report from the responsible relative concerning the patient's functioning. Hospital control patients were visited by the nurse one month after hospital release, and these same instruments were administered at that time.

In all, 204 patients were involved in the project. Of these, the 57 drug home care patients, 41 placebo home care cases, and 54 hospital controls were followed for a period ranging from 9 months at the least to 30 months at the maximum. In addition, 29 ambulatory drug home care cases and 23 ambulatory placebo home care patients were in the project for from 6 to 27 months.

The principal substantive findings concerning these 152 state hospital and 52 ambulatory schizophrenics were these:

1. Over 77 percent of the state hospital drug home care patients but only some 34 percent of the placebo cases remained in the community throughout their participation in the project. All controls, of course, were hospitalized. Not only did the program thus prevent hospitalization and save a considerable amount of patient bed time but this saving can also be translated into the possibility of more intensive care for the fewer patients hospitalized.

2. There was no appreciable attrition in the success of the patients over time at home. Drug and placebo home patients in the project for a longer time period were no less successful than those in the program for shorter periods of time. Thus, it is fair to speak of prevention of hospitalization as such rather than merely of delay in institutionalization.

3. Patients who failed and had to be hospitalized usually failed soon after acceptance into the program. Nearly all failures occurred within six months.

4. Even after an average initial hospitalization of 83 days and the presumable remission of the grosser symptoms, the hospital controls failed more often at home after release than did the drug home care patients.

5. Failure in home care was frequently of the "last straw" variety. Either patient behavior was so bizarre or dangerous as to be intolerable or the responsible relatives could no longer cope with the patient and his needs. Changes in the family situation resulting in a lack of supervision of the patient occasionally precipitated failure.

6. On the symptom and instrumental role level, patients improved in mental status, psychological test performance, domestic functioning, and social participation. These gains were considerable. In all of the many very specific measures, home care patients were functioning as well or better than the hospital control cases.

7. Most of the improvement in performance occurred in the patient's first six months in the study. Thereafter, functioning improved very little, if at all. In other words, once the acute signs and symptoms abated and functioning returned to a pre-episode level, there was little more gain made.

8. At their best, these chronically impaired patients still showed considerable problems in performing at what might be termed an adequate level. Both on the instrumental role performance level and on the psychological symptom level, the home care patients (and the controls) were still exhibiting rather low quality performance.

9. The ambulatory drug and placebo patients tended to corroborate in almost every respect the results obtained with the state hospital patients. Nearly 76 percent of the drug and 61 percent of the placebo cases succeeded on home care. Length of time on the project was not a major correlate of failure. In instances of hospitalization, failure occurred early and the precipitants were generally of the same nature. Functioning improved but most of the gains in the psychiatric, psychological, and social functioning measures were registered between intake and the sixth month's testing. Not much further improvement was exhibited from the sixth to the eighteenth, twenty-fourth, or twenty-seventh month evaluations.

4

Study Design and Procedures

The data on the outcome of mental hospitalization involved two primary cohorts of subjects: former patients and the comparison group of women who were their neighbors. In this chapter, the variables under study, the pattern of data collection, and the selection of patient subjects and their significant others will be described. The comparison group of normal women will be presented in Chapter 7 and the methods for their selection, data collection, and analysis will be discussed.

THE KEY VARIABLES

The design of the study revolved around three major foci for assessing the outcome of psychiatric hospitalization: first, to study the effects of social and psychiatric variables on posthospital performance; second, to ascertain the possible factors precipitating rehospitalization; and third, to compare patient performance with that of a control group of normal women. Since performance in the community was of central concern for all three aspects of the study, the performance measures are discussed first.

PERFORMANCE IN THE COMMUNITY: DOMESTIC, SOCIAL, AND PSYCHOLOGICAL MEASURES

Those acquainted with the literature on roles, role performance, expectations, and sex roles, in particular, well know the lack of empirically established norms by which to judge role performance. What can be found in this literature are numerous analyses and impressionistic assessments of "acceptable," "normative," "expected" behavior from men and women in American society. Above all, a concern with changing definitions and blurring of sex role differences is predominant. The general recognition that female and male role behavior cannot be adequately defined has led to the need for empirically establishing what the distinctive role expectations are, which areas of behavior are mutually exclusive, and which overlap. The research task to accomplish this is clearly difficult. Barring the actual collection of data on sex role norms, those interested in assessing role performance have one alternative: that is to make certain assumptions on experiential, logical bases, while at the same time drawing on competent analyses by perceptive observers. This was done, as the measures of role performance and role expectations to be described reveal. It was assumed that a "core" sex role for the American female is still identifiable in terms of areas of responsibility relegated to her rather than to the male.

The key dependent variables in this research were first, the ability to avoid rehospitalization and second, the ability of the former patient to perform adequately in the community. In order to assess posthospital performance, three measures were utilized.[1] These are described only briefly here. Readers interested in these specific measures and their scoring should check Table 1 in Appendix B.

1. *Domestic performance* contained items dealing with routine household tasks and care of children.[2] If the patient was either unable

[1] At first, an attempt was made to assess performance in terms of ability to hold a job after hospitalization. In this area difficulty was encountered since only one third of the entire patient group held jobs within the three years before hospitalization. Thus any measure of work performance would have had restricted applicability. For two thirds of the study group not employed, one may conclude that holding a job had not been part of their more recent life pattern. This was most characteristic of the married patients. Therefore, it was decided to omit the work area from the assessment of performance.

[2] For some purposes, the two items concerning children were omitted and a five item scale was used. Scoring details on all performance and expectation measures are presented in Tables 1 and 2 in Appendix B. In order to obtain criterion groups, patients were ranked on each performance and expectation measure in terms of total scores and then divided into approximate thirds (tied scores were grouped together). This division of patients into levels permitted contrast between high and low groups, albeit in relative terms.

to perform tasks or if she needed help from others she received a lower score than if she managed entirely on her own.

2. *Social participation* was a composite measure derived by judging the patient in terms of her significant other.[3] The items included leisure activities, such as watching television and reading the newspaper, as well as interpersonal behavior, such as visiting friends and relatives.

3. *Psychological functioning* included a list of 32 items each describing behavior symptomatic of impaired functioning. The more symptoms the patient manifested sometimes or often, the lower her score, and therefore, the poorer the level of her psychological functioning.[4]

4. In addition to the individual performance measures, an *index of total performance* in terms of high, moderate, and low level performers was developed on the basis of the three major performance aspects: domestic performance level, social participation, and psychological functioning.[5] The total performance score was derived by adding the patient's score on these three measures. This index of performance permits discussion of performance level as a multidimensional phenomenon encompassing the major behavioral areas considered important in this study.

---

[3] Two separate measures of social participation were developed: one based on the woman's own report of her participation, the second was a composite measure based on the significant other's report of both his and his relative's participation. Both measures discriminated comparably between criterion groups of high and low participators, and between patient and control women. Therefore, only one, the composite measure was used since it derives from significant other reports of performance as do the domestic and psychological functioning measures. Examples of social participation items and the detailed scoring system are presented in Appendix B, Table 1 on scoring.

[4] Adaptation of these items was done with permission by Dr. Lorr and with the consent of Howard Freeman and Ozzie Simmons. Information on the Lorr Scale is obtainable from Dr. Maurice Lorr, Neuropsychiatric Research Laboratory, Veterans Administration, Washington, D. C.

[5] Using a corrected contingency coefficient, the correlation between psychological functioning and social participation $= .28$ ($p < 0.05$); between psychological functioning and domestic performance, $C = .44$ ($p < 0.01$); between social participation and domestic performance, $C = .20$ (N.S.); between the index of total performance and psychological functioning, $C = .77$ ($p < 0.01$); total performance and domestic performance, $C = .54$ ($p < 0.01$). Because of these significant intercorrelations among measures, the index of total performance was used as an overall performance indicator.

POSSIBLE FACTORS AFFECTING OUTCOME

The selection of independent variables for study was based on the assumption that the outcome of psychiatric hospitalization might be linked to two major sources of influence: psychiatric factors and social factors. Experiences related to illness and to hospitalization must be taken into account in evaluating posthospital performance and the ability to avoid readmission since surely the key goal of hospitalization is to ameliorate if not to cure the illness. Thus, a primary issue is the efficacy of treatment in a mental hospital. Has hospitalization made it possible for the former patient to succeed in performing adequately and remaining indefinitely in the community? The many psychiatric variables available from hospital records of the former patient's experience were utilized in order to assess their relationship to outcome. These included the number of psychiatric hospitalizations, diagnosis, length of hospitalization, ward assignment, illness duration, type of hospital treatment received, type of release, prognosis at discharge, extent of out-patient care, and degree of impairment at admission and at discharge.

The second set of independent variables consisted of social factors potentially important in outcome both as judged from other researches and from a basic sociological standpoint. Here were included the descriptive social attributes of age, race, religion, and urban-rural residence; the familial variables—marital status, living arrangements after discharge, number and ages of children; social class level measured by a modification of the Warner Index of Status Characteristics as well as by the Hollingshead Two Factor Index;[6]

[6] See W. Lloyd Warner, Marchia Meeker and Kenneth Eells, *Social Class in America* (Gloucester, Massachusetts, Peter Smith, 1957); and August B. Hollingshead, *Two Factor Index of Social Position* (New Haven, 1957). The Warner Index of Status Characteristics was modified to include three dimensions: the former patient's education, house type, and dwelling area, weighted 5, 4, and 3 respectively and multiplied by the scale from 1 to 7 for each dimension to yield I.S.C. scores from 12–84. Warner recommends using occupation rather than education, but since not all our respondents were married women, the husband's occupation could not be used meaningfully. Source of income also had to be ruled out for the I.S.C. due to the difficulty in getting reliable information. A comparative analysis of *married* patient social class levels as measured by the I.S.C. and the Hollingshead Two Factor Index (which utilizes husband's education and occupation) resulted in equivalent class rankings on the two measures. For this reason and because of the greater simplicity of the Hollingshead Index, we used the latter exclusively for the more refined comparisons

and four other measures of expectations for behavior. The expectation measures were each based on a series of items used additively as a total score. These measures reflect the social psychological viewpoint that an individual's behavior is to some degree determined by the expectations held by his significant others.[7] The individual, whether he is sick or well, behaves in terms of the standards he has learned and which are viewed for him as adequate, normal, socially acceptable behavior. The four types of expectations utilized as independent variables were (1) the patient's self-expectations, (2) the significant other's expectations, (3) the agreement in expectations between patient and significant other, and (4) tolerance of deviance. The first three measures involved areas of social behavior, such as expectations for the woman's domestic performance, her social participation, and work performance. The fourth one, tolerance of deviance, referred to expectations of deviant versus normal psychological functioning. More details on these measures and their scoring may be found in Appendix B.

Three structured interview schedules were pretested and developed for use with each of the three categories of subjects: one schedule for interviewing community patients (the Patient Schedule), a second schedule for interviewing the significant other of community patients (the S.O. Schedule), the third for use with the significant other of rehospitalized patients (the S.O.R. Schedule). Each interview schedule is presented in Appendix A.

The schedules used for interviewing significant others of community and returnee patients included the aforementioned measures to elicit the patient's posthospital performance in terms of domestic activities, social participation, and psychological functioning. Significant others were also asked about their interpersonal relations with the patient, their expectations of her, their willingness to tolerate devi-

---

between married patients and married controls described in Chapter 7, since in these subsamples we had consistent data for husband's occupation and education.

[7] Alfred Lindesmith and Anselm Strauss, *Social Psychology* (New York, Holt, Rinehart and Winston, rev. ed., 1956); Neal Gross, Ward S. Mason and Alexander McEachern, *Explorations in Role Analysis* (New York, John Wiley and Sons, 1958); and William A. Rushing, "The Role Concept: Assumptions and Their Methodological Implications," *Sociology and Social Research,* Vol. 49 (October 1964), pp. 46–57. See Howard E. Freeman and Ozzie G. Simmons, *The Mental Patient Comes Home* (New York, John Wiley and Sons, 1963), who used a measure of expectations similar to ours.

ance, as well as a number of background items. Questions were arranged in a sequence meaningful for the structured interview situation. The schedule for interviewing patients was particularly concerned with her family and personal background, her self-expectations, and leisure activities. After each interview, patient and significant other were rated on socioeconomic characteristics, deportment of the respondent during the interview, and attitude toward the hospital, using a form separate from the interview schedules.

THE SHORT TERM HOSPITAL SETTING

The patients studied had been treated at the Columbus Psychiatric Institute and Hospital, one of several receiving hospitals opened in Ohio during the late 1940's and 1950's. The original act authorizing receiving hospitals specified that these "shall be used for the observation, care and treatment of the mentally ill and especially for those whose condition is incipient, mild or of possible short duration." But by 1950, research into origins, causes, and treatment of mental disorder was specified as indispensible to maximizing this short term approach. The Columbus Psychiatric Institute and Hospital was opened in 1951, and until July, 1961 when the hospital came wholly under the jurisdiction of The Ohio State University College of Medicine, it was a joint venture of the State Department of Mental Hygiene and the University.

In 1958, at the inception of the outcome study, the hospital had 126 beds divided into two male wards and three female wards. Over 90 percent of all admissions were voluntary and over two thirds of the patients were first admissions. The hospital handled all types of psychiatric problems in its basic role as a short term treatment center for adults, with an average length of stay of 45 days during the late 1950's. Since hospital policy emphasized the training of professional personnel, patients who were judged to need long term treatment or custodial care were typically transferred to Columbus State Hospital and other prolonged care institutions. The research division of the Columbus Psychiatric Institute and Hospital concentrated on basic research studies involving the biochemical, physiological, psychological, and sociological aspects of mental illness. The outcome study took shape amid a much larger sociological research enterprise on patient care, including ward behavior of patients, work satisfaction of mental health professionals, hospital organization, and home care of schizophrenics.

Until this study began, the hospital had no systematic follow-up program for released patients. Contact with some patients was maintained through out-patient visits with individual hospital psychiatrists for varying periods. The generally unstructured character of out-patient treatment was reflected in the lack of records kept by the hospital for such contacts. Thus, this outcome study was actively encouraged by the hospital administration and by the entire clinical staff. Every opportunity was provided to explain the study and enlist the support of all hospital professionals particularly at staff meetings.[8]

SOURCES OF DATA ON FORMER PATIENTS

HOSPITAL AND PSYCHIATRIC HISTORIES

Information dealing with the patient's diagnosis, illness, and treatment history was taken from the hospital records. A standardized form was developed in order to codify the many aspects of the patient's hospital stay, including the number of previous admissions, length of time spent in this and other mental hospitals, symptoms manifested at admission, degree of impairment at admission and discharge, behavior on the ward, type of treatment received, relatives who kept in touch with the patient during hospitalization, diagnosis, prognosis, and many other relevant items about the illness and hospital treatment history. The form was filled out by graduate student research assistants and was based primarily on therapist and nursing records kept during the hospitalization. Standardized instructions were used for completing the hospital record form; each form was then checked carefully by a second coder to ensure its accuracy. The hospital record provided not only data on treatment and illness, but also served as a basis for selecting the significant other, and for clues on possible problems in successfully interviewing the patient and her significant other.

---

[8] A notice to psychiatric residents as well as all letters to patients, their relatives, and physicians, interview schedules, and rating forms used in the entire study are found in Appendix A.

THE FIRST INTERVIEW

For women who remained in the community, both the patient and a significant other were contacted for interviews. Usually the closest relative in the patient's household was designated as the significant other. For married women, this meant the husband. Where no husband was available, a mother, sister, or daughter (18 years or older) in the patient's household was selected, in that order of preference. Where those household relatives were not available, another household person whom the patient considered close was chosen. In 20 percent of the cases the former patient designated a significant other outside her household for interview.

Former patients and their significant others were usually very cooperative. Many families took the follow-up interviews as evidence that the hospital maintained interest in the welfare of its former patients. Only a few families resented being contacted. In the first wave of interviews, there were a total of 23 cases in which only partial or no interview data could be obtained, or a loss of 8 percent. Compared with other follow-up studies in particular, and with interview-based research in general, this is an extremely high response rate. This success must be attributed, at least in part, to the fact that the follow-up was accepted by all concerned as a new hospital program to maintain contact with former patients and to learn how they were doing in the community.

Although respondents were contacted approximately six months after release, the number of days between discharge and the actual follow-up interview ranged from 160 to 240 days; the average elapsed time was 189 days. The decision to use a six month period was based on the dual interest in conserving as many patients as possible while concurrently maximizing the number of readmissions. In many outcome studies, one or two years elapsed before follow-up, thereby incurring a loss of cases through geographic mobility. Six months was also considered adequate time for patients to indicate the nature of their community adjustment. This reasoning was largely confirmed by checking rehospitalization records at the State Department of Mental Hygiene and in private mental hospitals in the area; it was found that the highest number of readmissions occurred within six months after discharge. From that time on until seven years later, each year showed a decreasing proportion of readmissions from the total patient sample studied.[9]

If the woman was still in the community at six months after release, a letter addressed to her was sent on official hospital stationery and signed by the hospital superintendent. The letter explained the follow-up as a new program for keeping in touch with former patients to see how they were doing in the community (a copy of this letter is in Appendix A). Interviews were requested with both the patient and her closest relative. The tone of the letter suggested that such a follow-up program would be of value to the former patient herself as well as a contribution to understanding and care of other and future patients. If it was known that the patient had been readmitted before the six month follow-up, a letter similar to that sent to community patients was sent to a significant other of the patient requesting the follow-up interview. In a few cases the interviewer learned of the patient's rehospitalization upon arrival at the home and then interviewed only the significant other. In all cases, a stamped reply card was enclosed with the letter so that the respondent could suggest a convenient time for the interviewer's visit.

Hospital records on each patient were searched carefully to find the name of a referring physician or family doctor. At the same time as patients were sought, a letter was sent to each known family doctor describing the study, informing him of the planned interview, and asking him to notify study personnel if the interview might be considered harmful to his patient. Many respondents might not have been so cooperative if their family physicians had not approved the program and in some instances urged their patients to participate. In a very few cases, because of the patient's condition or attitude, the doctor recommended against the interview.

Although graduate students and public health nurses had been

---

[9] This rate of readmission holds whether one considers number of *patients* readmitted *or* actual number of *readmissions*. Details on this point are presented in Chapter 5 on Rehospitalization. Cf. J. M. Wanklin, D. F. Fleming, Carol Buck and G. E. Hobbs, "Discharge and Readmission Among Mental Hospital Patients," *A.M.A. Archives of Neurology and Psychiatry,* Vol. 76 (December 1956), pp. 660–669, who found readmission rates highest at 4 to 6 months after discharge; and Benjamin Pasamanick, Frank Scarpitti and Simon Dinitz, *Schizophrenics in The Community* (New York, Appleton-Century-Crofts, 1967), who report that among schizophrenics in a home care program the highest percent of failures occurred within six months after acceptance into the program.

considered, the choice of psychiatric social workers as interviewers was deemed best for study purposes. Ability to handle former patients and their families would entail the knowledge and skills of persons professionally associated with the mentally disturbed. In retrospect, the choice was in general a happy one. Originally, full time social workers were sought, but since it was impossible to obtain competent persons on a short term basis, ten psychiatric social workers, employed full time in hospitals or clinics in the city, were hired on a part time basis to work on their own time, especially evenings and weekends.[10] The practicability of this plan lay in the fact that interviews would frequently be with husbands or working women who could not be reached during the daytime.

Interviewers were given three training sessions devoted to explaining the study objectives and describing their role. Detailed written and standardized instructions were provided and discussed concerning completion of the structured schedules. During the course of this training, each social worker was assigned an interview with a former patient and her significant other who were not in the study sample. This provided pretest data and also gave the interviewers practice in the use of the schedules. The test cases also enabled the investigators to become personally acquainted with interviewers so that it was possible to use an interviewer according to his suitability with respondents. Some could locate and contact a mobile lower class person who broke repeated appointments while others were expert at managing the adamant, hostile, resentful person for whom the hospital had negative meanings. As the study progressed, difficult cases were reassigned from one interviewer to another who might succeed in completing the interview.

Problems and questions were discussed and solved insofar as possible before the actual data collection began. But throughout the study, emerging problems were worked out with each interviewer

---

[10] We are grateful for the suggestion of Howard Freeman and Ozzie Simmons to use this part time arrangement. Social workers were selected from the membership list of the local chapter of the National Association of Social Workers. Of the five men and five women who began the interviewing, eight remained until interviews were completed for the patient sample. One male interviewer was dropped after he proved unable successfully to complete interviews. A female Negro social worker withdrew after several interviews because she was uncomfortable with both white and Negro respondents.

either by phone or in direct discussion with the administrative assistant and with the authors. It was found that the interviewers frequently needed encouragement, a sympathetic ear, and advice. Sustaining interviewer morale was a challenge when respondents were hostile, vituperative, or drugged, and when many visits to the patient's house were fruitless. The administrative assistant was extremely competent in this role; she also prodded interviewers to complete difficult or incomplete cases. Every attempt was made to expedite the interviewer's task in locating elusive respondents and obtaining their cooperation. The good rapport between interviewers and the office staff was sustained because no problem obvious to either was left unsolved.

The interview time with the patient varied between 25 minutes and an hour. The interview with the significant other took from 40 minutes to an hour and a half. The interviews were held separately so that each respondent would feel free to express himself. In the few instances when a respondent was absolutely unwilling to be interviewed at home, arrangements were made for meeting at the hospital or in offices specially designated for this purpose.

An early decision to soft-pedal the research focus of the follow-up and to emphasize the study as an experimental hospital program turned out to be sound. Interviewers and other project staff were encouraged to interpret the follow-up as something to be taken for granted by participants and in which their help was crucial. This approach seemed to put respondents at ease and reinforced the idea that the patient was not being singled out for unpleasant reasons. It was never a policy to deny the research aspect of the project if this were raised by the respondent. For those who were interested, interviewers explained the research focus of the study in more detail. Otherwise the use of the term *research* was avoided; the hospital letterhead and the superintendent's signature symbolized hospital sponsorship of the follow-up program.

Interviewers were prepared to refer patients who might clearly need further psychiatric treatment to the hospital or to encourage them to seek other psychiatric care when it was deemed essential. It turned out that few of the community patients and their families sought such help; in fact, few could be considered disoriented. Excessive suspicion or paranoid reactions may have motivated some who refused the interview, but among those patients who cooperated in the study, few problems in understanding or answering questions arose. This should be viewed not merely as a tribute to the respondents but also as evidence of the devotion of the interviewers, all of whom displayed ingenuity, flexibility, and great competence in carrying out the home interviews. In fact, after the completion of interviews with former patients and their significant others and the control group of nonpatients, no differences were noted in the interviewing process peculiar to respondents who had been patients.

PSYCHIATRIC ASSESSMENT OF PERFORMANCE

In order to have a clinical evaluation of the level or adequacy of posthospital patient functioning, independent of the more sociologically oriented one derived from the significant other, a random sample of former patients was asked to cooperate by presenting themselves for a psychiatric interview. The social worker scheduled an appointment for the psychiatric assessment usually within one week after the follow-up interview. Two hospital psychiatrists were involved in these evaluations and former patients were assigned to one or the other randomly. Neither psychiatrist was aware of the patient's previous history except as he may have deemed it advisable to ascertain this during the course of the interview.

The 246 community patients who had avoided rehospitalization represented the pool from which 119 women were requested, on a random basis, to return to the University Health Center for a psychiatric assessment. Despite the great deal of encouragement given to former patients and their families by the study staff, only 55 percent of those contacted cooperated in the psychiatric assessment program; the 65 patients comprised 26 percent of the community patients. The remainder either refused, cancelled, or simply failed to keep scheduled appointments. This occurred in spite of the fact that respondents knew they would be reimbursed for transportation costs to and from the hospital, for baby sitter fees, and any other expenses a patient and her family might incur in keeping the appointment.

Each of the physicians interviewed the patients without prior access to case materials. At the conclusion of the interview, which usually exceeded one hour in duration, a Lorr Psychiatric Rating Scale Form, Part I, was filled out by the examining physician for each of his cases.[11] In addition, the psychiatrist rated the degree of psychiatric impairment characterizing the patient as he perceived it at the time. Finally, the physician specified the diagnosis to be given the patient ranging from no mental illness present through the usual psychiatric categories.

As noted earlier, relatives of the patients (usually husbands) had also evaluated the psychological functioning of the patients. Each significant other had rated the patient on 32 items of psychological functioning. Of these 32 items, 17 paralleled those in the Lorr Scale. Hence, it was possible to relate skilled psychiatric judgments on these items to those of the less skilled but more familiar ones of the significant others. The psychiatric assessment data, whose purpose was to cross-check the data derived from interview schedules, did indeed serve to substantiate the latter. Patients found to function well in terms of the significant other's evaluation of their social, domestic, and psychological functioning were very likely to be rated as minimally impaired by the psychiatrist. The extent to which this medical evaluation supported the sociological one is described in a note on validity presented in Appendix A.

THE SECOND INTERVIEW

The second follow-up served the important purpose of ascertaining what changes occurred in performance after another year or more had elapsed since hospitalization. The second interviews took place about 18 months after release and about a year after the first follow-up interviews. This time a sample of 33 community patients was interviewed, all of them women who had been diagnosed as schizophrenic during their hospitalization.[12] Item and total performance

---

[11] The Lorr Psychiatric Rating Scale, Part I, contains 42 items pertaining to behavioral and psychological functioning. Each item presents the possibility of rating the degree of variation from a norm population. We departed very slightly from the procedure specified in the manual of instructions. Two items, 14 and 26, which deal with physical disability were excluded. Our total score, based on discrepancies from the item norms, became 40 for no visible impairment to 151 for complete and total disability. Also omitted from analysis were the factor scores since these served no useful purpose in this particular study.

[12] Interviews with the former patient and her significant other were completed in 37 cases. In 15, partial or no data at all could be obtained: in two cases only the significant other was interviewed, in five cases only the patient was interviewed, three were refusals, and five were lost because the patient had left the state. Thus of the 52 interviews attempted, 71.2 percent were com-

scores were compared across the two time periods. The general and major finding was that little change had occurred for most patients in the social, domestic, and psychological performance areas. T-tests between mean scores for the 33 schizophrenics in the three performance areas and in total performance for the two time periods yielded no significant differences. For many patients there were minor fluctuations—total score differences of several units between the two time periods. For only about five of the schizophrenic women were performance changes sufficiently great to reflect meaningful improvement or deterioration in their condition—two improved and three declined considerably. (See Appendix B, Tables 4, 5, and 6 for details.)

In domestic performance, there was no change at all for at least two thirds of the former patients. Analysis of the patients who became worse in domestic performance indicated that, in this area of performance, decline was largely characteristic of these chronic schizophrenics who had more mental hospital admissions and more out-patient care, were older and less well educated than the patients who improved or did not change. These characteristics cannot be said to apply to the patients who declined in social participation or psychological functioning.

In social participation more variation occurred from first to second follow-up than in any other area. There was a noticeable difference in performance for 39 percent of the women. Caution in interpreting the variation in leisure participation should be exercised, since it was difficult to ascertain how much of the change was due to irrelevant factors and how much was clearly indicative of the patient's condition.

In the area of psychological functioning, little change was evident.[13] The greatest changes were in somatic and depression symp-

---

pleted, representing a loss of cases considerably higher than for the first follow-up. But a further four patients who were hospitalized at the time of the second follow-up had to be omitted, leaving 33 usable cases in the reinterviews. The fact that only schizophrenic patients were involved may partly account for the less cooperative reaction to the second interview by some patients and their families.

[13] Correlations between first and second follow-up performance scores were high and significant for all areas except psychological functioning. For domestic performance $r = .53$, $p < 0.01$; for social participation, $r = .68$, $p < 0.01$; for psychological functioning, $r = .12$, N.S.; for total performance, $r = .54$, $p < 0.01$. This result of little change in overall psychological functioning must be reported despite the low and nonsignificant correlation. The

toms—and these fluctuations reflected both worsening and improvement. However, changes for the worse were proportionately higher in the mild and somatic-type symptoms. Improvement, however, was greater in the more severe symptom areas, such as motor difficulties, withdrawal tendencies, listlessness, insomnia, eating problems, paranoia, and hallucinatory behavior.

It must be concluded, then, that performance levels for a potentially volatile category of former patients—schizophrenics—did not change significantly beyond six months after discharge.[14] For the minority of "changeable" patients, the direction of change was inconsistent; some patients had improved in all areas, some degenerated in all areas. At the same time, for many patients, slight variations occurred in both directions—in some items of behavior their performance level was higher, in some, lower than earlier.

The importance of these findings, derived from a comparison of the performance levels 6 months and approximately 18 months after hospitalization, is two-fold. First, whatever else is involved, a high degree of reliability of the performance measures may be inferred. Considering the fact that at least one year elapsed between the two waves of interviews, the fact of similarity of responses both times is all the more meaningful. The rather high correlation coefficients appeared indicative of the reliability of the measures and supported the results from an earlier attempt to assess the reliability of instruments by repeating nine interviews with former patients only (see Appendix A, Note on Reliability.) Waiting over one year to repeat interviews did not lower reliability substantially.

A second inference to be drawn involves the time at which posthospital performance is measured. It will be recalled that the initial reasons for choosing six months as the follow-up time were: (1) to

---

low correlation value may be attributed to the high variability possible in the 32 item psychological functioning measure. The virtually identical mean scores for both time periods point to the low incidence of change in psychological functioning, as do the item frequencies. What changes did occur were predominantly in the milder somatic and depression symptoms representing fluctuations in 11 of the 32 symptom items.

[14] It is interesting to note that significant attitudinal changes had not occurred—tolerance of deviance, the patient's own expectations and those of her significant other remained substantially the same. Furthermore, readmissions among the schizophrenics comprised 37 percent, a rate of return not notably different than that for the whole cohort of former patients.

minimize the loss of former patients who might leave the community and state, and (2) to wait long enough after discharge to assess posthospital performance. The experience with the follow-up interviews at six months led to the belief that this strategy had been correct. However, the similarity of responses between the six month and 18 month interviews added even greater weight to the value of the six month follow-up. Since performance did not seem to change greatly once a former patient had been in the community for six months, there was little to be gained by delaying the first posthospital contact beyond that time. Further, the increased loss of cases in the second follow-up weighed against such delay.

SELECTION OF THE PATIENTS

The overall plan for the outcome study involved the initial designation of a sample of female patients. These women comprised a purposive sample of patients consecutively discharged from a short term psychiatric hospital during the eight month period from December 1, 1958 to July 31, 1959.[15]

SUBSAMPLES

As shown in Figure 4.1, the study group of 287 patients was distinguished into two subgroups—those who had remained in the community for six months after discharge (community patients) and those who had been readmitted to a mental hospital within that period (returnees). From among the community patients a small sample was assessed psychiatrically within a few weeks of the follow-up interview. Further, from among the community patients, a small sample of schizophrenics, living in the county area surrounding the hospital, was approached for a repeat interview at two years after discharge; this was the second follow-up. A group of late returnees was identified from among community patients. These women had been readmitted to a mental hospital at least once between six months and seven years after discharge from the study hospitalization. Information about

[15] Purposive sampling is a nonprobability method. See Claire Selltiz, Marie Jahoda, Morton Deutsch and Stuart Cook, *Research Methods in Social Relations* (New York, Holt, Rinehart and Winston, rev. ed., 1959), p. 520.

STUDY DESIGN AND PROCEDURES 71

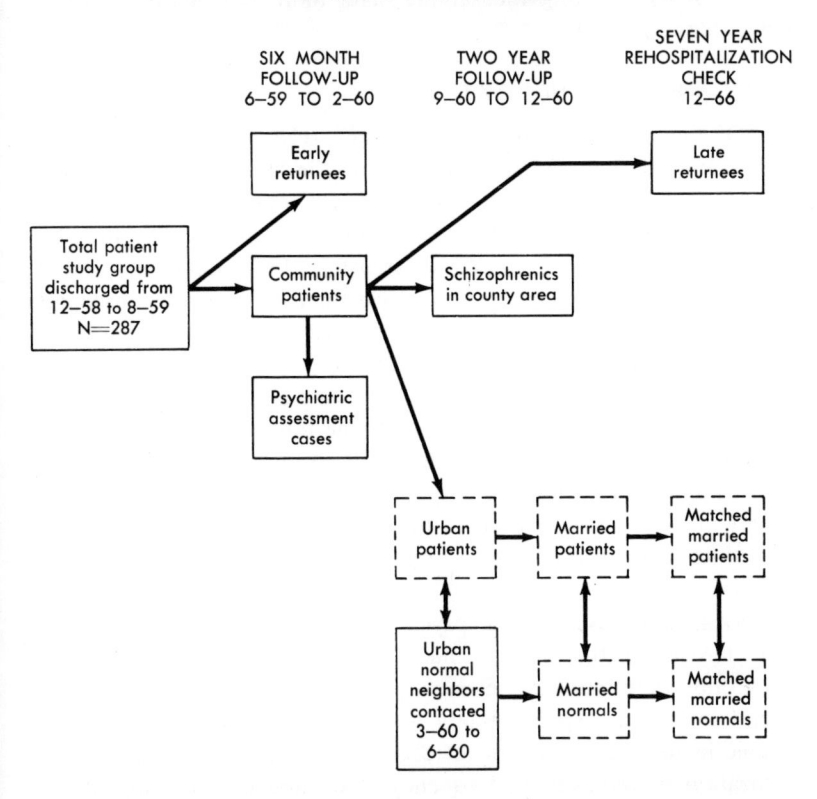

FIGURE 4.1. FLOW CHART SHOWING SPECIFIC SAMPLES
AND TIME OF DATA COLLECTION

| | SIX MONTH
FOLLOW-UP
6-59 TO 2-60 | TWO YEAR
FOLLOW-UP
9-60 TO 12-60 | SEVEN YEAR
REHOSPITALIZATION
CHECK
12-66 |

Note: Solid line boxes indicate samples contacted for interview. Broken line boxes show reduced samples for which data were available from earlier interviews and hospitalization records.

these "late" returnees was obtained from official hospital and state records.

Those community patients living in the immediate urban area were designated for matching with a comparison group of normal women. The control group of normal neighbors was in fact selected only for matching with patients who had demonstrated that they could remain in the community. Thus one month after completion of the six month follow-up, the patients' normal neighbors living about ten house numbers away were contacted for interview. From these two samples, urban patients and their normal neighbors, two successive sample pairs were distinguished, first by including married women only, then by equating the sample pairs more stringently on other social characteristics.

STUDY AND NONSTUDY PATIENTS

Of the total of 376 female patients released during the eight month study period, 287 were included in the follow-up. The remaining 89 cases were omitted for either of two reasons: (1) they were returned to an address outside the 13 county area served by the hospital[16] (33 cases) or (2) they were transferred to another hospital or readmitted to a mental institution in less than 15 days after discharge (51 cases). The remaining five nonstudy cases included three patients who had died in the six month period following discharge, and two patients who were released twice during the study period but were followed up only once. For purposes of the follow-up, then, a patient was defined as discharged if she "left bed" to return to the community and remained there for 15 days or more. Thus, patients released against medical advice, absent without leave, or placed on trial visit, as well as those formally discharged by the hospital staff were included.

In a comparison of the psychiatric and the social background characteristics of the 287 patients studied with the 89 excluded, the two groups were found to be similar in many respects but different in several important aspects. Study and nonstudy patients were comparable in the type of treatment they received during the study hospitalization as well as in the frequency of alcoholism as a complication in their cases. They were similar also in age, religion, race, and education. However, the two categories of discharged patients differed significantly in the following respects: a higher proportion of study patients were married rather than single, widowed, or separated; the diagnosis of a psychosis was more frequent among nonstudy patients while the neuroses and personality disorders were relatively more common in the study group; nonstudy patients had typically stayed less than a month at the short term treatment hospital while study

---

[16] Columbus Psychiatric Institute and Hospital served the following thirteen counties in Ohio: Champaign, Clark, Delaware, Fairfield, Fayette, Franklin, Licking, Logan, Madison, Marion, Morrow, Pickaway, Union. Over 70 percent of the patients were from Franklin County, which includes the Greater Columbus Area.

patients had stayed closer to two months; finally, study patients were overwhelmingly voluntary and first admissions compared with the greater percentage of nonvoluntary and multiple admissions in the nonstudy group (see Table 3 in Appendix B). It appears, then, that by the exclusion of these patients and especially of the transfers, more of the chronic and severe cases of the state hospital type were omitted from the study.[17] However, the rationale for excluding patients with community tenure of less than two weeks was based on pretest interviews which had indicated that relatives found it difficult to assess the patient's role performance during so short a community stay.

DESCRIPTION OF THE STUDY PATIENTS

PSYCHIATRIC CHARACTERISTICS: ILLNESS AND PREVIOUS TREATMENT

At admission to the hospital (for the study hospitalization), a therapist, usually a psychiatric resident, had evaluated the patient's condition. At this point in their lives, two thirds of the women had never before been patients in a mental hospital (see Table 4.1). The remaining one third had been hospitalized in a mental institution at least once before. Although typically their first admission, the former patients were found by the admitting therapist to have been sick for six years on the average. Since admissions among this sample were voluntary in 97 percent of the cases, it may be speculated that in fact some serious signs and symptoms must have precipitated the hospitalization. Judging by therapists' ratings of the degree of impairment at admission, these were indeed sick women. Three quarters were rated as moderately or severely impaired, about one fifth were considered mild cases, and only a handful appeared to be just minimally impaired.

Despite the relatively severe impairment reflected by the therapists' ratings, the diagnoses given the former patients indicated the wide range of illness types represented. By far the largest single cate-

[17] The authors recognize that by omission of these 51 early failures, the more severely and chronically ill, we have loaded the case somewhat for adequate role performance as a variable in avoiding readmission, and we have increased the likelihood of finding good performers among the community patients.

Table 4.1. Psychiatric Characteristics of All Former Patients in the Study (in Percentages)[1]

Diagnosis		Prognosis at discharge	
Acute or chronic brain		Favorable	21
syndromes	11	Guarded	68
Functional psychotic	35	Unfavorable	11
Psychoneurotic	41	Impairment at admission	
Characterological	13	Minimal	6
Alcoholism or addiction		Mild	20
Yes	11	Moderate or severe	74
No	89	Impairment at discharge	
Number of previous admissions		Minimal	39
None	66	Mild	25
One or more	34	Moderate or severe	36
Hospital treatment		Posthospital care	
Received drugs	41	Psychiatric	28
No drugs	59	Nonpsychiatric	49
Received EST	14	None	23
No EST	86	Posthospital drugs	
Type of release		Tranquilizers or sedation	24
Maximum benefit	60	Other	31
Trial visit	16	None	45
Left against medical advice	24		

[1] N = 287 except in a few cases with missing data.

gory involved the psychoneuroses (41 percent). About one third were classified as psychotic, including mainly three types: schizophrenic, involutional psychotic, and manic depressive reactions. Another 11 percent were diagnosed as organically damaged with acute or chronic brain syndromes, including those associated with intoxication by alcohol, drugs or poison, and those associated with trauma, circulatory disturbance, convulsive disorder, senility, metabolism, and diseases of unknown causes. Another 13 percent involved personality disturbance and psychophysiologic complaints. In no case was alcoholism or drug addiction the sole diagnosis, since, in fact, hospital policy was to avoid such cases. Instead, alcoholism and addictions were associated with some other psychiatric diagnosis, usually with the organic categories for roughly 11 percent of the patients.

Characteristic of the short duration treatment policy, these patients stayed in the hospital 52 days on the average. But although a hospitalization of between one and two months was modal, 15 community patients were in the hospital for less than one week, while the longest stays were recorded for eight patients whose hospitalizations lasted about six months each. During hospitalization, the course of treatment could include one of four care types or some combination of these, chemotherapy, electroshock therapy, psychotherapy, and milieu therapy. Interestingly enough, the prescription and course of therapies could easily be known for the first two, but not for the other two. In the attempt to learn which patients received which therapies, it was found that every patient had been seen for some amount of time, however short, by a psychiatric resident, but how much time and with what frequency could not be ascertained even by highly intensive scrutiny of daily and summary records. For these reasons, only reports on the reliably designated therapies received by the former patients are given here.

Forty-one percent had received chemotherapy, consisting largely of tranquilizers, but some sedatives and stimulants were also included. The remaining women received no psychotropic drugs. To a relatively small percentage (14 percent), EST had been administered. Among the several types of discharges, the largest proportion of patients (60 percent) were released as improved or as having achieved "maximum hospital benefit." Another 16 percent were considered to be back home in the community on a trial visit, on which basis they could be readmitted without further paper work if that were necessary. Twenty-four percent had left the hospital without the therapist's consent: they were either AWOL or had deliberately contravened medical advice against discharge by signing themselves out.

Before a patient left the hospital, her condition was evaluated by her therapist. This assessment included specification of the degree of remaining psychiatric impairment and likely future condition. Therapists' ratings of these women were unfavorable for 11 percent, favorable for 21 percent and guarded for all the rest. At discharge, their therapists regarded 36 percent as still moderately or severely impaired, 25 percent as mildly impaired, and 39 percent as evidencing minimal or no remaining impairment.

To determine the extent of after-care services rendered these still substantially impaired patients, significant others were asked whether the former patient was under the care of a professional person during her community tenure, how many such contacts the patient may have had, and whether she had received any drug treatment during this time. It appeared that most former patients did receive some degree of posthospital care and from a variety of sources, mainly nonpsychiatric. For example, only 20 percent were receiving out-patient care from the hospital itself; 8 percent were being treated through community psychiatric clinics or private psychiatrists. Nearly half depended on nonpsychiatric sources, mainly a family doctor, but also ministers, social workers, or other nonmedical practitioners. A little over half the patients had received some type of drug treatment from these various sources: 24 percent received tranquilizers or sedatives, while 31 percent were treated mainly with other, presumably nonpsychoactive drugs. Thus, some form and amount of after-care was available to most of the community patients, but rarely in any regular or systematic fashion.

SOCIAL CHARACTERISTICS:
PERSONAL AND FAMILY BACKGROUND

In religion, race, and area of residence, the patients were predominantly Protestant, white, and urban—80 percent or more fit these characteristics (see Table 4.2). A wide range of ages was represented, from the youngest at 14 to the oldest at 77 years, but over two-thirds of this group were between 20 and 50; the average age was 41 years. In terms of their socioeconomic characteristics, the former patients included roughly equal proportions of lower class and middle class women. Judging from the distribution of scores on the modified Index of Status Characteristics, the patients were predominantly lower middle (35 percent) and upper lower class (38 percent). In terms of educational level, half of the group had one or more years of high school education, one fifth had some college, and a little over a quarter had completed grade school or less.

The patient was typically a married woman, living with her husband in a conjugal or nuclear family context, and mainly a housewife. More exactly, 63 percent of this group were married and 46 percent had children. The remainder of the patients were nearly equally distributed among these four marital statuses: single, divorced, separated, and widowed. One third of the women had worked at some time within the three years preceding hospitalization. In most cases, the

Table 4.2. Social Characteristics of All Former Patients in the Study (in Percentages)[1]

Race		Marital status	
White	86	Married	63
Negro	14	Divorced	11
Religion		Separated	7
Protestant	81	Widowed	9
Catholic and other	19	Single	10
Residence		Family type	
Urban	84	Conjugal	59
Rural	16	Parental	9
Age		Other	32
10-19	4	Relationship of significant	
20-29	21	other to patient	
30-49	49	Husband	61
50-59	12	Others: child, other kin,	
60+ years	14	nonkin	39
Socioeconomic status (ISC)		Household composition	
Upper middle	16	Significant other in house	81
Lower middle	35	No significant other in house	19
Upper lower	38	Patient's children in house	46
Lower lower	11	No patient's children in house	54
Education		Adult females in house	33
College, 1+ years	20	No adult females in house	67
High school, 1+ years	51	Adult males in house	79
Grade school	29	No adult males in house	21

[1] N = 287 except for a few cases with missing data.

former patient was not expected to be a breadwinner even in the event of the significant other's inability to work. Significant others were asked: "If the person you consider as the chief breadwinner became unemployed for some reason, who would you then count on as the chief breadwinner?" Close to 70 percent cited persons other than the former patient who would act as substitute breadwinners.

While for married women the household usually contained only the conjugal family members, wide variation obtained in the remaining cases. Of the former patients not living in conjugal families, 9 percent were living with one or both parents. Another 32 percent were residing in a variety of other contexts: with a brother or sister, son or daughter over age 16, and assorted relatives—aunts, uncles, nieces, nephews; a few with nonrelatives; the remainder lived alone in a rented room, apartment, or house.

The selection of subjects and the collection of data described in this chapter were designed to serve the general goal in this study of evaluating the outcome of short term mental hospitalization. We chose to attack the problem of evaluation in terms of the following questions: (1) What psychiatric and social variables characterized patients who were rehospitalized? (2) What psychiatric and social variables were related to successful functioning in the community? (3) How did former patients compare in their posthospital performance with normal women? In the three chapters that follow, each question is spelled out in detail, and the relevant findings are presented.

5

Rehospitalization: Illness or Rejection?

From a sociological perspective, readmission to a mental hospital signifies the patient's failure to adjust satisfactorily to the demands of family and community. Hospitalization and rehospitalization are taken as evidence of societal rejection and functional impairment. Total institutions such as mental hospitals, prisons, and training schools are seen as repositories for society's rejects—the misfits, the maladjusted, the dangerous and bizarre who cannot be integrated constructively in day-to-day life. These misfits are often only the victims of narrowly circumscribed behavioral standards and definitions. In a world that is urban, industrialized, automated, fast moving, and ever changing, the maladjusted have no place; they cannot compete. The one solution for them is confinement. This rationale is basic to the tolerance of deviance concept which other researchers and students of deviant behavior have presented in explaining institutionalization. The thesis is that, in effect, relatives, neighbors, and employers press for institutional confinement of the person who deviates.[1]

---

[1] Howard E. Freeman and Ozzie G. Simmons, *The Mental Patient Comes Home* (New York, John Wiley and Sons, 1963); Edwin Lemert, "Legal Commitment and Social Control," *Sociology and Social Research*, Vol. 30 (1946), pp. 370–378; and Dorothy Miller and William Dawson, *Worlds That Fail, Part II, Disbanded Worlds: A Study of Returns to the Mental Hospital* (State of California, Department of Mental Hygiene, Research Monograph No. 7, 1965).

Thus, a key criterion in the outcome of mental hospitalization involves the former patient's ability to avoid later readmissions. In this sense, success means remaining out of hospital while failure is signified by subsequent rehospitalization. In this chapter, attention centers on the failures, especially the early returnees, (those readmitted within six months), as well as on the total category of former patients readmitted within seven years of the study hospitalization. It was assumed early in the study that most of the potential returnees would be rehospitalized within six months, especially since other researchers reported this pattern.[2] Moreover, a distinction was made between early (pre-six months) and late readmission (post-six months) in order to learn whether the two sets of returnees were similar: did like factors operate in the readmission of both groups? First, some statistics on rehospitalization will be presented. Following this, the crucially precipitating factors will be examined.

Table 5.1. Number and Percentage of 92 Patients First Readmitted During Specified Periods After Discharge from the Study Hospitalization

Readmission Period	Number of Patients Readmitted	Percent Readmitted (Cumulative)
Discharge to 3 months	25[1]	27
4 to 6 months	16[1]	44
7 to 12 months	12	57
13 to 18 months	8	66
19 to 24 months	10	77
Within 3 years	6	84
Within 4 years	5	89
Within 5 years	5	95
Within 6 years	1	96
Within 7 years	4	100

[1] Early returnees.

[2] Cf. J. M. Wanklin, D. F. Fleming, Carol Buck and G. E. Hobbs, "Discharge and Readmission Among Mental Hospital Patients," *A.M.A. Archives of Neurology and Psychiatry,* Vol. 76 (December 1956), pp. 660–669; Miller and Dawson, *op. cit.;* and Benjamin Pasamanick, Frank Scarpitti and Simon Dinitz, *Schizophrenics in the Community* (New York, Appleton-Century-Crofts, 1967).

RATES OF ADMISSION

The early assumption that rehospitalization would occur most frequently within the six month period after discharge was only partly borne out. Thirty-two percent of the entire patient cohort had been readmitted at least once within seven years. If the percent of patients who first returned to hospital within six months is considered, it will be seen, as in Table 5.1, that the 41 early returnees composed 44 percent of the total 92 patients eventually readmitted over a seven year period; by one year after discharge, 57 percent, and by two years, 77 percent had been readmitted. However, the largest single number of returnees, 25 patients, were readmitted within three months and the 41 early returnees within six months. Thus it is clear that the rate of returning patients was higher those first six months than at any subsequent time. However, it was at twelve months after release that more than half of those destined to return actually became returnees.

If the *frequency of readmissions* to mental hospitals is considered (rather than the number of patients readmitted), there is strong evidence that the highest rate of return indeed clustered in the six month posthospital period. As shown in Table 5.2, 24 percent of the 177 known rehospitalizations occurred in this period; at no other later time period did as high a percentage of readmissions occur. Although the returnees averaged two readmissions each, the best information indi-

Table 5.2. Frequency of Readmissions Following the Study Hospitalization for a Seven-year Period

Readmission Period	Number of Patients Readmitted	Percent Readmitted (Cumulative)
0 to 6 months	42	24
7 to 24 months	39	46
3 years	25	60
4 years	20	71
5 years	19	82
6 years	12	89
7 years	20	100
Total readmissions	177[1]	100

[1] Based on 177 separate known readmissions to a mental hospital for an N of 83 patients, of which 37 were early and 46 were late returnees. Information on readmissions for the total of 92 returnees was not available.

cated that about three quarters of these returned patients had had only one readmission in the seven year period. The remaining one quarter of all returnees were characterized by multiple readmissions—typically three or four. It seems then that a minority of the returnees accounted for the bulk of actual readmissions. For the majority of all the patients, the probability of rehospitalization decreased as a function of time—the longer a former patient had avoided return, the less likely she was to be readmitted.[3]

PSYCHIATRIC CHARACTERISTICS OF EARLY RETURNEES

The best predictors of rehospitalization were factors operative in the posthospital situation and most especially the patient's mental status. This finding only partly supports the thesis that *prior psychiatric and other medical aspects were less important in readmission than were social factors*. The data indicated that while the hospitalization experience itself was not predictive of who remained in the community, the former patient's psychological functioning—along with several social variables—was highly related to the risk of readmission.

Rehospitalized patients could not be differentiated from successful patients either in terms of their total number of previous admissions, the illness duration preceding hospitalization, in their length of hospital stay, their ward assignment, or in the extent of out-patient treatment after release (see Table 5.3). Two thirds of all patients, regardless of outcome, had been first admissions. Illness duration prior to hospitalization was an average of 5.4 years for rehospitalized patients compared with 6.2 years for community patients. These differences were not statistically significant. In terms of the treatment received during the study hospitalization, returnees and community

---

[3] The 92 returnees of the original 287 patient cohort probably represent an underestimate of the *actual* number of returnees. Estimates of readmissions were based on more exhaustive checks up to two years after the study hospitalization. The exact number of returnees beyond two years was more difficult to establish at the seven year check point. Furthermore, because of the initial study restriction that patients remain out of hospital at least 15 days, another 51 *immediate* returnees had been automatically excluded. These were the patients who either transferred to another mental hospital or who were readmitted within two weeks. If these 51 cases were added to the 92 study returnees, the readmission rate for the whole cohort of discharges would be about 40 percent—much the same rate reported by other studies.

Table 5.3. Psychiatric Characteristics of Returnees and Community Patients[1]

Psychiatric Characteristics	Early Returnees (N = 41)	Community Patients (N = 246)
Nonpsychotic diagnoses[2]	44	55
Alcoholism or drug addiction	17	10
Illness duration (mean in years)	5	6
Length of hospitalization (mean in days)	59	51
First admissions	63	67
Received drugs in hospital	49	40
Received EST in hospital	15	14
Maximum benefit release	56	61
Guarded prognosis at discharge	75	68
Moderate-severe impairment at admission	73	75
Moderate-severe impairment at discharge	33	37
Received posthospital psychiatric care	35	27
Received posthospital psychiatric drugs[3]	43	21

[1] In percentages except for means where indicated; N's vary from 41 and 246 in a few cases where data were missing.

[2] Includes organic, psychoneurotic, personality disturbance, and psychophysiologic diagnoses.

[3] Using chi square, $p < 0.01$.

patients were similar. Neither treatment with electroconvulsive therapy nor with drugs related appreciably to subsequent readmission.

There was little doubt that hospital diagnosis emerged as important in predicting readmission. But this result is based on gross trends rather than on strong statistical significance. Returnees were clearly overrepresented among diagnoses indicating either acute or chronic brain syndromes. The percentages of psychotic and psychoneurotic patients did not differ appreciably. *Hence, only a diagnosis of organic damage could be considered a crucial indicator of readmission within six months of discharge.* Closely connected with the major diagnosis was the presence or absence of addiction symptoms. As expected, the ability to avoid readmission was to some extent tied to lack of alcoholism or drug addiction. Only 10 percent of former patients had a history of addiction compared with 17 percent of the returnees.

Judging from the findings on diagnostic differences between returnees and community patients, there was some indication that returnees represented the more severely impaired patients. There was support for such an interpretation in the tendency for returnees to have been hospitalized longer (59 days on the average compared with 51 days for successful community patients). Returnees had also more frequently availed themselves of psychiatric help sources during their brief community stay than did community patients, and significantly more returnees received chemotherapy between hospitalizations. Forty-three percent compared with the 21 percent of community patients received drugs after release.

The type of discharge granted the patients differed significantly. Among returnees, 27 percent had been released on trial visit as contrasted with 14 percent of community patients. Apparently, there was some doubt on the part of the hospital staff as to the ability of one quarter of the returnees to function in the community. But the therapists' inability to predict outcome accurately was best demonstrated by their prognostic ratings of the patients at discharge. Favorable prognoses were given to 19 percent of the returnees, a percentage not very different from the 21 percent of former patients in the same prognostic category.

SOCIAL CHARACTERISTICS OF EARLY RETURNEES

Of these five demographic characteristics—age, race, religion, urban-rural residence, and social class—none appeared to have any marked relationship to rehospitalization. As shown in Table 5.4, those patients who returned to a hospital did not differ greatly from former patients in the community with respect to these characteristics. However, it is interesting to note certain trends of difference between rehospitalized and former patients.

Consideration of background factors such as race and religion indicated some tendency for rehospitalized patients to be white rather than Negro and to include more Catholics than the community patient group. Patients with rural backgrounds were more frequently found in the readmitted group than in the community group. In general, however, the entire group of patients in the study was predominantly

Table 5.4. Social Characteristics of Returnees and Community Patients[1]

Social Characteristics	Early Returnees (N = 41)	Community Patients (N = 246)
Age (mean in years)	41	41
Religion: Protestant	76	82
Race: White	93	85
Urban residence	78	85
Married	69	62
Living in a conjugal family	59	59
Husband as significant other	62	60
Significant other in household	80	81
Patient's children in household	49	44
Adult males in household	79	78
Adult females in household	41	30
Middle class patients	61	49
High school education	61	50
In fair or poor house types	48	59
Average dwelling area	42	41

[1] In percentages except for age. N's vary from 41 and 246 in a few cases because of missing data.

white, urban and Protestant, and the predominance of these characteristics applied to both rehospitalized and former patients. The slight differences in the readmitted group appeared to be due to chance variations rather than meaningful trends.

Social class level, like the above-mentioned factors, did not clearly distinguish returnee from community patients. But the distribution of patients on class-related variables showed a somewhat greater likelihood for rehospitalized patients to be lower middle class. Former patients, on the other hand, were more likely to be of lower class background than those who reentered a hospital. It has been proposed that lower class persons, in general, wait longer before seeking treatment than middle and upper class persons. This delay in seeking treatment by lower class persons might explain their tendency to remain in the community, although they may be as sick as higher class persons who seek readmission sooner. The same variables which cause the initial delay in seeking treatment are probably also involved in the greater tendency for lower class patients to delay seeking further treatment.

THE FAMILY SITUATION

Clearly, gross descriptive attributes of the patient and her family did not associate significantly with readmission. Next to be considered, then, is the family context—the situation prevailing in the patient's household. When the relationship between readmission and household composition was assessed statistically, no significant differences appeared between returnees and former patients. However, certain factors seemed to be more operative for the rehospitalized group. A somewhat greater percentage of married women were readmitted than remained in the community. Whether the patient lived alone without other adults or within a family context did not seem to affect readmission. Nor did it matter whether any adult males lived with her. On the other hand, the presence of both adult females and the patient's children in the household were more characteristic of readmitted than community patients.

SIGNIFICANT OTHER'S EXPECTATIONS AND READMISSION

For the period that the patient was in the community before being rehospitalized, she was subject to the feelings, expectations, and attitudes of the family members with whom she lived. The reactions to her former mental patient status and to having her in their midst may have played a role in her ability to remain in the community. A wide range of general attitudes was presumably involved, including conceptions of what mental illness entails and whether it is curable, a view of the mental hospital as a treatment setting or as a mere custodial institution.[4] More specific attitudes may have centered on the

[4] See for example, Elena Padilla, Jack Elinson and Marion Perkins, "Some Aspects of the Public Image of Mental Health Professionals and the Acceptance of Community Mental Health Services," Paper presented at the annual meeting of the American Public Health Association, Chicago, 1965; and Jum Nunnally, "The Communication of Mental Health Information: A Comparison of the Opinions of Experts and the Public with Mass Media Presentations," *Behavioral Science*, Vol. 2 (July 1957), pp. 222–230.

family member who had been a patient. Is she recovered or still sick? How shall we treat her? What can be expected of her now? Can we manage to keep her home?

Of immediate concern here are the expectations for patient behavior between hospitalizations with a view to understanding how these expectations may have related to readmission. It has been suggested that, in the family situation, the manifestations of abnormal behavior and the consequent inability to live up to familial expectations are likely to lead to institutionalization of the deviant person.[5] Thus, rehospitalization may be understood as the result of the family's high role expectations and unwillingness to have a deviant member at home, rather than in terms of how ill the patient may be. High expectations, especially if these are unreasonable, may reflect the family's refusal to have any but an adequately performing member in their midst.

The evidence for the patients readmitted within six months of discharge largely refuted such an assumption about familial intolerance of deviant behavior. When rehospitalized and community patients were compared on the expectations held by their respective significant others, it was found that returnees had been subject to consistently lower expectations between hospitalizations than were community patients since discharge. In other words, the expectations for returnees were lower in all areas and not higher as the tolerance hypothesis would predict. As shown in Table 5.5, significant others of returnees had a mean expectation score of 30 compared with the significantly higher score of 36 for relatives of community patients. On all expectation items, except the two involving child care and one concerned with family shopping, significant others of community patients held higher expectations than those held for the returnees. Most of the usual social and domestic activities had been significantly less ex-

[5] See Edwin Lemert, *op. cit.;* J. Sanbourne Bockoven, "Some Relationships between Cultural Attitudes Toward Individuality and Care of the Mentally Ill: An Historical Study," in Milton Greenblatt, *et al., The Patient and the Mental Hospital* (Glencoe, Illinois, The Free Press, 1957), pp. 517–526; and Ozzie Simmons and Howard Freeman, "Mental Patients in the Community: Family Settings and Performance Levels," *American Sociological Review*, Vol. 23 (1958), pp.147–154. Cf. also T. P. Rees, who pointed out the possible benefits to patients if they can be tolerated and treated in the community instead of being cut off and isolated during treatment. See "Some Observations on the Psychiatric Patient, the Mental Hospital and the Community," in Milton Greenblatt *et al., op. cit.*, pp. 527–529.

Table 5.5. Percentage of Significant Others of Returnees and Community Patients Who Expected Specific Activities

Activities	Expected of Returnees (N = 37)	Expected of Community Patients (N = 231)	P[1]
Dust, sweep, and other usual cleaning	68	86	0.01
Help with the family shopping	65	80	
Entertain people at home	38	75	0.01
Dress and take care of herself	89	98	0.05
Handle the grocery money	43	71	0.01
Prepare morning and evening meals	62	84	0.01
Take care of laundry and mending	57	83	0.01
Dress and bathe the children[2]	100	97	
Make sure the children get to school on time[3]	72	98	
Go visit friends and relatives	49	89	0.01
Get along with family members	76	97	0.01
Get along with the neighbors	68	94	0.01
Go to parties and other social activities	30	65	0.01
Hold a job full time or part time	8	33	0.01
Mean significant other expectations score	30	36	0.01[4]

[1] Based on chi square with 1 df.
[2] Based on N = 9 for returnees and N = 68 community patients with preschool children.
[3] Based on N = 18 returnees and N = 84 community patients with school age children.
[4] Critical ratio between mean scores.

Source: Adapted from Shirley Angrist, Simon Dinitz, Mark Lefton and Benjamin Pasamanick, "Rehospitalization of Female Mental Patients," *Archives of General Psychiatry, 4* (April, 1961), p. 365, by permission of The American Medical Association.

pected of returnees. Even so, the routine self-care and household tasks and the ability to get along with people were more frequently expected of returnees than were behaviors such as entertaining people at home, going to visit others, and holding a job. This tendency to expect just routine task performance and little social participation outside the home was reflected in comments made by relatives of rehospitalized patients:

The only thing I insisted on was that she try to keep herself cleaned up.

I didn't think she should take part in any religious or social groups because she just didn't feel like seeing people.

Thus, the expectations of the significant others appeared to be far from demanding or excessively high.

Several important implications of this finding deserve mention. Firstly, the hypothesis that readmission was due to high rather than low expectations did not appear to apply to this group of returnees. Secondly, there is a circularity involved in interpreting such a finding. The circularity stems from the fact that significant others of rehospitalized patients were interviewed *after* the readmission occurred. This means that the view held of the patient may have changed consequent to the change in her status from community patient to rehospitalized patient. Once the woman was rehospitalized, the significant other may have modified his expectations from those held while she was home. The relative might conceivably report lower expectations once readmission has occurred even though his actual expectations were likely to have been higher while the woman was home. The difficulty here lies in retrospective reporting of what he expected while she was home. Since she had been readmitted, the relative may feel the patient neither performed well while home, nor could he expect much of her, (the definition of the period between hospitalizations was colored by the fact of readmission), which may itself imply the patient's failure to make a satisfactory adjustment. This problem of interpretation also suggests that the proposition that high expectations are associated with return cannot be tested after readmission but should ideally be tested *before* rehospitalization occurs. In this way, the *post hoc* definition of the patient would largely be avoided.

Thirdly, it is interesting to note that the pattern of expectations for rehospitalized patients differed from that for community patients. Most community patients were expected to perform the basic domestic and social activities. On the other hand, the rehospitalized group was subject to varying expectations—some behaviors were frequently expected, while others were expected only by a small percent of significant others. This, taken in combination with the generally lower expectations held for readmitted patients, suggests that a realistic mode of accommodation may have been operating for community patients and rehospitalized patients alike. The higher expectations for the group remaining in the community may have reflected the greater ability of these patients to perform their roles; perhaps they were not only the better role performers but they may also have been less sick than the patients who went back to a hospital. The level of expectations held for the respective groups might thus mirror the realistic condition and status of each group. Furthermore, the consistent pattern of high expectations for former patients may suggest that, in general, the woman who could remain in the community was expected to do well in all areas of her role, and she may, in fact, have been able to live up to those expectations. The readmitted woman may have been able to do well in some areas but not in others; if this was so, the expectations of her significant other could reflect his accommodation to her actual deficits. Or he may more readily have demanded behaviors which were easier to perform, such as the cooking and cleaning, getting along with household members, and taking care of herself, while excusing those which required contact with nonhousehold members. In either case, it is suggested that this accommodation factor or corrosion process may explain both the lower level and the inconsistency of expectations held for readmitted patients.

PERFORMANCE, ILLNESS, AND REHOSPITALIZATION

Thus far, the analysis has shown that role expectations may have played an important part, but familial factors had only a very tenuous connection and treatment aspects no part at all in rehospitalization. But none of these variables reflect the woman's actual ability to perform in the community—the extent to which she performed socially and domestically and her psychological condition between readmissions. At this point it is necessary to evaluate whether the woman's ability to carry out her role had anything to do with returning to hospital.[6] Could the patient destined to become an early returnee perform as well in the community as the former patient who avoided readmission? Was readmission mostly a matter of low expectations

---

[6] In this context, posthospital performance becomes an independent variable potentially operative in rehospitalization. The reader is reminded that posthospital performance is a dependent outcome variable in the following chapter on social and psychiatric variables affecting performance.

and more intolerant significant others, for example, or was there objective verification of the returnee's inability to perform satisfactorily during her short community tenure?

The three measures of performance described in Chapter 4 were used to assess posthospital performance both for community and rehospitalized patients. For both groups, significant others reported whether the patient had performed each of a series of domestic tasks and social activities and exhibited specific intrapsychic symptoms. In the area of domestic performance, comparison of rehospitalized and former patients indicated that although the readmitted group tended to perform somewhat less well on all tasks than the patients who remained in the community, their overall performance did not differ significantly from that of community patients. In fact, the two patient groups tended to be high performers in the same areas (see Appendix B, Table 7). Thus, taking care of laundry, preparing meals, and cleaning house were generally well performed by both rehospitalized and nonrehospitalized women. With regard to social participation, only slight and far from significant differences emerged between the two groups. On the whole, as shown in Appendix B, Table 8, the returnee was comparable in her social participation to the community patient. The readmitted patient was noticeably less active in but one activity—having friends to her home.

Of the three performance areas, it was in psychological functioning that the two groups differed most clearly and dramatically. The rehospitalized patients manifested more abnormal symptoms and more of these women had each symptom than the community patients. Of the 32 symptom items, 23 significantly differentiated the returnees from nonreturnees (see Table 5.6). Compared with the mean psychological functioning score of 86 for community patients, returnees had a mean of only 75, a highly significant difference. As compared to the community patients, returnees manifested the more severely disordered behaviors, such as paranoia, hallucinations, antisocial behavior including excessive swearing, sexual misbehavior, disorientation, and suicidal or homicidal behavior. Returnees exhibited these extreme symptoms *as well as* the postural awkwardness, restlessness, somatic preoccupations, depression, and anxiety typifying the community patients. *It appears then that the readmitted group as a whole had exhibited more deviant behavior, a wider range of symp-*

Table 5.6. Percentage of Returnees and Community Patients Manifesting Specific Psychological Symptoms

Symptoms	Returnees (N = 38)	Community Patients (N = 228)	P[1]
Made no sense when talking	53	15	0.01
Walked, sat or stood awkwardly	40	11	0.01
Moved around restlessly	90	56	0.01
Swore, cursed often compared to other women	37	19	0.05
Always seemed worn out or tired	90	74	
Tried to hit or hurt someone	16	9	
Lacked control of toilet habits	3	5	
Said she hears voices	29	4	0.01
Did not want to see people	82	35	0.01
Just hung around the house doing nothing	61	36	0.01
Tried to hurt or kill herself	21	4	0.01
Got drunk often	24	7	0.01
Got grouchy or bad-tempered	63	59	
Misbehaved sexually	11	6	
Needed coaxing to do what is expected of her	53	28	0.01
Had trouble going to sleep	84	53	0.01
Took many pills	50	17	0.01
Needed help dressing, bathing or going to the toilet	13	3	0.05
Did not know what went on around her	40	7	0.01
Acted tense or nervous	97	76	0.01
Thought she is sinful or evil compared to other people	40	12	0.01
Thought people want to control or harm her	37	18	0.05
Worried about her bodily organs	37	29	
Mumbled or talked to herself	13	12	
Tried to get her way by saying she has pains	34	15	0.05
Got depressed suddenly	84	56	0.01
Said she sees people who are not there	24	2	0.01
Worried about her health	58	50	
Teased and picked on people	8	14	
Thought people are watching her or talking about her	42	22	0.05
Expected bad things to happen in the future without good reason	55	20	0.01
Did not eat well	68	33	0.01
Mean psychological functioning score	75	86	0.01[2]

[1] Based on chi square with 1 df.
[2] Based on critical ratio between means.

Source: Adapted from Shirley Angrist, Simon Dinitz, Mark Lefton, Benjamin Pasamanick, "Rehospitalization of Female Mental Patients," *Archives of General Psychiatry, 4* (April, 1961), p. 367 by permission of the American Medical Association; and adapted from Simon Dinitz, Shirley Angrist, Mark Lefton and Benjamin Pasamanick, "The Posthospital Psychological Functioning of Former Mental Hospital Patients," *Mental Hygiene, 45* (October, 1961), p. 585. By permission of The National Association for Mental Health.

toms, and had manifested more extreme or acutely disordered symptoms than the former patients who avoided readmission.[7]

Support for the finding that readmission tended to select patients with a greater number of and more florid symptoms came from the relationship of diagnosis to both performance and readmission. It was assumed for this purpose that the diagnosis describing the woman's illness during the study hospitalization could be taken as an index of the type and severity of her illness.[8] Indeed, it was found that the type of diagnosis was highly related to both readmission and performance level (see Appendix B, Table 9). The rehospitalized group more often than the former patient group included organic disorders and less often included the characterological or milder disorders. Hence, a diagnosis of organic damage was a predictor of rehospitalization. Unfortunately other diagnoses failed to differentiate readmitted from former patients so clearly. But one conclusion is clear: the rehospitalized patient was more likely to have been diagnosed as having a

---

[7] At this point, it is interesting to consider the relationship to readmission of each performance measure. The inability of the social participation and domestic performance measures to discriminate rehospitalized from former patients, while psychiatric functioning did yield such differences, may be interpreted in at least two ways. The measures used here were perhaps not valid or appropriate; or they may have been ineffective because they tapped more than one type of activity or dimension. Whatever their methodological defects, the two measures may well reflect the comparative irrelevance of social and domestic activities for measuring patient performance. It can be argued that the woman who manifested few symptoms was performing well, regardless of whether she cooked, cleaned, watched TV, or visited with the neighbors. That is to say, the social and domestic activities were not crucial or central indicators of the patient's condition (see Tables 7 and 8 in Appendix B). Whereas role performance did not differentiate returnees from community patients, it was psychological functioning which revealed the distinctions between readmission versus community tenure for the patient sample. It appears, therefore, that even if the woman did not perform adequately in her domestic duties or social obligations, she would not likely be rehospitalized unless she also exhibited a number of abnormal symptoms or some especially striking deviant behaviors. High risk for readmission appeared to characterize the individual whose behaviors were highly unusual or bizarre, or of an episodic nature, with lower readmission risk for those with chronic low level symptoms (*e.g.,* the process schizophrenics).

[8] Of course, it cannot be certain that the diagnosis was correct when it was made, or that it applied after release. It is safe to assume, however, that posthospital symptoms, when they existed, were likely to be similar to those manifested when the diagnosis was made. Since we are dealing with gross diagnostic categories rather than specific ones, such an assumption is not likely to be far out of line.

more severe disorder *during* treatment and was also found to be functioning less well than the community patient *after* treatment.

THE SIGNIFICANT OTHER'S VIEW OF READMISSION

Aside from assessing the association between readmission, performance and illness in a quantitative framework, the views held by relatives of returnees were also elicited concerning the events that led to rehospitalization. Significant others were asked what they considered to be the *main* reasons for readmission. This provided a baseline for determining the extent of congruence between these perceived precipitators of readmission and the actual psychological condition of the returnee while she was still in the community.

When asked which symptoms may have led to readmission, relatives described the whole range of deviant behaviors, mild and severe. Some women were rehospitalized for such comparatively mild symptoms as "headaches," others because they "just could not cope with everyday living." The symptoms thought to cause readmission included somatic problems, delusional behavior, nervousness, depression or other forms of withdrawal, alcohol or drug intoxication, and other specific bizarre behaviors. Of these reasons, episodic and drastic incidents were commonly reported as the chief precipitants to return:

She walked around naked with just a straw hat on, staring at the sky.

My wife woke up during the night and wouldn't talk. She didn't seem to know what was going on. Before that she had seemed fine.

She just didn't act right. She was very nervous and would sit in one chair for a long time and then walk back and forth all the time.

I thought she should go back to the hospital because of her terrible temper and I worried she might hurt the babies when she was all riled up.

About one quarter of the patients were returned for extreme and unmanageable behaviors involving specific attempts to hurt themselves or others.

It is interesting to note that the patient was most often rehospitalized for the same kind of symptoms that she was reported as manifesting before readmission. Both as a group and in the individual case, the symptoms characteristic of the rehospitalized patient's psychological functioning were also thought to be the reasons that led to readmission. Of all the patients described as manifesting a given symptom between admissions, over half were readmitted for that symptom. The tendency was, however, for a smaller number of symptoms than the patient actually exhibited to be considered as contributary causes of return.

It was also true in most instances that not a single dramatic episode, but a cluster of bizarre behaviors was seen by relatives as leading to readmission:

> She copied stuff from the Bible and talked of killing others. She was also afraid someone would kill her.

> My sister tore off her clothing and refused to dress. She has a terrible temper and it got worse because of being alone so much.

> She was sleepless and depressed over the noises in the highway construction. She took too many pills, and when under the influence of drugs she didn't know what went on.

Significant others were likely to describe such clusters of problems in most cases, and they specified single main reasons for readmission only because they were encouraged to do so. Thus even episodic factors rarely involved single items of deviant behavior; more often a series of problematic behaviors by the patient was considered as the factor in rehospitalization.

Thus, as a group, returnees were indeed sicker and poorer role performers than those remaining in the community. There were some, however, who performed socially and domestically as well as good performers in the community. These patients also manifested few symptoms and frequently their behavior was as "normal" as that of those community patients whose psychological functioning showed little deviant behavior. Contrarily, there were community patients who were as inadequate in all performance areas as rehospitalized patients. Thus, while, as a whole, rehospitalization selected sicker and more poorly functioning individuals, it also included a small number of good performers who were readmitted in spite of adequate role performance. When the *main* reasons for return given by relatives were studied, there was some evidence to suggest that the high performing returnee was likely to have manifested one of the more drastic and less tolerable symptoms. What seems to have occurred for this group was a single incident or a series of behaviors critical and frightening enough to the family to warrant readmission.[9] There is little doubt that this critical reactive episode triggered readmission for the high level performer. Without such an episode, rehospitalization might not have occurred for some time, if at all.

It was psychological functioning that differentiated the returnees from poor performers who remained in the community. Both returnees and poor community performers tended to have an overrepresentation of organic cases and after release they manifested a large number of abnormal symptoms. And both groups were generally low in overall psychological functioning. *However, it was the specific nature of the symptoms manifested* that differentiated them. The readmitted group was high in delusional and hallucinatory behavior, in suicidal attempts, and in disoriented behavior. The low performers tended to suffer from chronic and low level symptoms such as excessive worries over health and bodily organs, irritability, and incontinence. In effect, then, the rehospitalized group was characterized by acute and florid signs and symptoms while the low performers who remained at home evidenced less acute problems which are often difficult to manage but rarely threatening or anxiety provoking in character.

DIFFERENCES BETWEEN EARLY AND LATE RETURNEES

As interesting as the comparison between the returnees and the low performers who remained at home is the contrast between early and late rehospitalization. This section is concerned with the extent to which women who were rehospitalized beyond the six month follow-up were similar to or different from those readmitted earlier.

Among the series of psychiatric characteristics only the type of discharge from the study hospitalization differentiated the 51 late from the 41 early returnees (see Table 5.7). Nearly half of the early returnees had either left hospital against medical advice or on trial visit. On the other hand, of the later returnees, 75 percent had been dis-

---

[9] Cf. Scheff's concept of "residual deviance" as the explanatory factor in the definition of the person as mentally ill. See Thomas J. Scheff, *Being Mentally Ill: A Sociological Theory* (Chicago, Aldine Publishing Company, 1966).

Table 5.7. Psychiatric Characteristics of Patients Rehospitalized Before and After Six Months from the Original Discharge (in Percentages)[1]

Psychiatric Characteristics	Early Returnees	Late Returnees
Nonpsychotic diagnoses	44	39
Alcoholism or drug addiction	17	14
Illness duration: less than one year	36	54
Length of hospitalization: 45 or more days	54	53
First admissions	63	69
Received drugs in hospital	49	53
Received EST in hospital	15	16
Maximum benefit release[2]	56	75
Guarded prognosis at discharge	73	75
Moderate-severe impairment at admission	73	77
Moderate-severe impairment at discharge	33	38

[1] For returnees before six months N = 41 and after six months N = 51 except for smaller N's in a few cases due to missing data.

[2] Using chi square with 2 df, $p < 0.05$.

charged under the official MHB heading (they had received maximum hospital benefit, and this was usually construed as prognostically hopeful). In line with this difference was the tendency for late returnees to have had a shorter history of illness at the time of the study hospitalization compared with early returnees. One might say, then, that the later returnees had better outcome potential than those returning earlier.

The background characteristics appeared to distinguish the two groups of readmitted patients in two areas: social class and familial status. As shown in Table 5.8, the late returnees were significantly less well educated than their early counterparts. Among the latter, 26 percent had some college and 61 percent had some high school education; by comparison, 41 percent of late returnees had only grade school education. There was a significant clustering of Protestants among the late group compared with a higher percent of Catholics in the early group. Insofar as the proportion of Negroes was greater among the late returnees, one might hypothesize that race and religion

Table 5.8. Social Characteristics of Patients Rehospitalized Before and After Six Months from the Original Discharge (in Percentages)[1]

Social Characteristics	Early Returnees	Late Returnees
Age: 30 to 49 years old	62	56
Religion: Protestant[2]	76	94
Race: White	93	82
Urban residence	78	75
Married	69	52
Living in a conjugal family	59	50
Husband as significant other	62	49
Patient's children in household	49	42
Adult males in household	80	72
Adult females in household	44	44
Grade school education[3]	13	41

[1] For returnees before six months N = 41 and after six months N = 51 except for smaller N's in a few cases due to missing data.

[2] Using chi square with 2 df, $p < 0.05$

[3] Using chi square with 2 df, $p < 0.01$

may be class related for this sample of patients, so that later returns were more selective of lower class rather than middle class women.

The familial characteristics of late returnees indicated a trend for them more often to be unmarried (single, widowed, divorced, and separated) contrasted with the higher proportion of married women in the early returnee category. Fewer, of course, lived in conjugal settings, and in less than half of the cases was a husband the significant other. These results might be interpreted to mean that perhaps lower class and nonconjugal families were more willing to keep former patients at home and for a longer time before seeking readmission. Further, the unmarried women may have been able to delay readmission because fewer pressures would be exerted on them to perform or to seek further treatment—if the married patients were deficient, their need for further treatment might well have stemmed from the exigencies of domestic responsibilities.

Most crucial of all was the fact that the later returnees were clearly better performers while in the community between hospitalizations as indicated by significantly higher mean scores in the total performance and psychological functioning indices. The tendency held also for social and domestic performance as shown in Table 5.9.

The post-six month group of returnees compared favorably with the *total* community patient group in their performance level. *They particularly resembled moderate performers* in the community. Thus, unlike the low performance levels of the early returnees, the later returnees came from the group of former patients who had functioned fairly well and had been exposed to high expectations while in the

Table 5.9. Mean Scores on Four Performance Measures for Early and Late Returnees

	Early Returnees (N = 38)	Late Returnees (N = 49)	P[1]
Domestic performance	15.7	16.6	
Social participation	53.2	56.8	
Psychological functioning	75.2	85.5	0.01
Total performance	143.7	158.9	0.01

[1] Based on critical ratio between means.

community.[10] The low performers, whose illness was of a chronic nature, did not constitute more than a small percentage of community patients who were later readmitted. In a sense, one could attribute this to their very chronicity—the chronically ill patient and her family had probably adjusted to her limited functioning and made appropriate allowances for it. Moderate and high performers, contrarily, continued to be subject to relapse for which their significant others were either unprepared or which they could not or would not tolerate.

The findings on rehospitalization are important for several reasons. From the point of view of explaining readmission or the ability

[10] The mean expectation score held by significant others of early returnees was 29.5 compared with a mean of 36.2 for late returnees, which difference was significant at $p. < 0.01$.

to avoid it, it is interesting that many former patients can remain in the community as long as seven years before needing further hospitalization and that their relatives do not rush to readmit them. Indeed, the data show that relatives view readmission as a last resort for behavior which cannot be handled without medical help. Such patients may be well suited to systematic out-patient care or a home care program. These types of community facilities might then help the patient to avoid or to ameliorate the episodes which necessitate institutionalization. From a treatment standpoint, it suggests that patients whose relapse does occur early should have been hospitalized initially for a longer period. This raises the important issue of the efficacy of short term hospitalization. Of the original study group of 287 patients, 32 percent were readmitted at least once within seven years of discharge. These women *obviously* needed further treatment. It is possible, then, that the short term treatment setting is inadequate for a substantial proportion of mental patients and that other forms of intensive therapy are called for in such cases. For example, the notion of the day hospital (where patients spend daytime hours and return home in the evening as they might from a job) may be relevant here. Or again, the idea of the halfway house, which makes the transition from institution to community more gradual and systematic, is another alternative. The dichotomous institutions of long term custodial state hospital contrasted with the short term intensive therapy hospital leave large gaps in the needed continuum of treatment modes. Hopefully, the emerging community mental health facilities will fill this gap.

6

Factors Affecting Posthospital Performance

In this chapter, the concern is with the question: what social and psychiatric variables play a part in the level of posthospital performance of the former patients? It was shown in the preceding chapter that 86 percent of the former patients could avoid readmission for a reasonable length of time—six months in this case—but their ability to function in the community covered a wide range from low to high level performance socially, domestically, and psychologically. It becomes important to know what contributed to or fostered this variation in performance level. Furthermore, did the hospitalization experience including treatment received and length of stay have any bearing on posthospital performance or was it the set of social conditions operative in the former patients' community context that influenced performance level, or perhaps both?

Problems in differential diagnosis by therapists, the prevalence of trial-and-error nonspecific treatment, and emerging evidence that living arrangements and other social conditions after release may relate to outcome contributed to skepticism about the effects of psychiatric variables on posthospital performance. Both in existing treatment facilities and for the developing community mental health centers, it is clearly desirable to be able to predict patients' behavior prospectively so that valid and useful decisions can be made about readiness for release and appropriate types of after-care. The difficulty in predicting posthospital adjustment derives in part from the lack of understanding of the etiology of most of the mental diseases. It also derives partly, however, from the diversity of objective and subjective factors—prehospital, hospital, and posthospital—which seem to play some role, singly and in combination, in determining posthospital performance.

The foci of interest in this chapter are described by the following questions:

1. Is there a relationship between posthospital performance level and the following psychiatric variables: diagnosis, illness duration, number of admissions, length of hospitalization, type of hospital treatment, ward assignment, type of release, prognosis at discharge, degree of impairment at admission, degree of remaining impairment at discharge, type and extent of outpatient care after discharge?

2. Is there a relationship between posthospital performance level and the following personal and family characteristics of the former patients: religion, race, place of residence, age, family type, marital status, and the presence of adult males and females and children in the household?

3. Is there a relationship between posthospital performance level and indicators of social class, such as the modified Warner Index of Status Characteristics, the former patient's education, house type, dwelling area, and the Hollingshead Two Factor Index of Social Position?

4. Is there a relationship between posthospital performance level and the role expectations for the former patient, including the woman's own expectations for her social and domestic performance, the significant other's expectations, and the extent of their agreement on these role expectations?

5. Is there a relationship between posthospital performance level and the significant other's tolerance of deviance, that is, the extent to which he is willing to keep at home a former patient who manifests abnormal behavior?

PSYCHIATRIC VARIABLES AND POSTHOSPITAL PERFORMANCE

In the series of twelve psychiatric variables analyzed for their relationship to posthospital performance, only one variable was conspicuous for its signal significance (see Table 6.1). This was the association between the diagnoses assigned to the former patients during hospitalization and three of the four performance measures; only social participation was unrelated to diagnosis. It will be recalled that patients were distinguished into arbitrary thirds according to their performance scores. The contrast of low performers in the community with moderate and high performers lay primarily in their frequency of organic diagnoses. Thus the key psychiatric characteristic of low performers was the preponderance of the organic syndromes whereas high level community patients had functional and nonpsychotic disorders primarily. A related pattern of relationship but not a significant one was the tendency for alcoholism and addiction to occur only rarely among high performers and to characterize mainly low performers.

In the realm of treatment received by former patients, three variables bore some association to posthospital performance. These involved both inhospital and posthospital care. Drug therapy was received during hospitalization by low performers more frequently than high performers. Only one third of the high performers had been treated with drugs compared with half of the low performers. The type of care received between discharge and the follow-up time served to distinguish low from high level patients. Thus, psychiatric care either from the hospital's outpatient clinic or private sources was utilized by 32 percent of high performers but only by 18 percent of the low performers. In contrast, care from nonpsychiatric sources, such as general practitioners and nonmedical persons, was reported for 62 percent of the low community patients compared with 48 percent of high performers. Although no exact data were obtained on the type of out-patient treatment these women received, there was some indication that those receiving psychoactive and assorted nonpsychiatric drugs were predominantly the low performers.[1]

For the remaining psychiatric variables studied, no relationships to posthospital performance approached statistical significance, but

---

[1] We found it difficult to obtain systematic, reliable, and valid information on the extent and types of care patients received in the community. This was probably a function of both respondents' ignorance about specific drugs and dosages and the insufficiency of the questions. Thus, we hesitate to place much confidence in these figures on after-care.

Table 6.1. Psychiatric Variables Associated with Posthospital Performance[1]

	Performance Measure			
Variables	Total Performance	Domestic Performance	Social Participation	Psychological Functioning
Diagnosis	++	+	−	++
Posthospital treatment	+	−	++	+
Posthospital drugs	++	−	−	++
Hospital drug treatment	+	−	+	−
Hospital EST	−	−	−	+
Ward assignment	−	−	−	−
Impairment at discharge	−	+	−	−
Impairment at admission	−	−	−	−
Type of discharge	−	−	−	−
Prognosis at discharge	−	−	−	−
Number of admissions	−	−	−	−
Illness duration	−	−	−	−
Length of hospital stay	−	−	−	−
Alcoholism or drug addiction	−	−	−	−

[1] Relationships between pairs of variables are indicated with ++ for $p < 0.01$, + for $p < 0.05$, and − for no statistical significance.

some trends were evident. For example, low performers tended to have been sick for a longer period before admission, to have more previous admissions, to have been hospitalized for somewhat less time, to have left hospital more often against medical advice, to have less favorable prognoses, and to have more severe impairment at discharge from the hospital.

It must be concluded then that the expected lack of relation between psychiatric variables and community performance was supported overwhelmingly with the sole exception of diagnosis. *There is little doubt that hospital diagnosis is crucial in predicting posthospital performance.* Essentially, a diagnosis of organic impairment is an excellent predictor of poor posthospital performance while diagnoses of other than the psychoses are predictive of higher level functioning. By comparison, the treatment received during hospitalization did not relate to later performance. One would expect hospital drug therapy to facilitate later performance, and particularly since it is a comparatively major mode of treatment to be able to show its ameliorative if not curative value. That this appeared not to be the case among the former patients suggests a likely practice of treating the more impaired patients with drugs.

Although ward assignment ordinarily cannot be construed as a relevant psychiatric variable in posthospital performance, earlier evidence from the hospital studied pointed to the contrary.[2] Since patients were typically assigned randomly to three hospital wards on the basis of available space and were subjected to widely different ward treatment procedures, ward assignment could be considered an indirect measure of treatment and hence a potentially meaningful medical factor in outcome. It has been reported elsewhere that the three wards housing women did in fact differ widely in policies and practices of care and treatment. It was shown that these differences had little bearing on the overt behavior of patients on any of the wards. Now, to this must be added the result that ward differences have little significance for posthospital performance.

[2] See, for example, Benjamin Pasamanick, Simon Dinitz and Mark Lefton, "Psychiatric Orientation and Its Relation to Diagnosis and Treatment in a Mental Hospital," *American Journal of Psychiatry,* Vol. 116 (August 1959), pp. 127–132.

SOCIAL BACKGROUND CHARACTERISTICS AND POSTHOSPITAL PERFORMANCE

Whereas it has been shown so far that the psychiatric variables, excepting diagnosis, were at best weakly connected with posthospital performance, the results to be reported in this section indicate that stronger ties existed between the former patient's background characteristics and her performance in the community. Particular reference is made here to the important role of the familial setting in which the former patient lived since hospitalization.

The social characteristics which bore no relevance for posthospital performance among the community patients were the strictly demographic variables of religion, race, residence, and age. As shown in Table 6.2 the predominantly Protestant, white, urban character of the sample did not yield any striking differences among low, moderate, and high performers. No single performance area related to religion or urban background. There was some tendency for race to associate with total performance so that Negro women clustered in the moderate and high categories and whites in the low category, but this was probably because Negro women at the hospital were of disproportionately higher socioeconomic status than white women. There was also a trend for older women to be among the low performers whose mean age was 43.5 years compared with the average age of 40 years for high performers. This age trend was most operative in social participation so that more activity characterized the younger women.

Consideration of the family context in which the former patient lived indicated that a series of interrelated factors operated as important elements in the woman's level of posthospital performance. *The former patient's marital status, and accordingly, the type of family of which she was a part, the composition of her household, and her particular role in it—all had consequences for performance.* Other studies have previously shown that former patients who are married are better performers than patients in other marital categories.[3] This

---

[3] Howard E. Freeman and Ozzie G. Simmons, *The Mental Patient Comes Home* (New York, John Wiley and Sons, 1963); Leta M. Adler, "The Relationship of Marital Status to Incidence of and Recovery from Mental Illness," *Social Forces*, Vol. 32 (December 1953), pp. 185–194. Cf. also the evidence that married patients, especially females, have higher release rates and lower readmission rates compared to nonmarried patients; this may be viewed as indirect evidence of higher performance and higher expectations for the married. See Philip H. Person, Jr., *Hospitalized Mental Patients and the Outcome of Hospitalization* (Washington, D.C., The American University, 1964).

Table 6.2. Social Variables Associated with Posthospital Performance[1]

	Performance Measure			
Variables	Total Performance	Domestic Performance	Social Participation	Psychological Functioning
Patient's ISC score	++	+	++	++
Patient's house type	++	−	++	++
Patient's dwelling area	++	−	++	+
Patient's education	++	++	+	−
Significant other's education	++	−	+	−
Marital status	++	++	++	−
Family type	++	++	++	−
Relationship of significant other to patient	++	++	++	−
Number of adult females in household	++	++	+	−
Significant other in household	+	+	++	−
Children in household	++	++	++	−
Number adult males in household	−	−	++	−
Race	+	−	−	−
Age	−	−	++	−
Religion	−	−	−	−
Urban-rural residence	−	−	−	−

[1] Relationships between pairs of variables are indicated with ++ for $p < 0.01$, + for $p < 0.05$, and − for no statistical significance.

has been interpreted by Freeman and Simmons, for example, to mean that wives of psychotic patients are less accepting or less tolerant of deviant behavior and have higher expectations for the patient's performance than do mothers. The patient is then obliged to live up to these expectations or he is returned to the hospital. A second explanation has also been posited, namely, that sicker patients are handicapped in finding a mate and therefore fail to marry or else they cannot remain married. These two explanations are not necessarily incompatible, and data from the present study tend to support both interpretations.

In order to test the thesis that married patients tended to be less ill at both admission and at discharge than were those single, divorced, and separated, an analysis was made using (1) the therapists' ratings of patient psychiatric impairment at admission and at discharge and also their prognosis of outcome, and (2) four scales (schizophrenia, psychasthenia, depression, hysteria) of the Minnesota Multiphasic Personality Inventory (MMPI)—a diagnostic test routinely administered at admission and discharge. A second analysis compared the MMPI results, the rating of psychiatric impairment at admission, and at discharge, and the prognoses given patients returning to one of several types of living arrangement, conjugal, parental, sibling, child, nonkin, alone. The results of these analyses indicated that neither the degree of psychiatric disability at admission, nor at discharge, as rated by the therapist, were at all related either to whether the patients were married or nonmarried or to the type of household to which they were returned. The same held for the MMPI results and the psychiatrist's prognosis of case outcome.

Thus, marital status and living arrangements after discharge were not selective of more seriously impaired patients. Yet these same variables were found to be very highly related to posthospital performance. Married patients were found to be underrepresented among the low and overrepresented among the high performers. Eighty percent of the high performers were married compared with 47 percent in the low category. Over half of the low performers were single, widowed, divorced, or separated, even though these marital categories made up only a third of all the former patients. Stated somewhat differently, the high level performer was found to be living in a conjugal family with her husband, rather than with parents, adult children, siblings, other relatives, or alone. Under all living arrangements other than the conjugal setting, former patients performed at a lower level.

Of the several nonmarried categories of community patients, the widows—who were close to 60 years old, likely to suffer from chronic brain syndromes, and usually living alone, with an adult child, or other kin—had the lowest total performance scores and were particularly lowest in the psychological and social participation areas. The single women did moderately well in the latter two areas but were poor in domestic performance. The divorced and separated compared favorably with the married in their psychological condition but ranked somewhat below them in domestic performance and social participation; still, these women from dissolved marriages were the best performers of the nonmarried community patients, while the widowed women ranked lowest. Lest this performance disadvantage of the nonmarried patients be doubted, let it be said here that these former patients could not perform at the level of the nonmarried in the control group of normal women. The control group performed at a higher level in all three performance areas, but especially in domestic and psychological functioning.[4]

[4] A more detailed description of the nonmarried former patients and their neighbors is presented in Shirley Angrist, Simon Dinitz, Mark Lefton and Benjamin Pasamanick, "The Unmarried Woman After Psychiatric Treatment," *Mental Hygiene,* Vol. 51 (April 1967), pp. 175–181. It is important to add one note concerning the familial variables. There was a consistent pattern for each of the family characteristics to be significantly associated with domestic performance and social participation but not with psychological functioning; this is evident in Table 6.2. The higher scores for married patients on performance may partly reflect bias in the items composing the domestic performance measure perhaps due to emphasis on household tasks, family activities, and care of children. But care was taken to stipulate to respondents that all items referred to the patient's household, regardless of her marital status or with whom she lived. If a patient lived alone, items dealing with meals, laundry, and cleaning were taken to refer to the patient's provision for her meals, having laundry done, dusting, and sweeping her room or apartment. Where a patient had no children, the two items on care of children were given the middle weight for that item. Thus the investigators felt reasonably confident that this potential bias was foreseen and provided for. Since social participation related to the family variables just as did domestic performance, the issue may instead involve the independence of the patient's psychological condition from the household context, so that symptoms may have troubled the former patient because of the nature of her illness rather than because of the specifics of relationships. This interpretation will find support in a subsequent section where it is indicated that the role expectations of the former patient herself and her significant other affected primarily domestic and social performance areas, while minimally relating to the patient's psychological functioning.

Further consideration of the family situation yielded the general finding that when no role replacements were available for the former patient and when household members were directly dependent on her role performance, the woman tended to be a high performer. Thus, the presence of adult females other than the patient was associated with low performance generally, especially in the domestic and social areas. By contrast, when adult males (including the husband) lived in the household, the former patient was likely to be a high performer, most notably in the extent of her social participation. Similarly, women with children under the age of 16 at home were significantly higher in performance than childless ones. Finally, the fact that the former patient was employed or that she would be employed if the usual breadwinner were unable to work was associated with higher performance levels primarily in the domestic realm. The pattern which emerged from these disparate factors indicated the importance for the former patient of the nuclear family, particularly one including young children; no other women except the patient herself were available to carry out the usual homemaking responsibilities.

Thus, the results so far appear to support the notion that high level performers predominated in conjugal settings because husbands would rehospitalize low level performers while other significant others would be accepting of low performers. The issue here revolves around the idea that spouses tolerate deviant behavior significantly less than other relatives. Lest these results be interpreted directly and immediately in this way, it must be pointed out now that a distinction needs to be maintained between tolerance as a generic explanatory concept and the measure of tolerance used here, which referred to the significant other's willingness to house a former patient who manifests abnormal symptoms. In the latter sense, it will be reported later that no familial variables were related significantly to tolerance of deviance. At this point, it can be said that although wives performed better than widows, divorcees, and single women, one should not conclude that husbands were simply intolerant of low performance in the sense of symptom manifestation. It will be shown shortly that role expectations as well as the patient's performance level played a part in the significant other's view of her.

SOCIAL CLASS AND POSTHOSPITAL PERFORMANCE

Traditionally in American sociology, social class has been invoked as a key explanatory variable in behavior. It has been used to describe or explain a variety of attitudes, aspirations, and behaviors in terms of their class relatedness, such as leisure pursuits, educational aspirations, occupational choice, authoritarianism, voting behavior. Of concern here is the possible association of social class to the whole constellation of illness and health in American society including the incidence and prevalence of certain diseases at given social levels, the manner and machinery for treating the sick, and the chances of good outcome after treatment. In particular, the mental disorders have been shown to be differentially prevalent among the social class categories so that members of the lower class have been high risks for mental illness, for less adequate treatment access, and for questionable outcome.[5] If, as has been suggested, class has to do with tolerance of deviant behavior, then it may affect the community performance of women who have been treated for mental disorders.[6] In other words, one would expect lower class persons to be more accepting of abnormal or unusual behavior while middle class persons should be less tolerant of the bizarre or unusual. Thus, poorly performing patients in middle class families should be unable to remain in the community; their relatives would be expected to rehospitalize them more readily. In this way, middle class women who remain in the community must be adequate performers compared with lower class former patients who would be tolerated by their families even if they performed poorly.

In this section, the issue of class as a variable in posthospital performance will be presented in two ways—first, in terms of the general findings for all community patients, and second in terms of a more refined analysis which isolated a homogeneous segment of mar-

---

[5] August B. Hollingshead and Frederick C. Redlich, *Social Class and Mental Illness* (New York, John Wiley and Sons, 1958); and Leo Srole, Thomas Langner, Stanley Michael, Marvin Opler and Thomas Rennie, *Mental Health in the Metropolis: The Midtown Manhattan Study* (New York, McGraw-Hill, 1962).

[6] Howard E. Freeman and Ozzie G. Simmons, *op. cit.*

ried patients from the larger sample. It will be shown that at a crude level, social class appeared to associate with posthospital performance, but in the light of more refined analyses this result could not be accepted at face value.

The general picture relating class with performance for community patients was one of a consistently significant association between the two sets of variables (see Table 6.2). To begin with, the patient's score on the Warner Index of Status Characteristics related to all areas of performance, so that higher performance characterized the higher status former patients. Whereas the high performers were typically middle class, low performers tended to have lower ISC scores. Much the same pattern of relationship held for other more specific indicators of social class. The former patients who were low performers clustered in the lower educational level, having received mainly grade school or high school educations compared with the higher proportion of high performers who received some college education. Reference to the specific seven point scales making up the ISC, that is, dwelling area, house type, and education, yielded the same results—higher status on each variable associated with higher performance.

However, the relationship of social class to posthospital performance changed when a more refined analysis was carried out with a homogeneous group of married community patients. The intention was to eliminate possible biases introduced into the larger community patient sample from the fact that women who were single, divorced, widowed, or separated had been judged both for social class estimation and for performance identically with married women.[7] By restricting attention to married women, the relationship between social class and posthospital performance received its severest test. This was so simply because the married patients had already proved to be

[7] Since the ISC and the Hollingshead ISP yielded comparable social class breaks for the women studied, the ISP was used whenever data for only married women were analyzed because of the ease of computing and utilizing the ISP. When the sample was limited to married former patients, several other limiting conditions were introduced. Only those women were included who were white, functionally rather than organically impaired, not addicted to alcohol or drugs, living with husband, and both the former patient and her husband had been interviewed. The narrowed sample consisted of 62 women representing 43.7 percent of the married community patients and 25 percent of the total 246 community patients. These 62 women were assigned scores on the Hollingshead Two Factor Index of Social Position on the basis of the husband's occupation and education.

better performers. If social class level could differentiate among these generally good performers, it would pass such a test. In fact, it did not. Using both Pearsonian correlations and the t-test between mean scores, no association was found between any performance area and social class level.[8]

Can one then conclude that social class is unrelated to performance? At this point it appears that class played no *direct* part in posthospital performance. It will shortly be demonstrated that class did operate to influence performance *indirectly* through the class-related role expectations held up for the former patient.

ROLE EXPECTATIONS AND POSTHOSPITAL PERFORMANCE

It is a key proposition of sociological theories of behavior that behavior is related to expectations. In role theories, especially, the proposition prevails that individuals know how to perform their roles largely in terms of the expectations they themselves associate with their roles as well as the expectations held up for them by important persons with whom they regularly interact.[9] This proposition consists of two not always explicit assumptions. First, in any reciprocal relationship each of the actors adjusts his performance to the perceived expectations of the other. Were this not so, there would cease to be any rationale for the continuation of the relationship and behavior would become idiosyncratic. Second, the expectations of others are founded not only on common and shared experiences with the actor but on the ability of the actor to perform his role. Since this ability may at times be impaired to a greater or lesser extent, the expecta-

---

[8] The Pearsonian r values between the ISP scores and each performance area were: $r = .13$ with domestic performance, $r = .09$ with social participation, $r = .05$ with psychological functioning, $r = .12$ with total performance.

[9] See for example, Edwin J. Thomas and Bruce J. Biddle, "Basic Concepts for Classifying the Phenomena of Role," *Role Theory* (New York, John Wiley and Sons, 1966), pp. 23–45; Theodore R. Sarbin, "Role Theory," in Gardner Lindzey, Ed., *Handbook of Social Psychology* (Cambridge, Massachusetts, Addison-Wesley, 1954), pp. 223–258; William A. Rushing, "The Role Concept: Assumptions and Their Methodological Implications," *Sociology and Social Research*, Vol. 49 (October 1964), pp. 46–55; Neal Gross, Ward S. Mason and Alexander W. McEachern, *Explorations in Role Analysis* (New York, John Wiley and Sons, 1958); and Robert K. Merton, "The Role-Set: Problems in Sociological Theory," *British Journal of Sociology*, Vol. 8 (June 1957), pp. 106–121.

tions of others with regard to the performance of the person should continually be in a limited state of flux: it is possible for the significant others to expect more or less of the actor over time and within limits. In short, the assumption is that not only does performance tend to measure up to expectations but conversely, expectations also tend to reflect performance. In these reciprocal relations between actor and significant others, it is therefore impossible to specify which of the two variables—expectations and performance—is independent and which dependent except in operational terms.

It was assumed that such a process of interpersonal relations should be relevant also to former mental patients—that their behavior ought to be generally consistent with the expectations appropriate for their roles as women, housewives, and mothers. Further, the significant other's expectations may not coincide with the former patient's own expectations; his views and comprehension of what could be reasonably expected of her might differ. They may indeed disagree on what must be done by the woman and what can be feasibly omitted by her. Therefore, the interest in expectations and performance was extended to include the former patient's self-expectations, her significant other's expectations, and the extent of their agreement or disagreement.

Further, role expectations as a variable may implicate other variables, including the social class dimension of role behavior and the illness dimension. The way in which family members treat their relative who has recently left a mental hospital is likely to reflect diffuse and class-related attitudes about mental illness, about mental hospitals, the specific hospital staff members and treatment policies, and the severity and duration of the patient's illness prior to, during, and after hospitalization. Ideas about her former mental patient status, reactions to having her at home, and the reliance on her for specific family functions should be involved in the expectations for her performance: can she take care of the house, see people, go shopping? Will she stay inactive for awhile or perhaps act strangely again? Therefore, the whole set of psychiatric and social factors that might affect any relationship between expectations and performance were taken into account, especially since some of these factors were shown earlier to affect posthospital performance. When the findings for the association of each type of expectations—the former patient's self-expectations, those of her significant other, and their expectation agreement—have been presented, those intervening psychiatric and social variables which related to expectations and mediated between expectations and performance will be described.

THE FORMER PATIENT'S SELF-EXPECTATIONS

How did these self-expectations of the patient correlate with her performance level? The findings indicated that the two variables were closely associated: *the high level performer tended to have high expectations, and conversely, low expectations characterized the low level performers.* Furthermore, the relationship held for all areas of performance, except for psychological functioning.[10] For the criterion groups of high and low performers, it was found that their mean scores on patient expectations differed significantly on all four measures of performance. High performers had higher mean expectations scores than did low performers. In fact, high performers fully expected to perform all types of activities compared with the lesser expectations of low performers (see Table 6.3). Thus the high performers in the community expected to be doing housecleaning, family shopping, entertaining people at home, handling grocery money, preparing meals, visiting friends or relatives, and attending social activities to a significantly greater degree than did the low performers. However, high and low performers were similar in their self-expectations concerning personal care, care of children, getting along with people; they were even comparable in the proportions of those who expected to be working outside the home.

Ten of the 14 expectations could be matched with actual performance items. When these items were compared for each patient as in Table 6.4, it was found that the woman who carried out most of the domestic and social tasks was also likely to feel that she should do these things: the woman who felt she ought to carry out these behaviors was, in fact, likely to do so. One woman explained:

> I feel I should be doing everything for my own mental health.

[10] Using a contingency coefficient as a measure of correlation, patient expectations correlated with each performance area as follows: with domestic performance $C = .54$, $p < 0.01$; with social participation $C = .31$, $p < 0.05$; with total performance $C = .42$, $p < 0.01$; with psychological functioning $C = .20$ which was not statistically significant.

Table 6.3. Percentage of High and Low Performers Who Expected to Perform Each Item

Item	High Performers (N = 74)	Low Performers (N = 76)	P
Dust, sweep, and do other usual cleaning	99	86	0.01
Help with the family shopping	96	80	0.01
Entertain people at home	87	57	0.01
Dress and take care of herself	100	99	
Handle the grocery money	87	59	0.01
Prepare morning and evening meals	95	83	0.05
Take care of laundry and mending	96	88	
Dress and bathe the children[1]	100	80	
Make sure the children get to school on time[2]	100	91	
Visit friends or relatives	95	76	0.01
Get along with family members	99	92	
Get along with the neighbors	100	93	
Go to parties and other social activities	77	51	0.01
Hold a job full time or part time	39	41	
Mean score on patient expectations	38	35	0.01

[1] Based on N = 41 of high and low performers with preschool children in the household.
[2] Based on N = 58 of high and low performers with school age children in the household.

Conversely, the woman who had difficulty performing well was less likely to hold high expectations for her own performance. This was expressed variously by two women:

> No, I can't entertain because I'm not at ease yet.

> I feel I should get out of the house more, but I can't due to lack of finances, all the housework, and the children.

While high performers expected to be doing everything except hold a job, the expectations of low performers were high only in some areas: getting along with family and neighbors, care of children and self, and domestic chores, but not formal social activities.

The generally high congruence between what the patient expected of herself and the tasks she actually performed (as reported by

Table 6.4. Percentage of Community Patients Who Expected to Perform and Actually Performed Specific Items[1]

Item	Expected and Performed	Did Not Expect Did Not Perform	Expected Did Not Perform	Did Not Expect, Performed
Dust, sweep, and other usual cleaning	65	6	29	0
Help with family shopping	36	9	54	0
Handle the grocery money	48	23	27	2
Prepare morning and evening meals	68	9	22	0
Take care of laundry and mending	70	7	22	1
Dress and bathe the children	85	0	12	3
Make sure the children get to school on time	83	1	15	1
Entertain people at home	60	7	17	16
Visit friends and relatives	82	6	6	6
Hold a job full time or part time	24	58	16	2

[1] N for the first five items is 224; N = 67 for item six; N = 88 for item seven; N = 227 for the last three items.

the significant other) was evident from the fact that over 60 percent of the women felt they should do the house cleaning, meal preparation, laundry, look after their children, and visit friends or relatives—and they did in fact carry out these behaviors. But in other areas, neither the performance nor the expectations were high: namely, in handling grocery money and holding a job. It is very probable that for many of these women, handling money was not a part of their usual role just as working outside the home was not part of their current life pattern. On the other hand, child care responsibilities were most frequently both expected and performed. It is also likely that the inability to perform certain tasks may have led to a modification of expectations, so that those items were not expected which could not be carried out because of the patient's condition.

This overall congruence between expectations and performance was not present for a minority of patients in several areas, as shown in Table 6.4. Some of the community patients performed well in most areas despite their professed lack of expectations; for example, 16 percent did not feel they needed to entertain and yet they did so. The other type of discrepancy between expectations and performance was the reverse case—in which the expectations were not matched by performance. In general, however, the pattern of relationships between performance and expectations held for most of the former patients, so that the higher the former patient's expectations for her role performance, the higher her actual performance level.

SIGNIFICANT OTHER'S EXPECTATIONS

Significant others tended to expect more in the domestic sphere and less in the social and job spheres; this was a realistic reflection of what the former patients actually did. They performed most actively in the domestic tasks around the house and in care of children when they had any. Nevertheless, social activities were not neglected, and in this respect the women also closely approached the level of activity expected by the significant other. The pattern of association reported above for self-expectations and performance held also for the significant other's expectations and the former patient's performance. *High performers were subject to expectations that were significantly higher than the expectations held by relatives of low performers.* The woman who carried out the various behaviors was generally also expected to do them. Conversely, the poor performer was less likely to be expected to perform well. A significant other stated:

> If she continues to improve, I'd expect her to do these things, but not now.

The greatest contrast in the expectations held up for low and high performers was in the whole range of domestic responsibilities, such as housecleaning, shopping, preparing meals, getting laundry done, caring for children, as well as in social participation involving having people over to the house, visiting with friends and relatives, and participating in social activities (see Appendix B, Tables 10 and 11). The three items on which significant others made no distinction between good or poor performance by the former patient included a basic expectation held up for nearly all the women—that she take care of her personal needs—and the little expected items that she hold a job and get the children off to school.[11]

So far it has been shown that expectations and performance were tied together but it has not been indicated which is the cause or which is the effect in this coupling. The findings provide strong support for the assumption enunciated earlier that a process of interaction and mutual influence appears to operate between what an individual is capable of doing and what is expected of him by those with whom

---

[11] There is an important indication that the relationship between significant other expectations and total performance was largely a function of the close association between expectations and the specific area of domestic performance. Using contingency coefficient as the measure of association, significant others' expectations were found to correlate significantly and positively with the index of total performance ($C = .50$, $p < 0.01$ and with domestic performance ($C = .67$, $p < 0.01$). The close connection between the role-related expectations of the significant other and the woman's domestic performance warrants comment particularly because no such relationship was obtained with social participation or psychological functioning. Two explanations have plausibility. One interpretation indicates that since the expectations measure tapped largely domestic behaviors, the performance and expectations items were overlapping and perhaps contaminated by each other. However, although social participation activities were also included in it, the expectations measure still did not appear related to actual social participation. A second interpretation points to the possibility that instrumental role expectations were indeed closely linked to instrumental role performance. In that sense, psychological functioning may not have been relevant directly to role performance, and social participation may have been only secondarily relevant compared with the centrality of the woman's domestic responsibilities in her role performance.

he interacts. Thus the behavior of former patients was adjusted to the expectations of significant others, while others in turn modified their expectations in terms of the individual's characteristics and abilities. It appears that self-expectations related to performance in the same manner so that women who expected to perform adequately actually did so. Can one then conclude that the two sets of expectations, self- and other, were either the same or very similar since both related positively to performance? This question is considered next.

AGREEMENT IN EXPECTATIONS

Agreement in outlook and attitudes has for some time been considered by sociologists to be a crucial variable in satisfactory interpersonal relations. Such a viewpoint especially has been built into studies of marital adjustment.[12] However, sociologists have taken a second look at the role of harmony in interaction, and some have questioned whether agreement can be assumed to be functional in interpersonal and group relations.[13] It is the purpose of this section to report findings on the relation between agreement in expectations and performance, without making any prior assumptions whether agreement itself is a desirable end in the interaction of the former patient with her significant other.

Unlike the separate measures of self- and significant other's expectations, the measure of expectation agreement yielded only a trend of association with performance. In general, the pattern was for high agreement to be related to high performance in all areas. However, the clearest association was with domestic performance.[14] The strong relationship of expectation agreement to domestic performance was consistent with the pattern of association reported for self- and significant other expectations with domestic performance. Just as expec-

[12] Cf. Ernest W. Burgess and Harvey J. Locke, *The Family* (New York, American Book Company, 1945), and more recently, Nathan Hurvitz, "The Measurement of Marital Strain," *American Journal of Sociology,* Vol. 65 (May 1960), pp. 610–615.

[13] Cf. Lewis Coser on the *Functions of Social Conflict* (Glencoe, Illinois, The Free Press, 1956), who points to the overemphasis on agreement and harmony in social interaction. Cf. also Neal Gross, *et al., op. cit.,* who urge sociologists not to assume that agreement in expectations exists among actors in a role-set.

[14] The contingency coefficient was .46, $p < 0.01$. No statistically significant association was obtained for expectation agreement with social participation, psychological functioning, or total performance.

tations per se appeared crucially centered on the woman's domestic responsibilities, the degree of agreement in expectations between her and the significant other also focused on the primacy of homemaking tasks (see Table 6.5). Thus fulfillment of child care tasks was highly expected both by significant others and former patients, and in fact, these were the most frequently performed. Also fairly highly demanded by both sets of persons were the cleaning, cooking, and laundering tasks, and again these were typically carried out by most of the former patients. The main social activity to be highly expected

Table 6.5. Percentage of Former Patients and Their Significant Others Who Agreed on Specific Expectation Items[1]

	Agreed		Disagreed	
Item	Both Expected	Did Not Expect	Patient Expected More	Other Expected More
Dust, sweep, and other usual cleaning	86	4	9	1
Help with family shopping	77	8	12	3
Entertain people at home	64	13	12	11
Dress and take care of herself	98	1	1	0
Handle the grocery money	65	17	12	6
Prepare morning and evening meals	82	6	9	3
Take care of laundry and mending	82	7	10	1
Dress and bathe the children	94	1	2	3
Make sure the children get to school on time	93	2	5	0
Go visit friends and relatives	81	3	7	9
Get along with family members	94	1	2	3
Get along with the neighbors	91	1	5	3
Go to parties and other social activities	50	18	16	16
Hold a job full time or part time	28	56	12	4

[1] Based on N = 225 for all items except for item eight where N = 67 of former patients with preschool children and item nine where N = 88 of former patients with school age children in the household.

Source: Adapted from Simon Dinitz, Shirley Angrist, Mark Lefton, and Benjamin Pasamanick, "Instrumental Role Expectations and Posthospital Performance of Female Mental Patients," *Social Forces*, 40 (March, 1962), p. 251. By permission of University of North Carolina Press.

and performed was that the former patient go to visit friends and relatives. On the whole, then, there was a tendency for expectation agreement between patient and significant other to implicate those items which in fact the patient did perform, particularly in the domestic realm.

However, there emerged a striking difference in the relation of each set of expectations to the patient's performance. The significant other's expectations were more in line with the woman's actual performance than were her own expectations. Not only did she tend to expect more of herself than he did, but the significant other's expectations coincided more nearly with what she was able to do.[15] If the former patient put excessive demands on herself because she felt these things were required, she was obviously overestimating her significant other's expectations. In actuality, he seems to have been the more realistic appraiser of what she could do, insofar as his expectations corresponded more closely to her behavior.

EXPECTATIONS AND PERFORMANCE: INTERVENING VARIABLES

The relationship between performance and expectations could be simple and concise if it were not already clear that other factors were operating which themselves influenced expectations or performance or both for the former patients studied. A major factor affecting the expectations both of former patient and significant other was the patient's type of illness; a second set of variables involved the composition of the patient's household; third was the interrelation of social class and expectations.

The community patients' performance levels had been shown earlier to be related to the nature of their illnesses. That is, the diagnosis of an organic disease was significantly associated with low per-

[15] The authors are aware of the methodological pitfall embedded here. The possibility is considered that since the significant other's expectations and the patient's performance were *both* reported by the significant other, these measures may be contaminated rather than independent of each other; they would, therefore, logically be highly correlated. But it is relevant to note that patient expectations—which were reported by the patient herself—also associated highly with performance and significant other expectations, ($C = .42$ and $.79$, respectively, $p < 0.01$), indicating that the significant others' reporting may be accurate and not necessarily biased. This point was further supported by the psychiatrists' rating of functioning—an independent measure—which agreed with our performance assessment.

formance. It may now be observed that diagnosis also played a part in expectations—both the former patient and her significant other tended to have lower expectations for her performance if she was diagnosed as having an organic brain syndrome, while their expectations were moderate or high for the women diagnosed as psychoneurotic or characterologic. As summarized in Appendix B, Table 12, no other psychiatric variable was as significantly related to expectations; however, there were tendencies for other illness indicators to reinforce the association between diagnosis and expectations. For example, proportionately more patients subject to low expectations had been on drugs after hospitalization, had been rated as at least moderately impaired upon hospital discharge, and had been given unfavorable prognoses. Further, the patients subject to low expectations had been ill longer before admission, and cases complicated by addiction or intoxication also concentrated among them. Clearly, then, here is evidence for the general hypothesis that expectations may be influenced by the former patient's ability to perform. Thus, her illness condition may have affected the expectations held up for her; one cannot assume that behavior was solely a *resultant* of expectations.

The level of patient and significant other expectations could also be interpreted in terms of social characteristics as presented in Appendix B, Table 13. The patient's age was inversely related to expectations so that women subject to low expectations averaged 46 years compared with 40 years for the moderate and 37 years for the high expectation categories. The data also showed that husbands held higher expectations for their wives' performance than did any other types of significant others. Married community patients had higher expectations for their own role performance than single, divorced, separated, or widowed women. Conjugal households with young children present but lacking other adult females (who might act as role replacements) contained an overwhelming preponderance of the high expectation patients and significant others. In summary, it appears that high expectations for instrumental performance occurred precisely in those family situations in which adequate performance of the routine female role was most necessary. The lowest expectations existed in those households containing persons available to serve as role substitutes for the former patient. In this respect, *high expectations and high performance appear to be crucially interrelated with the need or demand for role performance: one performs when the obligations and the expectations to perform exist, or the expectations are held up for the person because no one else can execute these behaviors.*

Sociologists have long contended that expectations vary with social class factors such as education, occupation, and zone of residence. The present data certainly supported this contention. For example, college educated former patients and their significant others had a significantly higher level of expectations than did those with only a grade school education. Similarly, using the Warner ISC instrument as a measure of class, upper middle class persons had the highest, and lower class persons the lowest expectations for patient role performance; these relationships are summarized in Appendix B, Table 13. Since it was reported earlier that performance and class were similarly related so that higher performance characterized the middle class patients, this result might have been accepted as consistent and final. Instead, exploration in depth of the class-expectations-performance link was carried out by restricting attention to the married former patients who represented the generally good performers subject to high expectations.

For 62 married community patients and their husbands, it was found that social class correlated positively with the expectations of both patients and husbands.[16] Thus although for this refined sample class had not been associated with performance, class was linked with expectations. It was further found that among the expectation items, those dealing with domestic chores did not differentiate middle from working class respondents, while the social expectations largely contributed to the higher expectations held by middle class patients and their husbands. Given these facts, then: (1) that social class was not related to performance; (2) that social class was related to expectations; and (3) that expectations correlated significantly with performance—a major conclusion follows, that despite the absence of a statistically demonstrable relationship between social class and performance, these variables were nevertheless related to each other in a meaningful if not direct manner.

In an effort to assess the nature of this relationship to expectations, a further analysis was undertaken by construction of a typology

[16] For scores on the Hollingshead Index of Social Position and patients' expectations $r = .33$, $p < 0.01$, for ISP scores and husbands' expectations $r = .28$, $p < 0.05$.

based on the dichotomization of social class into middle and working class categories and total performance into high and low levels. Mean expectation scores were then computed for each of the cells derived: middle class-high performance; middle class-low performance; working class-high performance; and working class-low performance (see Table 6.6). *These results indicated that middle class women whether*

Table 6.6. Mean Expectation Scores of 62 Patients and Husbands by Middle and Working Class Positions and High and Low Performance Level

	Middle Class High Performance (N = 12)	Middle Class Low Performance (N = 9)	P[1]
Patients' Expectations	33.83	33.44	N.S.
Husbands' Expectations	33.92	33.11	N.S.

	Working Class High Performance (N = 19)	Working Class Low Performance (N = 22)	P[1]
Patients' Expectations	33.58	30.86	0.01
Husbands' Expectations	33.47	31.45	0.05

[1] Based on t-tests between means.

Source: From Mark Lefton, Shirley Angrist, Simon Dinitz, and Benjamin Pasamanick, "Social Class, Expectations and Performance of Mental Patients," *American Journal of Sociology, 68* (July, 1962), p. 85. By permission of the University of Chicago Press.

they were high or low performers were not subject to differential expectations—quite the contrary, wives and husbands of middle class status maintained high expectations despite the woman's low performance. By contrast the working class wives and husbands differed significantly in their role expectations—high expectations were held up for high performers but lower expectations for low performers. In short, *the expectations for middle class women appeared to be independent of performance, while those of working class women were a function of their ability to perform those very same activities.* Since the differences in expectation scores were due largely to the behaviors concerning social rather than strictly domestic activities as is evident from Appendix B, Table 14, these findings reflect the oft-documented middle class bias toward the purely social amenities of role performance. One wonders then whether the former patients accepted the class-related norms for role performance any less than do women in the general population. Perhaps both their role expectations and their performance were indeed representative of normal or never psychiatrically treated women. This issue is raised speculatively here. The question will be pursued in detail in Chapter 7 where the former patients will be systematically compared in all areas of performance with the control group of their normal neighbors.

TOLERANCE OF DEVIANCE AND POSTHOSPITAL PERFORMANCE

A principal concern in this study of outcome was the relationship between tolerance of deviance on the part of significant others and the former patient's ability to perform. By tolerance of deviance was meant the extent to which families were willing to keep at home one of their members who manifested abnormal symptoms. If a former patient who was unable to carry out instrumental role performance could remain in the community, then it was likely to be due to tolerance by significant others or to their expectation that some deviant behavior will occur.[17]

It has been argued that in an urban, industrial, fast-changing society, deviance—whether its form be crime, juvenile delinquency, pregnancy out of wedlock, or mental illness—becomes threatening and the deviant is burdensome to family members. Especially in the case of mental disorder, institutionalization may be an easy solution for behavior which in other periods of history or in other societies has been tolerated without undue discomfort to family or society.[18]

[17] See Howard E. Freeman and Ozzie G. Simmons, "Mental Patients in the Community: Family Settings and Performance Levels," *American Sociological Review*, Vol. 23 (April 1958), pp. 147–154; and Ozzie G. Simmons and Howard E. Freeman, "Familial Expectations and Posthospital Performance of Mental Patients," *Human Relations*, Vol. 12 (November 3, 1959), pp. 233–242.

[18] Edwin M. Lemert, "Legal Commitment and Social Control," *Sociology and Social Research*, Vol. 30 (May 1946), pp. 370–378; G. Morris Carstairs, "The Social Limits of Eccentricity: An English Study," in Marvin Opler, *Culture and Mental Health* (New York, Macmillan, 1959), pp. 373–389; and Joseph W. Eaton and Robert J. Weil, *Culture and Mental Disorders: A Comparative Study of the Hutterites and Other Populations* (Glencoe, Illinois, The Free Press, 1955).

Among the former patients studied there was a wide range of performance levels, as well as a range of role expectations to which these women had to adjust. Just as the former patient's performance was directly related to her significant other's role expectations, so also was her performance affected by his willingness to tolerate her abnormal symptoms. It was found that *high level performers in the community had relatives with low tolerance of deviance, while low level performers tended to have significant others willing to keep the former patient at home despite the symptoms she may have exhibited.*[19] Thus the extent to which families were willing to keep at home the former patient who manifested abnormal symptoms related importantly to the performance of the patient. A relationship existed also between the significant other's tolerance and his role expectations so that high expectations and low tolerance were associated as were low expectations and high tolerance.

Consideration of specific symptoms showed that significant others with high level performers at home were far less tolerant than those with low performers (see Table 6.7). For example, 54 percent of those whose relatives were high level performers said they would seek readmission of the patient if she was "always worn out or tired," while only 34 percent with low level performers would do so. Similarly, for depressive behavior, 87 percent with high performers at home were low in tolerance compared with 60 percent whose relatives were low performers. These differences in tolerance did not achieve statistical significance for only six items, although the trend remained consistent—these were symptoms either so severe as to be rare for the entire patient group, such as assault and attempted suicide, or so mild as to prevail throughout all performance levels as, for example, not eating well or grouchiness.

When significant others low in tolerance were compared with those high in tolerance in terms of the specific symptoms for which they would consult the hospital, a further finding was noteworthy: *although high tolerance relatives were significantly more tolerant*

---

[19] Tolerance of deviance was related in similar fashion to all performance measures. Using contingency coefficients to measure correlation between tolerance and each area of performance, it was found that for domestic performance $C = .28$, $p < 0.05$, for social participation $C = .30$, $p < 0.05$, both for psychological functioning and total performance $C = .48$, $p < 0.01$. Further, in each performance area, low and high performers had relatives whose mean tolerance scores were respectively high and low.

Table 6.7. Tolerance of Deviance and Posthospital Performance: Percentage of Significant Others with High and Low Performers Who Would Rehospitalize the Community Patient for Each Symptom

Symptom	High Performers (N = 76)	Low Performers (N = 79)	P[1]
Made no sense when talking	97	80	0.01
Always seemed worn out or tired	54	34	0.05
Tried to hit or hurt someone	97	89	
Just hung around the house doing nothing	78	47	0.01
Tried to hurt or kill herself	100	98	
Got grouchy or bad tempered	50	35	
Needed coaxing to do what's expected of her	63	30	0.01
Acted tense or nervous	51	34	0.05
Did not eat well	46	39	
Was hearing or seeing things	100	91	0.05
Could not control toilet habits	87	77	
Got drunk often	86	68	0.05
Too many pills	88	66	0.01
Stayed away from people	80	46	0.01
Misbehaved sexually	86	76	
Got depressed suddenly	87	60	0.01
Mumbled or talked to herself	95	70	0.01
Neglected household chores	53	33	0.05
Did not know what went on around her	99	89	0.05
Mean tolerance score[2]	27	34	0.01

[1] Based on chi square with 1 df.

[2] Based on critical ratio between mean scores.

of nearly all symptoms than low tolerance relatives, few relatives appeared willing to house a patient who manifested severe symptoms. If the patient was suicidal, homicidal, incontinent, hallucinatory, delusional or disoriented, even relatives who were, on the whole, accepting of deviance would insist on readmission; as Appendix B, Table 15 shows, 62 percent or more of high tolerance relatives would readmit the patient for such symptoms. Tolerant significant others would, however, be willing to keep the patient at home if she had somatic symptoms, depression, or antisocial tendencies. It is also pertinent to note that there was a consistent pattern in low tolerance. Those relatives who were unwilling to tolerate a woman who "made no sense when talking" were also unlikely to tolerate one who was "always worn out," or even one who was "grouchy or bad tempered." In other words, such significant others were unwilling to stand for either mild or extreme symptoms. And the contrast between those low and high in tolerance was striking—for example, the low tolerance relatives would more readily rehospitalize for minor symptoms, such as not eating well or acting tense (84 percent) but only 10 percent of high tolerance relatives would do so.

Validation for the relationship of performance level to tolerance was provided by a question asking significant others if they expected the patient to be rehospitalized. It was hypothesized that relatives high in tolerance with low performers at home would predict readmission, while high level performers with low tolerance significant others would not be expected to be readmitted. This indeed was the case. Twenty-three percent of significant others of low performers predicted the patient's readmission while only three percent of relatives with high performers expected rehospitalization to occur. Relatives with poorly functioning patients apparently anticipated readmission; they may have been realistically reacting to the fact that the low performer was sicker and therefore more likely to need further treatment. Where performance was high, relatives did not expect readmission to occur; this may similarly reflect their realistic assessment of the woman's good condition. Thus, low tolerance may mean that the former patient was well enough so that no abnormal behavior was expected, but if it did occur, rehospitalization would then be seriously considered.

Some evidence for this line of reasoning came from the interrelationship of diagnosis, tolerance, and performance. Using diagnosis as an indicator of illness severity, it was observed that both performance and tolerance were linked with the patient's illness. Thus low performers were sicker and generally had more tolerant relatives than high performers. Significant others high in tolerance tended to have a higher proportion of the organically impaired patients compared with the less tolerant significant others. To some degree those families with a severely impaired patient appeared to have accommodated to this fact, and they seemed to adjust to the illness over a period of time. Since the relationship of diagnosis with performance and tolerance resulted from overrepresentation of organic psychoses in the low performance-high tolerance group, removal of this diagnostic category eliminated the effect of diagnosis on both tolerance and performance. Even with diagnosis controlled, the relationship between performance and tolerance remained significant. Thus for the functional psychoses and the characterologic disturbances which composed the bulk of patient types studied, high performance was a correlate of low tolerance and low performance accompanied high tolerance.

Another issue connected with the intricate link among performance, illness, and tolerance concerns the extent to which expectations for role performance implicated tolerance of deviant behavior. It must be underscored that the meaning of tolerance in this study referred to expectations for normal or abnormal behavior in the psychological sense; that is, tolerance of deviance was measured by the extent to which significant others were willing to house a former patient who manifested psychiatric symptoms. There was, in fact, a tendency for tolerance and role expectations to be significantly related so that high expectations were concomitant with low tolerance on the part of significant others.[20]

Given the interrelationships among illness severity, performance level, tolerance, and expectations, one must question the suitability of accounting for performance merely as the resultant of either tolerance of deviance or role expectations. The evidence presented so far heavily supports the notion that instead of viewing expectations (whether for role performance or for abnormality) as strictly determinative of performance, performance should be viewed as affecting both the expectations and tolerance held by significant family members. Performance here refers to actual behavior over a period of time as well as to the assumed ability of the former patient to perform, that is to her condition or health status. By comparison, only a minor influence on tolerance was exerted by familial characteristics. Thus, married former patients, with no adult females in the household, with young children, and those from the middle class tended to be subject to low tolerance of deviant behavior, but these were trends and not relationships of statistical significance. The key feature in the association between tolerance and performance was clearly the patient's own con-

[20] The contingency coefficient was .33, $p < 0.01$; the relationships of tolerance to patient expectations and expectation agreement were positive but not significant statistically.

dition or ability to perform adequately. The finding that the tolerance of *all* significant others was lowest for severe symptoms underlines this point. In other words, no relative was disposed to keep at home a person who manifested extreme behavior; such persons were likely to be rehospitalized.

7

Former Patients and Their Neighbors

Undoubtedly the most distinctive feature and significant contribution of this investigation involved the systematic comparison of the performance of former mental patients with their neighbors. Up to now, social psychiatric research has been characterized by two distinct lines of inquiry: longitudinal efforts at evaluating case outcome after treatment and epidemiologic studies aimed at establishing the extent and distribution of abnormal functioning in a general population. The earlier chapters of this volume illustrate the longitudinal approach. In nearly all longitudinal research the patient is his own control. Baseline readings and data taken prior to the illness onset or hospitalization are used as the standards by which to judge functioning subsequent to treatment.[1] Valuable as this perspective is for both clinical practice and research, it is nevertheless sharply limited if there is no way of relating the status of the index case to that of an untreated control or other type of norm. Thus, it is possible to see great progress during and after treatment and still find that the patient's behavior was and remained considerably different from the norm.

A second line of social psychiatric inquiry has involved efforts

[1] See for example, Lee Gurel, "Release and Community Stay Criteria in Evaluating Psychiatric Treatment," in Paul Hoch and Joseph Zubin, Eds., *Psychopathology of Schizophrenia* (New York, Grune and Stratton, 1966), pp. 527–552; and Blaine E. McLaughlin, *Long-Term Results of Psychiatric Outpatient Treatment* (Springfield, Illinois, Charles C Thomas, 1965).

at establishing these much needed normative criteria of adequate performance through cross-sectional, as opposed to longitudinal, investigations. Prevalence studies of varying quality and merit have tried to determine the distribution of psychiatrically relevant symptoms in specified populations. The practical purpose of obtaining knowledge of the distribution of the extent and severity of these symptoms in a general population is as a yardstick against which the symptomatology in criterion groups at any point in time could be measured.[2]

Whatever the merits and defects inherent in symptom-determined performance standards and in attempts at following patients after psychiatric treatment, the joining of these separate concerns represents a logical and difficult step forward. In the present state of the art and science of psychiatry, this juxtaposition is necessary in assessing meaningfully the effectiveness of hospital treatment and the status of mental patients—relative to others—before and after such care.

Without belaboring the issue, the "felt need" to include a comparison group of normal or never psychiatrically treated women derived from the lack of an adequate and meaningful definition of mental illness. Without some sort of reasonably objective criteria for evaluating the performance of treated patients in the community—standards which can most readily be ascertained in comparison with never previously treated yet otherwise comparable persons—total reliance must be placed on insight into the symptom or illness aspects of functioning. While there is nothing inherently objectionable about studying intrapsychic functioning, the unreliability of such judgments is well known.[3] Worse still, focus on intrapsychic dynamics, as has already been suggested in the discussion of rehospitalization and elsewhere, does not necessarily predict or reveal the level of instrumental role performance. As Jahoda and others seeking some sort of meaningful definition of mental health and illness have observed, there is a dif-

[2] Cf. August B. Hollingshead and Frederick C. Redlich, *Social Class and Mental Illness* (New York, John Wiley and Sons, 1958); Leo Srole, Thomas Langner, Stanley Michael, Marvin Opler and Thomas Rennie, *Mental Health in the Metropolis: The Manhattan Midtown Study*, Vol. I (New York, McGraw-Hill, 1962); and Benjamin Pasamanick, Dean Roberts, Paul Lemkau and Dean Kreuger, "A Survey of Mental Disease in an Urban Population: I. Prevalence by Age, Sex and Severity of Impairment," *American Journal of Public Health,* Vol. 47 (1957), pp. 923–929.

[3] Benjamin Pasamanick and Leonard Ristine, "Differential Assessment of Posthospital Psychological Functioning: Evaluations by Psychiatrists and Relatives," *American Journal of Psychiatry*, Vol. 117 (July 1961), pp. 40–46.

ference between attributes and action, between covert and overt behavior.[4] Doubtless, a set of criteria which would subsume both levels would be most desirable; in the absence of such criteria, standards based on both the symptomatic and instrumental role performance levels are about the most that can presently be expected.

This discussion is particularly relevant in view of the present trends in patient management and mental health care. As ever more patients are treated within the context of community-centered mental health treatment facilities and remain at home alongside their less impaired or unimpaired neighbors, the need for more closely determining the dimensions of health and illness will be ever more crucial. Consider, for example, the issues involved in making decisions about so relatively simple a matter as the disposition of the treatment dropout. Should such a person be hospitalized, left alone, transferred to another service, or what? In other terms, what constitutes effective coping behavior, and how can it be measured?

In the not very distant past when mental health care consisted mainly of hospital ward confinement for protracted periods, the status of the patient was considerably easier to evaluate than it was in his or her incumbency in the community. For one thing, a criterion group of patients was always at hand, and each patient implicitly or explicitly could be and was rated in terms of the functioning of the others. In addition, the spectrum of functioning being rated was narrowly restricted. The complexities involved in everyday living and the stresses imposed by these problems were wholly absent. In the dependency situation fostered by the total institution, a patient's progress could be charted largely in terms of the absence or degree of presence of psychological symptoms. As a result, a much greater emphasis came to be placed on the symptom level than on the ability to perform instrumental roles, even if only on a minimally acceptable scale.

Once patients are returned home or are, by virtue of the new community facilities, never hospitalized to begin with, the reference group is no longer the confined patient but rather the next-door neighbor, the co-worker, or the other acceptably functioning persons

[4] Marie Jahoda, *Current Concepts of Positive Mental Health* (New York, Basic Books, 1958); and Frederick C. Redlich, "The Concept of Health in Psychiatry," in Alexander Leighton, John Clausen and Robert Wilson, Eds., *Explorations in Social Psychiatry* (New York, Basic Books, 1957), pp. 138–164.

of the same age, sex, race, marital status, and social class position. Instrumental role performance becomes almost as vital a criterion of adjustment as the range and severity of psychiatric symptoms. This then is the problem. How well do treated mental patients function in the community in relation to their normal or never previously treated neighbors? Stated a little differently, to what extent does the functioning of previously hospitalized patients reflect their neuropsychiatric status and problems, and to what extent does it reflect their specific family constellations? On the other hand, do the expectations for performance of husbands of normal women differ from those of husbands of formerly hospitalized women? Are husbands of normal women more or less sensitive, more or less tolerant, of mildly bizarre and deviant conduct, and of low level instrumental performance? Does previous hospitalization make a significant other more cognizant and accepting or merely more critical of the performance of a spouse or close relative?

THE NORMATIVE POPULATION

THE SELECTION OF CONTROLS

The decision to obtain a comparison population raised some rather difficult questions about the selection of control subjects, the instruments to be used, the methods of obtaining cooperation, and the interviewing process and related issues. The first and most immediate concern was to achieve as close a match in pertinent social characteristics with the former patients as possible, and particularly on those variables known to be operative in the definition of attitudes about and treatment of the mental disorders. Since such variables are primarily the socioeconomic, the decision was made to use the neighbors of the community patients as the comparison group. In this way, at least rough similarities in the life styles of the patients and controls could be expected.

Because of the difficulty and the comparatively high cost of locating neighbors for the rural patients, it was decided to limit the control group selection to the key urban area involved. Since rural residence was characteristic of less than 10 percent of the patient sample, concentration on an urban control group was not unreasonably limiting. Thus, controls were selected for community patients living in the Greater Columbus area defined as the boundaries of Franklin County.

Whenever a patient's home address was within the county limits, a control neighbor was to be chosen for her.

Two other restrictions on the designation of controls were imposed. First, *controls were to be selected only for patients who had been in the community for at least six months without return to a mental hospital.* Obviously, these were the women whose behavior could be judged more meaningfully in comparative fashion; returnees were thus excluded from the control selection procedure. Second, only in cases in which interviews had been successfully completed with both a former patient and her significant other was the patient eligible to be paired with a control.

The control group was initially defined as consisting of women from the households located ten numbers higher than the patient's address on the same street. As with the former patients, husbands were the first choice significant others, and female relatives in the household were the second choice. The chief sources for choosing the households of controls were the most recent city and suburban directories, supplemented by use of the criss-cross and telephone directories. From these sources most of the following information could be obtained: the name of the head of the household and his wife's name, whether he owned or rented the dwelling, names of other adult household residents, occupations of the residents, and telephone number. This was usually sufficient information to permit the sending of a letter to the control explaining the study and requesting an interview. The letter expedited the interviewer's task in locating respondents and obtaining their cooperation.

The residence ten numbers higher than the patient's and on the same street usually resulted in selection of a household two to four houses away from the patient on the same side of the street. It was anticipated, moreover, that the selection rule would need to provide for instances where there was no address exactly ten numbers higher than the patient's. A detailed set of operating procedures were developed whereby project staff could select controls under all possible circumstances. The same rules were used by interviewers when it became impossible to preselect a control; they made the choice by visiting the patient's street and determining in which residence to choose a control. Thus, for example, the address ten numbers lower than the patient's was selected if the address ten numbers higher did not exist because the street ended; if no residence was exactly ten numbers higher or lower, the nearest address above or below ten respectively was selected; businesses were skipped; if the residence chosen was next door to the patient, it was omitted and the household three residences away from the patient was substituted; where no addresses existed as on a few county roads, specific provisions were made to select the fifth dwelling north or east of the patient. (See Appendix A for the complete instructions to interviewers on the selection of controls.) Interviewers were permitted to substitute respondents only for specific reasons, such as finding a dwelling vacant, refusal to be interviewed after a visit to the respondent's residence, extended vacations on the part of assigned respondents, or if no woman 18 years or older was in the assigned household. When substitution was necessary, only two attempts to substitute respondents were authorized.

By execution of this exacting selection procedure, 171 patients were paired with controls. This number was further reduced to 157 because of inadequate interview data for three controls and the omission of 11 others who had previous treatment for mental disorder. These latter cases were excluded on the basis of information from one or all of the following: the control, her significant other, a detailed survey of the records at the State Department of Mental Hygiene, and the clinics and mental hospitals in the county.

THE INTERVIEWS

Almost all data on the control group were obtained in an interview with each woman and her significant other. In the process of planning this interview, it was clear that the approach which had been used in contacting former patients would be inappropriate for women who had never been treated for a mental disorder. It was, therefore, decided to define this part of the outcome study as a community survey on the health and functioning of women and to call it officially the Family Health Survey. Instead of specifying the survey's direct sponsorship by the psychiatric hospital—an affiliation that might bias respondents against the study—the relationship to the University Health Center and the study's financial support from the United States Public Health Service were emphasized. These points were explained both in the letter requesting the interview and by the interviewers who contacted the controls. Each interviewer carried a letter of introduction in case his identification should create a problem.

The designated householders living approximately ten house numbers away from the former patients were each sent a letter describing the health survey and requesting an interview. Whenever possible the letter was addressed to the woman, using her given name, for example, Mrs. Betty Smith.[5] When no female name was available, the letter was addressed to an assumed woman in the household, for example, Mrs. Robert Smith. A stamped reply card was enclosed with the letter so that an interview time convenient for the respondent could be indicated. If upon phoning or visiting the household, no persons to whom the letter was addressed could be found, the interviewer tried to ascertain who the household members were and requested an interview with a woman and her husband, daughter, sister, or other suitable significant other.

Six of the original psychiatric social workers who had interviewed the former patients and their relatives acted as interviewers for control respondents. A training session with these six interviewers was conducted to explain the Family Health Survey identity of this part of the project, the procedures to be followed in contacting controls and substituting respondents where necessary. Interviewers were equipped with detailed instructions for selecting control respondents. At the training session, interviewers were each assigned two pretest cases to provide practice in interviewing "normal" persons and to iron out potential procedural difficulties. The interviewing of controls took about four and a half months. As had been the case with the patient sample, most interviews were conducted during evenings and on weekends when respondents could be found at home.

INSTRUMENTS

Interviews with controls and their significant others were conducted with structured schedules which paralleled those used in the patient follow-up. The patient and significant other schedules were modified to exclude all items relevant only to the hospitalization and treatment experiences of the patients. The performance, expectations, tolerance, and background measures were left essentially intact. A few questions were altered to make them more appropriate. For example,

[5] The names mentioned here are fictitious.

while the significant other of the former patient was asked about the patient's work history, these questions were asked directly of the controls. For the woman's domestic performance, the patient's significant other was asked about the period of time since the patient left the hospital (the last time), while for controls, the time period was the last six months. In the questions concerning tolerance of deviance, the patient version included the phrase *"needs to go back to the hospital,"* while the control version substituted the words *"needs to get treatment."*

A final change in the instruments designed for the controls involved the inclusion of the Cornell Medical Index (women's form). This was done for two reasons: first, to support the study in the general health of women and second, to provide information on the control's medical history with indications of any earlier episodes or any treatment for mental disorder. In this way, it was possible to identify and exclude women in the control group who had experienced or been treated for some mental disorder. The control was asked to fill out the form herself during the time her significant other was being interviewed. Slightly more than two thirds of the controls completed the Cornell Medical Index.

Cooperation on the part of controls and their significant others far exceeded expectations. For patients, identification with the hospital made the interview official and less voluntary. For controls, a response rate typical of community surveys was anticipated, although there was the hope that identification with the university would contribute toward the acceptability of such an interview. Seventy-three percent of the respondents *originally* selected as controls were interviewed successfully. In another 23 percent of the cases, a second respondent had to be chosen as a control, because originally designated respondents refused the interview, the selected dwelling was vacant, or no woman was in the household. In four percent of the control cases, a third respondent had to be selected to substitute for the first two. Only three patient cases remained unmatched because of refusal on the part of three sets of respondents selected as controls to cooperate.

THE PATIENTS' NEIGHBORS

Despite these painstaking efforts and great success in obtaining 157 matched pairs, the two groups were found to be far from similar in attributes associated with instrumental role performance. Indeed, one of the principal findings is that no matter how carefully selected, former patients are likely to be significantly different from normal women. The reason for this is probably both cause and effect of psychiatric illness. Psychiatric disorders both select and produce a population substantially unlike a normal population. Apart from its consequences for this study and for epidemiologic investigations in general, the import of this finding has significant ramifications for community care and other management programs as well as for the early detection of vulnerable persons. The chief differences between patients and normal controls were in marital status, family type, living arrangements, and educational achievement. These areas more intimately and directly reflect competency in functioning than do some of the other socioeconomic attributes.

MARITAL STATUS AND FAMILY TYPE

The 157 control women were not significantly older or younger than their former patient counterparts (38 versus 42 years of age respectively). Nor were they different in racial or religious composition—about 80 percent in each group were white and Protestant. They were also predictably alike in socioeconomic status, as measured by the Hollingshead Two Factor Index of Social Position, and in house and neighborhood types which are related measures of social class. Neighbors and patients were mostly of working class background (Class IV in Hollingshead's distribution), with not inconsiderable numbers in the lowest social class group and in the middle and upper middle range in the distribution. Similarly, neighbors and patients were equally of urban background. Thus, the observed differences in marital status, family living arrangements, and educational attainment cannot be attributed to demographic considerations but must be linked to the origins and sequelae of the psychiatric illness.

Table 7.1 shows the marital status of the women in each cohort. Two striking differences are immediately apparent. While only 57 percent of the former patients were married, the figure for the controls was considerably higher at 82 percent. This disparity was equally clear in the far greater number of single women among the former patients (12 percent) and in those separated or divorced (21 percent of the patients and only 3 percent of the controls). Thus, incipient and actual psychiatric impairment may tend to affect mate selection

Table 7.1. Marital and Family Status of 157 Matched Pairs of Patients and Neighbors

	Percent Patients	Percent Neighbors
Marital status		
Married	57	82
Single	12	2
Widowed	10	13
Divorced or Separated	21	3
Family type (household)		
Conjugal	54	80
Parental	10	1
Parental-Conjugal	2	1
All Other	34	18
Significant other		
Husband	56	77
Relative	33	17
Nonkin	11	6

negatively, and after marriage, to result in a disproportionately high rate of marital dissolution.

One particularly important consequence of this difference in marital status concerned the person designated as the significant other. Thus, husbands constituted 56 percent of the significant others for the former patients but a very much higher proportion for the control women. Not only was this the case for husbands as significant others, it was also applicable to relatives in general. There were many more nonrelatives who served as significant others for the former patients. In terms of living arrangements, nearly twice as many of the former patients were living with nonkin, or alone, in comparison to the women in the control population. This obviously meant that the significant others for patients came from a pool of persons with lesser knowledge and intimacy with them than was the situation for the significant others of the control women.[6] The implications of this finding

[6] Again, one must confront the possibility that two factors operate to present the unmarried women as poorer performers. First, as indicated earlier, the patients may tend to be less marriageable and less able to remain married due to their psychiatric impairment. Second, the unmarried may simply be

should be tempered, however, with the observation that in about 80 percent of the cases in both cohorts, the significant other was living in the same household as the study subject.

EDUCATIONAL ATTAINMENT

In addition to the familial situation, the only other distinction between the 157 former patients and their neighbors was in educational achievement. Here again, incipient neuropsychiatric problems may have been responsible for the lesser grade level achievement of the former patients. Thus, nearly half of the former patients had attended high school, as contrasted to more than three fifths of the controls. Again, 28 percent of the patients, but only 19 percent of the normals, had achieved no more than a grade school diploma.

The net effect of these differences between the former patients and their normal neighbors tends to invalidate any simple comparisons of instrumental role performance levels, expectations, and tolerance for aberrant behavior. In view of the significant variations in marital status and family type, it is certainly not unrealistic to anticipate differential expectations about role performance in marriage and family life. The greater number of unmarrieds among the patients means that fewer had responsibilities typically associated with the female role. Similarly, the greater variety of significant others for the patients (husbands, parents, children, siblings, friends, and neighbors) at least introduces the possibility of differential perception, knowledge, and reporting of patient functioning. Despite these critical limitations, both cohorts probably reflect the universes from which they were drawn. The normal controls appear to be reasonably typical of the adult female population of the same age and socioeconomic status. In this sense, they do highlight the unique status of the patient in the community.

---

subject to lower expectations in instrumental role performance both because the child care and domestic responsibilities are not central or crucial to their roles, but also because their significant others are less competent to judge performance compared with the perspective of spouses. In the subsequent comparisons of patients and neighbors controlling for marital status, it will be evident that the neighbors (both married and unmarried) could perform better than the patients. But it was also found that internal comparison supports the performance superiority of the married over the unmarried normals; this parallels the marital status differences observed for former patients. For details on these data see "The Unmarried Woman After Psychiatric Treatment," *Mental Hygiene* (April 1967), pp. 175–181 by the present authors.

PSYCHOLOGICAL FUNCTIONING

The former patients, not unexpectedly, were evaluated by their significant others as much poorer functioners than the control women. The mean psychiatric functioning score was 86.7 for the former patient group and 91.1 for the controls—a very significant statistical difference. Reduced to a symptom level, this means that the patients were perceived as functioning more poorly on 29 of the 32 behaviors assessed by the inventory. On 21 of the 32 items, the patients were reported as functioning significantly more poorly. In only one instance were the control women reported to be functioning more poorly than the former patients. This symptom item concerned awkward physical movements (see Table 7.2).

While these findings indicate that the former patients were below par relative to the controls, closer examination suggests caution in drawing definitive conclusions. While patient-control differences were observed in 21 of the symptom areas, no such significant differences occurred on 11 of the symptom items. Six of the latter items pertain to extremely severe behaviors—hallucination, delusion, incontinence, incoherence, confusion, and disorientation. These behaviors were not very prevalent in either group. The remaining nondifferentiative symptoms concerned relatively mild problems—awkward movements, restlessness, grouchiness, and the manipulation of persons and situations using physical symptoms as an excuse. The surprise here was that so very many of the controls were reported to evidence these behaviors: 46 percent were described as restless, 59 percent worn out, 60 percent tense and nervous, and 57 percent grouchy. Stated more succinctly, the principal differences between patients and controls were not in the severe symptom range where the occurrence of such behaviors almost inevitably results in hospitalization. Nor was it in the mild or usual symptom range where normatively no definition of illness accrues. The real distinction concerned symptoms of a chronic nature which impede adequate functioning and are defined as being sufficiently disruptive to fall within the illness designation. Such symptoms include abusive language and excessive swearing, idleness, restlessness, insomnia, and health worries.

Table 7.2. Frequency of Psychological Symptom Manifestation of 157 Matched Pairs of Patients and Neighbors

Symptom	Percent Patients	Percent Neighbors	P
Makes no sense when talking	12	12	
Walks, sits, or stands awkwardly	12	18	
Moves around restlessly	56	46	
Swears, curses often compared to other women	22	5	0.01
Always seems worn out or tired	74	59	0.01
Tries to hit or hurt someone	10	1	0.01
Lacks control of toilet habits	5	4	
Says she hears voices	3	1	
Does not want to see people	34	22	0.05
Just hangs around the house doing nothing	34	16	0.01
Tries to hurt or kill herself	4	0	
Gets drunk often	8	1	0.05
Gets grouchy or bad tempered	58	57	
Misbehaves sexually	6	0	0.01
Needs coaxing to do what's expected of her	24	11	0.01
Has trouble going to sleep	50	27	0.01
Takes many pills	17	8	0.05
Needs help dressing, bathing, or going to the toilet	3	1	
Does not know what goes on around her	8	3	
Acts tense or nervous	77	60	0.01
Thinks she is sinful or evil compared to other people	12	1	0.01
Thinks people want to control or harm her	15	1	0.01
Worries about her bodily organs	23	13	0.05
Mumbles or talks to herself	10	4	0.05
Tries to get her way by saying she has pains	12	7	
Gets depressed suddenly	53	28	0.01
Says she sees people who are not there	1	1	
Worries about her health	43	23	0.01
Teases or picks on people	15	2	0.01
Thinks people are watching her or talking about her	17	3	0.01
Expects bad things to happen in the future without good reason	20	1	0.01
Does not eat well	35	14	0.01
Mean score	86.7	91.1	0.01

DOMESTIC PERFORMANCE

The results on the domestic performance measure reinforce the psychological functioning conclusions. The control women were reported able to assume and carry out normal household duties unaided far more often than the former patients. The mean scores based on all seven items were 18.4 for the controls and 15.0 for the former patients. This difference was, of course, statistically significant. More-

Table 7.3. Unaided Performance of Domestic Responsibilities of Matched Pairs of Patients and Neighbors

Item	Percent Patients	Percent Neighbors	P
Prepares morning and evening meals	69	88	0.01
Does grocery shopping	36	66	0.01
Handles grocery money	48	78	0.01
Dusts, sweeps, and does other usual cleaning	67	80	0.01
Takes care of laundry and mending	68	86	0.01
Dresses and bathes children[1]	85	83	
Makes sure children get to school on time[2]	85	94	
Mean score[3]	11.9	13.7	0.01

[1] Item applicable to 48 of the total former patients and to 60 of the total controls.
[2] Item applicable to 60 of the total former patients and to 62 of the total controls.
[3] The child care items are excluded.

over, when the two items dealing with child care duties were eliminated from consideration, the differences between patients and controls were maintained.[7] An interesting sidelight in this respect concerns the fact that former patients who had children living at home were as adequate in child care as comparable control women. This would seem to indicate that women who marry and have children are probably less impaired than patients who never marry or whose marriages are dissolved prior to the birth of any child (see Table 7.3).

The other interesting observation concerns the large number of

[7] These two child care items were removed in this analysis because of their inapplicability to a greater percentage of former patients who were unmarried.

normal neighbors who were reported as functioning poorly in their role as housewives. The performance of domestic tasks, perhaps more than any of the other measures, would seem to tap social class behavior rather than health or illness. Clearly, the middle class preoccupation with cleanliness, orderliness, and good housekeeping practices are not reflected in the functioning of some of the psychiatrically unimpaired lower class women.

SOCIAL PARTICIPATION

Of the three principal areas of functioning, only the social participation index failed to differentiate the patients and neighbors. The respective mean scores were 55.2 for the patients and 56.8 for the controls. Three of the 11 items favored the controls—visiting friends, daily newspaper reading, and time spent on hobbies. One activity—moviegoing—was more often engaged in by the former patients. These generally inconclusive findings are probably partly a function of the nature and insensitivity of the social participation inventory and of the possible effect of having fewer spouses as significant others. The inventory is based on the subject's involvement in various activities relative to that of the significant other. It is probable that a refined measure, independent of significant other participation, would have shown appreciably more variation in the type and amount of participation of the two sample groups.

SELF-EXPECTATIONS

The importance of expectations as a concomitant, if not determinant, of level of performance has been discussed elsewhere in this volume (pp. 113 to 126). Additional support of this relationship can be found in the results of the analysis of the expectations of the 157 successful former patients and their neighbors. The self-expectations measure, it will be recalled, consisted of 14 routine domestic and social behaviors. Not surprisingly the normal women expected considerably better performance of themselves in these tasks than did the former patients. The respective mean scores for controls and patients were 38.1 and 36.1.

An item breakdown indicated significant differences in expectations in eight of the 14 activities (see Appendix B, Table 16). Four of these eight concerned purely domestic activities such as housecleaning, handling of the grocery money, and meal preparation. These differences, of course, corroborate the reported inadequacies of the former patient group, relative to the controls, in the area of domestic performance. The other four items dealt with social participation. The controls expected more of themselves principally in the fulfilling of interpersonal social obligations such as entertaining at home and visiting others.

SIGNIFICANT OTHER EXPECTATIONS

Using the same checklist of activities and tasks, the significant others of the controls had the higher expectations (37.1 versus 35.8) for performance. Since they also had reported their relatives to be doing well in these duties, the expectations and performance were mutually reinforcing. The significant others of the controls focused on five of the 14 tasks or activities as differentiating the two groups. It is noteworthy that all five activities centered around household task performance rather than the fulfillment of social obligations (see Appendix B, Table 17).

TOLERANCE OF DEVIANCE

One final measure deserves mention. The significant other of each patient and control was asked to indicate whether he would contact a psychiatric facility or agency if the subject manifested any one of 19 symptoms indicative of neuropsychiatric problems. The thesis was that the significant others of the controls would be less tolerant of aberrance (having experienced it only hypothetically) than would the significant others of the patients. The results failed to sustain the hypothesis. The significant others of the patients and controls were equally tolerant or intolerant of these aberrant behaviors (see Appendix B, Table 18). The respective mean scores were 29.2 and 29.0. Moreover, it is clear that decisions to seek psychiatric care would not be taken lightly. The responses indicated that such aid would be requested only when the subject made no sense when talking, was manifestly confused and disoriented, hallucinatory, or assaultive or suicidal. There were some seemingly random variations on three of the 19 symptom items. The significant others of the former patients indicated greater tolerance of eating and elimination difficulties while the controls' significant others would more often countenance sexual misbehavior.

MARITAL STATUS AND PERFORMANCE

After much discussion of the import of these comparisons, there remained the distinct possibility that the sources of variation between the groups were familial—the unequal percentages of married women, husbands as significant others, and household configurations—rather than previous mental hospitalization and treatment. To eliminate this possibility more refined analysis was undertaken separately comparing the performance levels of unmarried patients with unmarried controls and of married patients with their married neighbors.

UNMARRIED PATIENTS AND THEIR NEIGHBORS

Since the unmarried former patients had emerged as poor performers compared with married patients, it was important to ascertain whether this was mainly due to their restricted opportunity to

Table 7.4. Comparison of Unmarried Patients with Their Unmarried Neighbors in Mean Performance Scores

Area of Performance	Unmarried Patients (N = 66)	Unmarried Neighbors (N = 29)	P[1]
Domestic performance	15.2	17.0	0.05
Social participation	51.7	52.4	
Psychological functioning	85.7	90.5	0.05

[1] Based on critical ratio between means.

perform the female role. If this were true, then both unmarried patients and their unmarried neighbors ought to perform at a similar level. *It is clear from the patient-neighbor comparison, however, that the unmarried patients performed at a lower level in all areas than their counterparts among the controls* (see Table 7.4). In psychological functioning the controls' superiority was inexorably evident: former patients manifested more assaultive and suicidal behavior, withdrawal, alcoholism, paranoia, depression, and nervousness. But single, widowed, divorced, and separated patients were also less able to visit friends, prepare their own meals, and keep their dwelling clean than their unmarried neighbors. It must be concluded, then, that among the unmarried women, former patient status was associated with a generally lower performance level than that characteristic of their normal neighbors.

MARRIED PATIENTS AND THEIR NEIGHBORS

The two groups of married women (91 patients and 128 controls) were very similar in all demographic aspects. There was not a single background factor of the 13 examined which significantly differentiated the two groups. Most important, however, this procedure practically eliminated the problem of varying significant others. In the case of the married former patients 92 percent of the significant others were husbands, and the vast majority of these men were living with their wives. By the same token, nearly 95 percent of the significant others for the control women were husbands living in the same household setting as their wives.

Psychological Functioning. The purification of the study groups by exclusion of all but married women permits even greater confidence in the validity of the finding that controls continued to maintain their clear-cut edge in psychological functioning. Using total scores, which subsume both number and severity of reported symptoms, the mean for the married former patients was 87.1 as against 91.1 for the married controls. The magnitude of this difference was, of course, statistically significant and very comparable to that obtained with the 157 total pairs. Furthermore, of the 32 symptom items, 16 statistically differentiated the two groups in favor of the controls. This is five fewer significant symptom items than in the previous contrast. These five items included idleness, malingering, pessimism, sexual misconduct, and tenseness. In these instances, however, as on all other symptoms rated, a higher percentage of patients than of controls were reported as manifesting the behavior.

These findings lend additional support to the proposition that even the less impaired married women among the former patients exhibit a broader spectrum of psychiatrically pertinent overt symptom manifestations than their neighbors. The two groups—previously treated women and their never previously treated neighbors—simply represent different population universes with regard to such symptom manifestation. *If the reporting of the significant others does in fact accurately portray the psychological status of the wives, it is perfectly evident that hospitalization and treatment failed to elevate the level of functioning of the former patients to that of their neighbors.* Given the chronicity and psychological deficits frequently associated with certain of the psychiatric disorders, the poorer functioning of treated patients is hardly surprising. The aspect that does occasion interest and concern is the considerable number of ostensibly normal married women who show various symptoms ranging from the very mild to the deeply serious. While many epidemiological studies have indicated the pervasiveness of psychiatric symptoms in the general population, it is nonetheless disquieting to replicate such results. On the other hand, this study does convincingly demonstrate that normals, troubled and beset as they may be, still function far better than former patients. This balanced perspective on the problem is necessary in order not to despair wholly of ever reaching some meaningful conception of the nature of mental illness.

Domestic Performance. The findings regarding the less adequate domestic performance of the former patients were conceivably distorted by the inclusion of single and otherwise nonmarried women. Now, however, since all subjects were married at the time of interview, the domestic performance comparison is better focused, and the results achieved of far greater importance. The mean scores on the five item domestic performance index was 12.7 for the expatients and 13.9 for the neighbors. This difference was statistically significant. Furthermore, of the five items, only the one dealing with housecleaning activities failed to differentiate the two married groups of women. But even in this particular sphere the controls were reported to be considerably better performers. In general, then, the married patients were decidedly inferior to their married neighbors in their ability to carry out the usual chores and responsibilities associated with the housewife role. Especially noteworthy was the fact that the greatest discrepancy between the two groups occurred in matters having to do with the handling of money and purchasing. For example, only 34 percent of the former patients were reported as able to handle the grocery shopping without some help—in contrast to 67 percent of the controls. By the same token, 54 percent of the 91 married former patients were able to handle the grocery money without aid of some kind as compared to 78 percent of their married neighbors. Here again, the significant other reports show that approximately a third of the normal neighbors are incapable of shopping or handling money. This fact is, perhaps, as important as the differences between the two groups of women. Clearly, there seems to be no greater consensus on what constitutes adequate handling of domestic responsibilities than on satisfactory psychological status.

Social Participation. In support of the earlier analysis of the total pairs of former patients and neighbors, the difference between the two married groups in terms of their social participation was minimal. There was but one type of activity which differentiated them —the former patients tended to go to the movies more frequently, relative to their husbands or significant others, than did the women in the comparison group. In addition, the married expatients engaged in more radio listening and television viewing than their neighbors. Apart from these passive pastimes, there was no other variation in their patterns of social participation.

Self- and Significant Other Expectations. Examination of the self-expectation data indicated that our fear of a built-in bias against the former patients was not wholly without warrant. When only those women who were married were compared, there was very little difference between the groups in terms of the expectations they held for their own behavior and functioning. The mean scores for the groups based on the entire series of expectation items differed little. These scores were 37.4 for the former patients and 38.4 for the controls. In addition, only two items on the expectations checklist indicated much variation. The neighbors more often expected to entertain at home and to visit friends and relatives. These clearly are the most critical aspects of social participation—interacting with others in or outside the home. In effect, expectations may well follow from performance in this respect. In any event, there was surely a high degree of concordance between expectations and actual performance.

The expectation pattern of the significant others paralleled that of the married women themselves. Not a single item differentiated the two groups of significant others, and the mean expectation scores were virtually identical—37.4 for the husbands of the former patients and 37.5 for those of the controls.

Tolerance of Deviance. The similarities between the married former patients and controls and their respective significant others with regard to expectations were supported by the responses having to do with tolerance of deviant behavior. There was virtually no difference in the mean tolerance scores registered by the significant others of both groups. These were 28.6 for the former patients and 28.5 for the controls. There were, however, three symptom items which did distinguish the significant others, and interestingly enough, these items were the same ones as in the total group comparison. The three items dealt with poor eating habits, incontinence, and sexual misbehavior. It is difficult, of course, to draw any conclusions based on these items. It is much safer to assess the meaning of the similarities—husbands were very much alike in their judgments of the relative importance of psychiatrically relevant behavior patterns.

FURTHER SAMPLE REFINEMENT

RESTRICTION OF THE SAMPLE

Even after the additional narrowing and purification of the former patient and neighbor groups, the findings remained unchanged. The former patients still manifested more psychiatrically relevant symptoms and were portrayed as being considerably less adequate in their performance of routine household tasks. On the other hand, the gap between them in these respects had narrowed measurably after the requirement of being married at the time of interview was imposed. Therefore, it seemed logical to add some final refinements in order to make certain that background variables did not contaminate these results. If, after the imposition of additional restrictions on the samples, the results continued to hold up, confidence in the observed differences between patients and normals would certainly increase. For the final test, then, both the patients and their control neighbors included only women who were: white, married, living with husband, and interviewed along with the significant other. Former patients also had to have been diagnosed as functionally rather than organically impaired at the time of hospitalization and free of alcohol and drug problem complications.

The effect of this process of adding additional criteria for sample inclusion was to shrink sample size considerably. This was especially painful after the tremendous effort to obtain large numbers of subjects for comparison. In numbers, 62 patients and 60 neighbors of the original 157 pairs were left. All subjects meeting the specified criteria were included rather than only those patients and controls who matched as neighbors. This, of course, is the reason for the unequal number of cases in the two populations. Not only were patients and neighbors now also alike in race, marital status, household composition, and interview completeness, but the two samples were also equivalent in other background characteristics. They were, for example, the same age, and their Hollingshead Index of Social Position scores were almost identical.

THE ADEQUACY OF PERFORMANCE

When the 62 patients and 60 neighbors were contrasted, two impressive findings emerged. First, the psychological performance measure continued to differentiate the two populations. *The successful patients continued to evidence more of, and to a greater extent, the various psychiatrically relevant symptoms in the checklist.* The mean scores—88.0 for the patients and 91.1 for the neighbors—were again significantly different. Second, no difference of any degree of magnitude was found in the domestic and social participation areas. Indeed, the 62 patients were reported to be doing every bit as well in these respects as their counterparts. For example, the mean domestic functioning scores for the former mental patients and their neighbors were 13.2 and 13.8, respectively; on the social participation inventory, the comparable average scores were 58.8 and 58.2. *Thus, as the expatients more closely approximated their controls in background, their instrumental role behavior approached, reached, and even surpassed that of their neighbors.* They still, however, could be distinguished from the normal women by their significantly greater symptom range and intensity.

THE LEVEL OF EXPECTATIONS

The imposition of more severe criteria did not alter the direction or magnitude of the findings on the softer measures such as expectations and tolerance. Again, three principal results were obtained. First, there continued to be absolutely no difference in the expectations for instrumental role performance on the part of the husbands. Both sets of husbands expected reasonably adequate domestic role performance but were considerably less demanding with regard to social participation. Second, and more important, the women neighbors held the significantly higher expectations for themselves. This was particularly pronounced in the social participation sphere. This is interesting because it confirms a not so implicit assumption in this work: the principal differences between the expatients and others are in the *quality* of performance and in the willingness and ability to perform the discretionary, as opposed to the mandatory obligations of the female role. All the women, irrespective of previous treatment, appear to accept the mandate of the domestic responsibilities incumbent in being a woman, even if their performance of these duties leaves something to be desired. The crucial distinction is in their willingness to expect of themselves involvement in activities which are somewhat more peripheral to the female role. Control women include in their expectations set interpersonal contacts and such activities as entertaining at home and visiting people. Former patients tend to exclude them. Because of either the illness itself or the stigma associated with previous treatment, former patients are likely to deemphasize these central interpersonal involvements in their life style.

Third, despite the moderately high correlation coefficients in the expectation scores of the index cases and their husbands in both groups ($r = +.59$ for neighbors and $+.41$ for patients), an interesting and suggestive pattern emerged. In the control group, the wives tended to expect more of themselves than did their husbands. This was most evident in the domestic and social participation realms. In the patient group, there was no directionality to the data. Husbands had a slightly higher level of expectations for social participation and wives for domestic duties.

THE FACTOR ANALYSIS

Up to now, the analysis has focused exclusively on the similarities and differences between patients and controls on the various measures used in the study. Initially, 157 former patients were compared with their normal neighbors. Later, only married patients were compared with married controls. Finally, severely restricted groups of patients and neighbors were contrasted. The successive steps provided even more definite evidence that only the psychological symptoms held up as distinguishing these populations from each other; instrumental role performance and the softer variables became less important as the subjects became more alike in social background characteristics. Such patient-control comparisons, though necessary and revealing, represent but one approach to the quest for empirical dimensions and standards for evaluating mental illness and health. Another way of approaching the problem is to begin with the interrelationships and patterning of the variables—independent, intervening, and dependent. To this end, a factor analysis was undertaken.

For the purposes of this analysis, both study groups were combined (N = 122) but were quantitatively distinguished in such a way so as to represent one of 11 variables under consideration (0 = former patient, 1 = control). Of the remaining ten variables, six were categorized as independent (social class, self-expectations, significant other expectations, tolerance of bizarre behavior, age of each subject, and having school age children). The remaining four variables were considered to be dependent. These included the psychological functioning, domestic performance, social participation, and total performance index scores.

Pearsonian correlations were computed for the 11 variables. A centroid factor analysis was conducted, and five factors were extracted from the 11 item matrix. These factors were graphically rotated, using simple structure for the location of axes. The resulting rotated orthogonal factors and their loadings are displayed in Table 7.5. Factor *A* may best be characterized as a *performance factor*. Although the highest loadings occurred on social participation and total performance, it is apparent that domestic and psychological functioning were also related, but to a lesser extent. Obviously, the most interesting feature of this factor is that not one of the postulated independent variables loaded to any extent, not even patient status. Factor *B* is most parsimoniously interpreted as an *expectation factor*. The highest loadings occurred on both husbands' expectations and especially self-expectations. There were moderately positive loadings on domestic and psychological performance and a moderately negative loading on social class. Curiously, the patient versus control item again failed to load significantly. In addition, the failure of social participation to load on this factor suggests that of the two dimensions of role performance considered, domestic performance was the far more important concomitant of expectations.

Factor *C,* a *specific factor,* had a high positive loading on age and a high negative loading on having school age children in the household. Psychological performance showed a moderately positive loading. No other item loaded on this factor. Factor D was the only one which distinguished the former patients from their controls. Since the controls were scored one and the patients zero, the relatively high positive loading represented an association between being a control and this factor. A moderately positive loading was observed on psychological performance and a moderately negative one on social class. Finally, Factor E emerged as a second specific factor. Only one variable—tolerance of psychologically bizarre behavior—loaded in a moderately negative fashion on this specific factor.

Table 7.5. Orthogonal Factors and Loadings

	Criteria	A	B	C	D	E	h^2
1.	Patient vs. control	10	15	−04	50	−10	0.294
2.	Social class	08	−30	00	−35	−10	0.229
3.	Husbands' expectations	13	64	02	−19	−05	0.466
4.	Self-expectations	00	81	01	03	19	0.693
5.	Tolerance	08	−08	26	−13	−42	0.274
6.	Age	07	−05	74	19	−04	0.593
7.	School age children	06	01	−81	−09	−05	0.670
8.	Domestic performance	42	44	03	00	−10	0.381
9.	Social participation	85	04	−18	−19	03	0.794
10.	Psychological performance	43	34	35	40	22	0.631
11.	Total performance index	74	08	02	11	09	0.575
	$\frac{\Sigma q^2}{n}$	0.153	0.137	0.130	0.062	0.028	(0.510)

Source: From Mark Lefton, Simon Dinitz, Shirley Angrist, and Benjamin Pasamanick, "Former Mental Patients and Their Neighbors: A Comparison of Performance Levels," *Journal of Health and Human Behavior*, 7 (Summer, 1966), p. 7. By permission of The American Sociological Association.

Thus, the factor analysis showed two things. First, it confirmed the positive relationship of the functioning variables to each other, and second, it reconfirmed that the relative absence of psychiatric symptoms is associated with control or neighbor status and patient status with poorer psychological functioning.

It must be concluded that the former patients in the community performed far less adequately than their normal neighbors. The patients' psychiatric condition was patently poorer even when they were highly equivalent to their neighbors in background characteristics. The successive refinement of patient-control comparisons, however, led to their comparability in instrumental role performance.

The paramount point that emerged from the matching procedures was the fundamental distinctiveness of the patient sample. It appears that patients are drawn from a population notably atypical demographically as well as psychiatrically. Thus, the notion of a normal control group must itself be questioned since the very process of matching tends to minimize the unique configuration of social-psychiatric characteristics of patients. Either as cause or effect of patient status, the total cohort of former patients appears less able to achieve success in two key areas of American life—family and education.

Furthermore, close matching by social characteristics leads to high comparability in role performance between former patients and their normal neighbors. However, in contrast to their neighbors, the former patients evidence distinctive psychiatric impairment. This suggests the likely possibility that instrumental role performance is a quite separate element of the former patient's functioning and not necessarily affected by an impaired psychiatric condition. At least for the acute reactive types of former patients in this study, such orthogonality of functioning aspects may be a common *modus vivendi*.

This unique and extensive series of comparisons between former mental patients and their never previously treated neighbors yielded three critical findings, a number of lesser results, and the thorny problem of interpreting and unifying these data. The implications of these findings both for evaluating performance of the mentally ill and for treating them will be discussed in the next chapter.

8

Summary, Issues, and Implications

The advent of energizing and tranquilizing drugs during the 1950's raised the happy possibility of short term treatment and long term community tenure for the mentally ill. This was the first step in a series leading to the current community mental health center idea that, for all but a few psychiatric patients, varieties of care should be community based with long lasting institutionalization as the exceptional treatment mode. The widespread use of chemotherapy resulted in rapid turnover of mental hospital patients. Thus the question arose of how to determine the usefulness of specific therapies and of hospitalization itself.

Several studies of outcome originated during this period taking as their premise that social variables operative after release are causal in outcome. It was assumed that failure to remain in the community might be understood in terms of unrealistically high demands to perform in the family setting and especially in terms of family members' unwillingness to tolerate even mildly disordered functioning or inadequate role performance. The study reported in this volume was also designed to test such a general hypothesis.

However, unlike other studies of outcome, this one introduced some critical innovations of emphasis and method. Since the special concern was to evaluate women's performance in the community, the adjustment of expatients was compared with that of their neighbors who had never been treated for mental disorders. Among several other unique features of this research (the focus on acute short term cases, use of independent psychiatric assessment of patients), this provision of a normative or comparison group against which to assess the adequacy of expatient performance yielded startling and important results.

The selection of subjects involved first the designation of a sample of 287 women patients who had been discharged from a short term mental hospital. These expatients were mainly Protestant, white, urban, married women from lower and middle class backgrounds. They had been diagnosed mainly as functional psychotic and psychoneurotic, but some organic cases were included. Second, 157 control subjects were chosen who were neighbors of the urban patients. Among the former patients, the 41 women who were readmitted between two weeks and six months after release were defined as returnees, while the remaining 246 women who had avoided readmission were designated as community patients. For all study respondents, both former patients and controls, a significant other in the household, typically the husband, was interviewed. Each woman who was a community patient or a control and her significant other were interviewed separately at home by a psychiatric social worker using a structured schedule. In the case of returnees, only a significant other was interviewed. The schedule contained measures of role performance, psychological functioning, expectations, and background characteristics. For the former patients, the first follow-up interview took place six months after release from the hospital. About one quarter of the community patients participated in a psychiatric assessment by a hospital psychiatrist within a few weeks after the home interview. Thirty-three schizophrenic patients and their significant others were reinterviewed two years after release in order to evaluate changes in functioning during their community tenure.

In this study, we tried to answer three important questions. First, what particular psychiatric and social factors influence hospital readmission, if and when it occurs? Second, what particular psychiatric and social factors contribute to adequate role performance on the part of those patients who successfully avoid rehospitalization for at least six months following discharge? Third, how well do former patients function at home compared with their normal neighbors?

In this chapter the capsulated results are presented; first, for the patient-neighbor comparison; then, for types of expatients who could remain in the community; third, for the returnees. The remainder of the chapter will present the major issues and implications stemming from these results.

SUMMARY OF KEY FINDINGS

FORMER PATIENTS AND THEIR NEIGHBORS

1. The effort to compare the performance levels of the community patients with those of normal women involved, to begin with, 157 patient subjects and their neighbors. The comparison of these two groups yielded differences in overall performance, but especially in the domestic and psychological areas, the normal neighbors emerged as superior performers.

2. When appropriate adjustments were made to account for group variability in demographic and background characteristics, the never treated women and the expatients were found to be similar in instrumental role performance. The only major difference observed between them occurred in psychological functioning.

3. Even in the comparison between highly equivalent groups of former patients and neighbors (matched on marital status, identity of the significant other and household composition), the psychiatric handicaps of the former patients were significantly greater.

4. In the areas of instrumental role performance, role expectations, and tolerance of deviant behavior, the matched groups of former patients and their normal neighbors manifested extremely similar profiles.

5. Furthermore, the matched groups of neighbors and expatients showed the same patterns of relationships on attitudinal variables: for both sets of women, high role expectations were held for the high level performers, and low tolerance of deviant behavior was characteristic of the significant others of high performers.

FORMER PATIENTS IN THE COMMUNITY

1. In general, the 246 (of the original 287) community patients, as a group, were found to be performing at higher levels than those achieved by the rehospitalized women. This superiority of community patients was notably significant in psychological functioning.

2. Among a series of twelve different psychiatric variables, only diagnosis related significantly to posthospital performance level. For-

mer patients who had been diagnosed as organically impaired were clearly more likely to be among the low performers after release, while the psychoneurotic and characterologic patients were high performers; functional psychotics tended to be distributed evenly among high, moderate, and low performers.

3. Of the several social variables thought to be critical concomitants of posthospital performance (social class, marital status, race, religion), only one, marital status, proved to be significantly and consistently associated with performance level. Married women were found to be clearly superior in performance to unmarried women in all areas.

4. In terms of attitudes, it was found that instrumental role expectations held by both the expatients and their significant others were positively and markedly related to performance in the social and domestic areas, while tolerance of deviant behavior was inversely related to psychological functioning. Despite these predicted associations, it was concluded that the expectation and tolerance variables could not be regarded as determinants of posthospital performance, but rather themselves may be reflective of actual performance abilities.

REHOSPITALIZED PATIENTS

1. A definite rehospitalization pattern emerged: the highest proportion of readmissions, 15 percent, occurred within the six months following discharge, and most of these, within the first three months. Rehospitalization continued to occur, but at a declining rate. Within two years, 25 percent (or 71 patients) had been readmitted at least once; at the end of seven years, 32 percent (92 subjects) were known to have been readmitted.

2. Virtually all readmissions, early or late, were found to be precipitated mainly by continued or recurrent psychiatric difficulties. Unexpectedly, the social factors originally viewed as significantly related to readmission were not important—particularly, social class level and familial status. Further, the assumption that readmission was the result of excessively high expectations on the one hand, and low tolerance of deviance on the other, was not borne out.

3. While psychiatric problems precipitated nearly all readmissions, the specific content and nature of the problems were quite different for the early than for the later returnees. *Early returnees* (readmitted within six months) were generally sicker, exhibiting a wider

range of symptoms both mild and severe. Furthermore, they were more often diagnosed as organically impaired and their symptoms, as more chronic. By contrast, the *later returnees* tended to exhibit an episodic illness pattern; their signs and symptoms were usually more acute, though fewer in number and narrower in range. They showed almost no organic impairment or addictions. Their level of overall functioning was generally higher than the early returnees, and in fact, compared favorably with that found in subjects who were not readmitted at all.

4. In addition to their distinctive psychological syndromes, the early and late returnees differed in role performance. For the early and more impaired returnees, social performance was notably poor. The later returnees, except for their more florid symptoms, seemed quite adequate in role activities.

SOME ISSUES FOR DISCUSSION

PERFORMANCE IN THE COMMUNITY: NORMAL AND ABNORMAL

Of the original study population of 287 former patients, 85 percent had succeeded in remaining in the community for at least six months. It was recognized from the start that judgments about their performance would remain relativistically dependent on other patients as a standard, unless performance could be gauged by "normal" standards. The comparison of the urban expatients with their never psychiatrically treated neighbors provided such a measure. Three outstanding findings from the comparative data on patients and neighbors warrant discussion. The *first* is epidemiological and indicates that the former patients as a group were atypical socially as well as psychiatrically when compared to their normal neighbors; *second,* even when the former patients and their neighbors were systematically matched to control for social and familial differences, the patients were reported as significantly poorer in psychological functioning; and *third,* the same variables related to high instrumental performance among patients were also concomitants of high performance among their neighbors. In fact, no major differences in performance or in expectations for performance were found between patients and their neighbors when relevant social and familial factors were controlled. Each of these findings will be considered and interpreted.

Expatients are different. If not the most significant result of the pairing of patients and their neighbors, then certainly one meriting serious consideration in all future epidemiological studies was the finding that expatients are different than their neighbors, so different, in fact, that one might well ponder whether certain demographic atypicalities are perhaps inherently characteristic of patient status; sufficiently different, indeed, so that there is some question about the legitimacy of expatient-neighbor comparisons for any purposes at all and particularly for establishing criteria and guidelines for defining mental illness.

Despite a systematic and successful procedure which did, indeed, pair patients with nearby neighbors, thereby controlling socioeconomic, racial, and other such background variations, patients were found to be unique in three respects: marital status, household configuration, and education. Former patients were disproportionately single, separated, or divorced. This, in turn, resulted in atypical living arrangements. Patients, too, had failed to achieve the educational levels of their normal neighbors.

Two explanations of these phenomena are reasonably plausible. First is that the incipient, prodromal and/or actual symptoms, signs, and patterns in mental illness hinder or even preclude the quality of interpersonal relationships that result in marriage. In the less likely event of marriage, the same problems become instrumental in its dissolution. The net effect, then, is to remove patients from normal households and to concentrate them in pathological families which can better tolerate their aberrations or in parental, kin, or sib family settings. More often, too, these patients end up living with another single person. In these arrangements, it is possible to participate and share without belonging, and hence, to be tolerated within limits. The point is that the illness precedes and determines the alienation and underachievement. The logic of this argument is that some sort of family setting will have to be created if patients are to be successfully treated in a community care program.

The alternative view is that previous psychiatric involvement, especially that just occurring in late adolescence or early adulthood, has so defined and stigmatized the patient that she eventually conceives of herself as an unworthy and inadequate marriage partner. Focusing on her perceived disabilities and inadequacies, she may, in fact, succeed in convincing those around her of her deviant status.

Once defined as mentally ill, the rest of the process follows naturally. She soon becomes the person she has been labeled and has defined for herself.[1]

Between these alternatives, we opt for the first as accounting for the greatest part of the variance. But whether one or the other explanation is preferred, or perhaps another not even mentioned here, the conclusion is the same. *Female expatients are not like their neighbors or, for that matter, like any randomly selected group of females in the community.* Psychiatric difficulties and societal definitions impede or preclude the establishment and maintenance of normal family relations. Since in American society the prestige of the female and her access to the opportunity structure is still tied to her status as wife and mother, the former patient is considerably handicapped by her singleness and atypical household living arrangements.

Finally, disregarding the barriers to social mobility conferred by race, and to a lesser degree by ethnicity, American ideology has encouraged the desire for upward social mobility. At the present time, education represents the principal institutional vehicle to such upward mobility. The former patients badly underachieved in this respect. This, of course, would lend credence to the thesis that the typically lower class status of patients admitted to public mental hospitals is not so much a matter of their having fallen in status but rather that they never rose, because sick people are simply unable to compete effectively. The behavioral concomitants of illness frustrate achievement, preventing upward social mobility. Even if privately treated patients, past and present, were to be included, the argument would be that the likelihood is still great that this population would be very heavily weighted with lower class cases. If the nonpsychotic treated cases were also removed, the remainder would unquestionably be selected from the bottom fifth, or even tenth, of the socioeconomic ladder.[2]

Expatients manifest psychological symptoms. Disregarding arguments concerning the validity and meaningfulness of the utilization of a symptom checklist to determine psychiatric disability, there is no

---

[1] See Thomas J. Scheff, *Being Mentally Ill* (Chicago, Aldine Publishing Company, 1966), pp. 84–101, for discussion of labeling.

[2] Cf. August B. Hollingshead and Frederick C. Redlich, *Social Class and Mental Illness* (New York, John Wiley and Sons, 1958).

question at all about the results. *No matter how restrictive the criteria by which patients and neighbors were paired, the patients invariably were rated as indicating a greater number of psychiatrically relevant signs and symptoms more often.* Indeed, the range and intensity of these symptoms differentiated the cohorts more reliably than any and all other measures. If consensus were ever to be achieved on the relevant nonacute and nonflorid signs and symptoms characteristic of the different neuropsychiatric disorders, the problem of determining their prevalence in the population would be a relatively simple one.

From the medical perspective, psychiatric disorders are basically chronic disorders requiring long range care and treatment. Sometimes the chronicity takes the form of low level, even minimal impairment and deterioration. Terms like *process schizophrenia* and *"burnt out" psychosis* are shorthand designations for these types of reactions.[3] Sometimes the low level chronicity is interspersed with episodic flare-ups and florid symptoms. While the community patients were not sick enough to warrant rehospitalization, they were in fact sick, at least sicker psychologically than their normal neighbors. This explanation is consistent with the fact that the community patients were previously hospitalized and presumably for manifestation of one or more bizarre symptoms. In addition, such manifestations were usually diagnosed as acute episodes, and the patient subjects were discharged after relatively short periods of hospitalization. This suggests that the major concern of the clinical staff is with the remission of those symptoms for which treatment was sought. Even if it is correct to assume that these former patients have remained in the community primarily because there was no recurrence of incapacitating symptoms, it does not necessarily follow that psychological difficulties have been eliminated. The psychiatric orientation, then, holds that the former patients remain at least minimally impaired and that the significant others' reports as well as the psychiatric evaluations are fairly accurate recordings of that fact.

The sociological perspective does not directly dispute this medical interpretation. Instead, the focus is on the definition of illness and its reporting. The basic argument is that the significant other of

[3] Leslie Phillips, "Social Competence, the Process-Reactive Distinction, and the Nature of Mental Disorder," in Paul Hoch and Joseph Zubin, *Psychopathology of Schizophrenia* (New York, Grune and Stratton, 1966), pp. 471–481.

the patient and the expatient herself are cognizant of the meaning of illness. Behavior that would be disregarded in others is linked to the illness. There is a preoccupation with symptoms and their interpretation. Significant others, therefore, are more prone to overreport, to confuse reactions to the stresses and strains of everyday life with mental illness. Conditioned, and in fact, schooled to be tolerant and supportive, significant others are presented with an illness context which colors their evaluations. They overreport out of symptom consciousness and preoccupation.

The significant others of the normal subjects are more innocent of the illness configuration. Tenseness, anxiety, sexual athleticism and misconduct, excessive imbibing, eating and sleeping problems, and other symptom manifestations are assessed as neither especially unusual or as necessarily requiring psychiatric intervention. Above all, the often unspoken preoccupation with mental illness characteristic of former patients and their relatives is unnecessary and extraneous to persons defined as normal. Normals would therefore tend to underreport symptom manifestations or to overlook them as unimportant. No doubt, these perspectives each account for some part of the difference in reported psychological functioning. Certainly future research can do a great deal to sort out the variations accounted for by the medical and sociological perspectives.

Expatients and neighbors are comparable in instrumental roles. The findings concerning instrumental role performance, principally the activities associated with the statuses of wife, mother, and homemaker, were equally consistent but in the opposite direction from those dealing with symptom manifestations. In the paired comparison, the 157 expatients were reported as less adequate than their normal neighbors. This performance gap narrowed considerably in the married pair comparison and disappeared entirely in the last analysis of the more highly equivalent groups. Finally, the factor analysis indicated the absence of any loading on domestic functioning by patient-control status.

One explanation postulates that the similarities in role performance between patients and neighbors hide more than they reveal because of the insensitivity of the instruments. What actually emerges as a portrait of instrumental role performance may not reflect true performance similarities but rather the criteria or standards by which significant others perceive and evaluate their wives' behavior.[4]

The several components of the married woman's role in American society have been traditionally based on the notion that family systems are universal, their structural properties similar, their basic functions virtually identical; hence, the features of required role performance are a general phenomenon rather than a unique one. In short, that the housewife prepare meals, take care of the cleaning chores, manage the shopping responsibilities, and so on, are expectations derived from a *general* conception of the family system. While there may be consensus about basic components of a role, the problem of discerning the specifics remains. A single illustration will suffice: for the woman of the house, to manage the cooking chores is a general expectation and is certainly an integral aspect of her role. But questions may be raised regarding cooking as a specific behavior pattern. For example: how elaborate are meals to be? Does the ability "to cook" include consideration of the number of meals to be cooked each day? For which particular members of the household? Is cooking viewed as an isolated activity or as a series of integrated behaviors involving other management responsibilities?

In addition we tend to assume that household tasks are easily identifiable as "housewife" as opposed to "husband" duties and responsibilities. In situational perspective, however, those assumptions become problematic. If one looks at shopping behavior, for example, the assumption of segmentalized responsibilities may be erroneous. The supermarket, automobile, frozen foods and the revolution in packaging have all combined to alter radically not only traditional patterns of timing and planning, but in many instances, make it

[4] In a recent work, Preiss and Ehrlich suggest that, "Part of the problem of identifying roles is also the problem of specifying the level of generality at which the sociologist-observer chooses to operate. To be concerned with the generality of the role performance is to be concerned with whether the observed behavior is predominantly status-centered or predominantly, for want of a better term, situationally-centered." (p. 165). Is a role better explained by the dictates of the system of which it is a part or by the peculiarities of any given system in which such behavior is relevant? Although both views of a particular role may be logically correct and empirically efficacious, there may indeed be a wide discrepancy between the results of any two investigations which proceed from one as opposed to the other perspective. See Jack J. Preiss and Howard J. Ehrlich, *Examination of Role Theory: Case of the State Police* (Lincoln, Nebraska, University of Nebraska Press, 1966).

extremely convenient, if not essential, for all members of the family to participate. Thus, the execution of certain household duties may be better characterized as shared behavior rather than the exclusive property of a single role incumbent. What may be true for shopping may also hold for other types of domestic activities—care of children, cleaning chores, and the routine tasks related to meal preparation. *Thus the reported similarities between community patients and their neighbors in role performance may have disguised qualitative differences between them in the situationally specific options of the domestic role.*

A second and more parsimonious explanation of these results is also methodological—*that as successively more stringent criteria were used to determine sample inclusion, the patients and controls became more closely paired on the relevant characteristics associated with instrumental role behavior.* Sick or well, the demands on married women with small children at home and no household help are not likely to be too different. Further, the more similar the patients and controls, the less disturbed the patients. In other words, the imposition of each additional set of criteria forced the selection of healthier and better functioning patients.

The argument has now come full circle. We must conclude that the original pairing of patients and neighbors was the soundest way to approach determining normative standards. However, the more criteria applied, the more selective the patient population and the closer to the controls in symptoms and performance.

THE CONTRIBUTION OF SOCIAL VARIABLES TO PERFORMANCE

This study was based on the sociological assumptions that (1) patient experiences are primarily social experiences, and (2) the social world to which the expatient returns is far more instrumental in his fate than any illness or treatment variables. The potency of marital and familial status, social class, and expectations as variables in performance for expatients and their normal neighbors alike substantiated this position. But the explanatory value of social factors either for distinguishing patients from nonpatients or community tenured expatients from returnees has to be discounted. *Thus, it must be argued that the criteria for assessing posthospital outcome should be viewed as distinct and independent.* In a subsequent section, the illness factor in outcome will be discussed. In what follows here, the contribution of social factors is considered.

Status and familial factors. The findings that illness figures strongly in distinguishing patients from nonpatients and returnees from nonreturnees do not, however, totally obliterate social factors in outcome. The firm fact that psychiatric patients stem from a totally different population than healthy persons warns against a drastic swing away from sociological explanations of outcome. Indeed, personal and familial background characteristics (education, marital and familial status) may indirectly influence outcome; such factors do appear to select out potential or incipient patients from nonpatients. In this sense, *status and familial factors may be crucial variables initially for selection and then later for outcome of treatment for mental illness*. The social characteristics clearly influence role performance of both sick and healthy persons. In that respect they can be *partly* predictive of posthospital performance.

Social variables of the attitudinal sort (role expectations and tolerance of deviance) were shown to affect performance similarly for both expatients and their neighbors. Thus, these social and subjective variables are also generically influential in performance. For this important generic contribution to understanding behavior, the social factors cannot be ignored.

Accommodation between performance and expectations. The important point about the patients who could remain in the community is that their performance levels varied widely. A substantial number of these women were performing no better, and in a few cases, worse than subjects who returned to the hospital; and at the high end of the spectrum, were former patients whose instrumental performance level was not only generally superior but no different from reports obtained on normal women. Psychiatrists have long held, and the results of epidemiological studies readily confirm, that there are many persons in the community who suffer from mental disorders severe enough to warrant hospitalization but are not hospitalized. Similarly, the findings about low community performers show that many *former patients* are tolerated by their families and other intimates even though rehospitalization may be medically advisable. While almost all community patients manifested many mild symptoms, the low performers suffered disproportionately from problems of disorientation, irrational fears, suicidal and destructive behavior, hallucinations, and incontinence. Furthermore, these women were much like the early rehospitalization cases in respect to the inadequacy of their role performance. Yet these obviously sick women were not readmitted.

It could be argued that despite relatively severe and persistent symptoms, they seemed to remain acceptable to their families, as long as there was no florid episode. Obviously the broader social context of which the patient is a part needs to be considered. Of specific concern is the interactional process which results in acceptance of these former patients as they are. For example, for any given family, to what extent was acceptance of the patient's low performance a normative and long term adjustment, regardless of the intrusion of mental illness, and to what extent was such tolerance engendered by the *contrast* between the acute symptoms precipitating hospitalization and the relatively less distressing posthospital manifestations?

One might speculate that a kind of corrosion is operating in the interaction of the patient with family members. Unlike the common assumption in role theories that performance is primarily determined by expectations of significant others, this study provides evidence of an *accommodation process* operative over time in the household context. In this view, interaction among household members involves an interplay between the actor's actual performance and the expectations held up for him. The better the performance, the more good performance is expected. *As performance (or the ability to perform) degenerates, the expectations of family members are corroded, so that they become accustomed to expect less of their relative.* In the prehospitalization period and again after release, it appears that such an accommodation is made to gradually diminishing performance.

The accommodation process involves not only the connection between performance and expectations but also the relation between two sets of expectations—the actor's and his significant other's. In the interplay between performance and behavioral expectations, the actor accommodates his expectations both to his lessening performance ability and to the accompanying reduction in the significant other's expectations. Thus the actor begins to expect less of himself as time goes on.

The evidence from this study strongly supports this inferred operation of an accommodation process. Just as role expectations and role performance were found to be highly related, so were the woman's self-expectations closely associated with her husband's. The most potent value of these results is their derivation from *both* the patient *and* the control group data. Because of this, the authors are confident in extending the accommodation hypothesis beyond the abnormal context of families containing a mental patient to the general family setting in which behavior and norms evolve in the day to day interaction process. We would argue that the accommodation process involves more than merely the labeling of deviance or mental illness behavior by both the significant others and the individual himself.[5] Because, unlike the total societal reaction to deviance, the family shows an ability to accommodate to actual behavior rather than only to ascribe, impute, or expect given kinds of behavior. Thus, families adapt to needs and peculiarities of their members, and many are inclined to make very significant adjustments for relatively long periods of time. In this sense, it is useful to separate the types of labelers or definers of deviant behavior. Unlike the more distant medical and legal officials, work colleagues, and even acquaintances, family members would less readily perceive and label residual deviance as mental illness. Spouses, parents, and other household relatives appear to retain a "normal," or at least a conforming view of their members for as long as possible.[6]

Some methodological alternatives. The importance of the accommodation hypothesis stems from its challenge of the traditional role

[5] Thomas Scheff, *op. cit.,* pp. 105–168.

[6] Our thanks go to Raymond F. Sletto who originally suggested that we view the close tie between performance and expectations as reflection of an accommodation process in the family. Distinctions between sets of labelers has been well described by many writers. See for example, David Mechanic, "Some Factors in Identifying and Defining Mental Illness," *Mental Hygiene,* Vol. 46 (January 1962), pp. 66–74; and Charlotte Schwartz, "Perspectives on Deviance—Wives' Definitions of Their Husbands' Mental Illness," *Psychiatry,* Vol. 20 (1957), pp. 275–291. See especially Saad Z. Nagi, "Some Conceptual Issues in Disability and Rehabilitation," in Marvin B. Sussman, Ed., *Sociology and Rehabilitation* (Washington, D.C., American Sociological Association, 1966), p. 105: "It can be argued that adaptations in the normal patterns of relationship among family members in response to a health condition actually constitute part of their normal roles. Therefore, in the context of these systems, it would seem conceptually unsound and empirically fruitless to approach sickness, illness, and disability as roles in themselves. They may be better defined as conditions, and analyzed in terms of their impacts on the performance of normal roles characteristic of the systems."

theories which weight expectations more heavily than behavior.[7] The stance taken here serves to bring new skepticism into old assumptions about behavior as effect rather than cause. It appears useful to consider here some research strategies for sorting out role performance from role expectations. To test out the possible primacy of behavior in determining expectations and to study the interaction between behavior and expectations, a first requirement is a longitudinal research design.

A key dilemma in interpreting the present study findings originates in the evaluation of both expatient and neighbor performance from the *reports* of significant others. Whether the women or their relatives report on performance there is a contamination effect. The possible overestimation of normals' and underestimation of expatients' functioning have been discussed earlier. A further problem in the reporting is that it likely reflects accommodation to and acceptance of behavior over a period of time. Neither can one gauge the observers' or interviewers' contribution to contamination in reported behaviors; the professional halo and functions identified with psychiatric social workers may have colored responses.

Among the methods that would permit elimination of these contaminants would be, first, the use of *direct observation* to describe and evaluate behavior, and second, the *parallel measurement* of psychophysiologic and chemical indices of behavior to validate the overt behavorial observation. Ideally, intervention experiments could be designed to permit longitudinal study of the interaction between significant other and patient. For example, in a community care clinic, significant relatives could be trained to behave toward the patient in specified ways. Or using job retraining and other rehabilitation methods, the subject's "new" behavior could be assessed for its effects on the significant other's expectations. Thus the behavior-expectations link can be experimentally isolated from matters of recidivism and rehospitalization. In fact, comparable research on the socialization process for children as well as adults should yield meaningful results of more generic value. For example, recent studies on the postnatal

---

[7] The broadest implications of this are documented and discussed in Dennis H. Wrong, "The Oversocialized Conception of Man in Modern Sociology," *American Sociological Review*, Vol. 26, No. 2 (April 1961), pp. 183–193.

development of infants provide evidence of immediate unique behavioral patterns in crying, perception of light and shade or texture, and feeding frequency, to all of which both the mother and the nurses must adjust. In specific research on families containing abnormal members, the assumption is implicit that familial adjustment is required to cope with the deviant.[8]

ILLNESS AS A PRECIPITATOR OF REHOSPITALIZATION

The assumption that the social variables (demographic, familial, and attitudinal) would affect readmission proved false. *First,* symptoms rather than social factors accounted for readmission. *Second,* whether readmission occurred within six months or as late as seven years after release, it appeared to stem from illness rather than social difficulties.

Outcome: performance versus readmission. This outcome study was designed in 1958. In line with the prevalent environmental explanations both of mental illness and of the social organization of psychiatric care, we opted for a sociological explanation of outcome. However, as the study progressed, changes occurred both in the prevailing societal climate and in our own thinking. As a result, our perspective has had to change concerning the crucial variables. *Just as it was argued earlier that social variables lack potency in distinguishing expatient from normal female role behavior, so now we reiterate the result that only psychiatric illness factors could separate returnees and community patients.* In the light of this finding, we concur with Freeman and Simmons when they suggest, "in order to understand the posthospital fate of the mental patient, it is essential that the analytic distinction between illness behavior and instrumental behavior be kept clear, and that the issues related to the illness not be

---

[8] Robert L. Fantz, "Origins of Form Perception," *Scientific American,* Vol. 204 (May 1961), p. 41, describes early infant pattern perception. Other studies reflect family adjustments to the "deviant" in their midst. See Bernard Farber and Julia L. McHale, "Marital Integration and Parents' Agreement on Satisfaction With Their Child's Behavior," *Marriage and Family Living* (February 1959), pp. 65–69; and Theodore Lidz, Alice R. Cornelison, Stephen Fleck and Dorothy Terry, "Schism and Skew in the Families of Schizophrenics," in Norman W. Bell and Ezra F. Vogel, Eds., *A Modern Introduction to the Family* (Glencoe, Illinois, The Free Press, 1960), pp. 595–607. See also Clark E. Vincent, "Mental Health and the Family," *Journal of Marriage and the Family,* Vol. 29 (February 1967), pp. 18–39.

confused with those related to inadequate instrumental role performance."[9]

The observed similarity in instrumental role performance between community patients and returnees suggests that psychological difficulties, at least the mild ones, may implicate only a segmentalized aspect of the total personality. Although a poor mental condition may indeed be indicative of illness, the illness may exert little influence on the overt routine forms of behavior. In short, psychopathology need not automatically imply social pathology. If this is so, the many efforts to define mental illness as deviant behavior show central inadequacies. The tendency to equate psychoneuroses with psychoses, or personal problems with mental disorder, or brain damage with problems of living, or anomia with psychological withdrawal dangerously ignores the multidimensionality of the mental disorders. One danger lies in blurring the line between the mentally healthy and the mentally ill. Thereby mental patients have been too readily viewed as social misfits, escapists, and malingerers; and the eccentric or nonconformist are viewed as emotionally disturbed or "sick."[10] A second hazard involves

[9] Howard E. Freeman and Ozzie G. Simmons, *The Mental Patient Comes Home* (New York, John Wiley and Sons, 1963), p. 213. In *Social Science and Social Pathology* (New York, Macmillan, 1959), p. 225, Barbara Wootton indicates that "As definitions of mental illness become ever vaguer or more deeply entangled in the accepted norms of social conduct, so does it become ever more evident that many of those who are labeled "mentally sick" acquire this label merely because in one way or another they have failed to manage their lives conformably with the demands of the social environment in which they find themselves . . . In such cases it is the antisocial behavior which is the precipitating factor that leads to mental treatment. But at the same time the fact of illness is itself inferred from this behavior for which it is also the excuse. But any disease, the morbidity of which is established *only* by the social failure that it involves, must rank as fundamentally different from those of which the symptoms are independent of social norms." Still others have argued that the distinction between psychological condition and instrumental role is not totally clear, since some behavioral areas fit in both domains. See Robert B. Ellsworth and W. H. Clayton, "Measurement of Improvement in Mental Illness," *Journal of Consulting Psychology,* Vol. 23 (1959), pp. 15–20.

[10] Shirley S. Angrist, "Mental Illness and Deviant Behavior: Unresolved Conceptual Problems," *Sociological Quarterly,* Vol. 7, No. 4 (Fall 1966), pp. 436–488. Benjamin Pasamanick has commented on the vast range of rates of prevalence resulting from the blurring of diagnostic categories and confused definitions of illness and health: "What is Mental Illness and How Can We Measure It?" Paper presented at Symposium on Definition and Measurement of Mental Health sponsored by The United States National Center for Health Statistics, Washington, D.C., March 7, 1966.

the already noted overreliance on social-environmental factors in explanations both of illness etiology and of posthospital outcome.

Limitations of the tolerance concept. Prior to the study, it was postulated that patients who performed poorly after discharge would be readmitted due to the low tolerance for their behavior shown by family members. Thus an inverse relationship was expected between patient performance and family tolerance. This was found. It was further supposed that some patients would be readmitted to hospital even though their performance level was not lower than others who remained at home. This second requirement was not demonstrated. In fact, the patients who were readmitted were lower in overall performance and especially in psychological functioning than those remaining in the community. The fact that returnees were decidedly sicker than community patients indicates that intrinsic features of the illness are of greater consequence in precipitating readmission than are the variations in the way significant others perceive, evaluate, or tolerate such illness.

Therefore, while the posited relationship between tolerance and performance was supported, its relationship with readmission has to be reevaluated. The findings reveal a great consensus among significant others regarding the signal importance of severe symptoms. The vast majority of both patients' and neighbors' significant others would seek hospitalization for a suicide attempt, incontinence, hallucinatory or delusional behavior. Thus it is noteworthy that they would readily seek treatment for their relative when needed. This suggests that traditional avoidance and stigma of mental hospitalization have been severely modified. Still, institutionalization is viewed only as a last resort not as a commonplace event.

This great latitude in tolerance by significant others indicates not only their own willingness to keep the former or potential patient at home, but also their perceptions of the "social limits of eccentricity."[11] Furthermore, it may again reflect the extent to which families adapt to the deviant or bizarre behavior of one of their members.

Repeated readmission for episodic cases. A substantial number of eventual returnees spent considerable time in the community and

[11] G. Morris Carstairs, "The Social Limits of Eccentricity: An English Study," in Marvin K. Opler, *Culture and Mental Health* (New York, Macmillan, 1959), pp. 373–389.

with their families. Analyses comparing the community functioning of early and late returnees showed that the *later returnees were fairly good role performers, as competent in performing domestic and social responsibilities as the average former patient who succeeded in remaining in the community for seven years.* Early returnees were typically characterized by disorders high in chronicity and severity and by low performance capacities. By contrast, later returnees were moderately successful role performers and their illness problems were more typically intermittent. During periods of symptom remission, they could function quite adequately. For all readmissions whether within six months or seven years, the evidence indicated that specific episodes, and acute or reactive disease phases prompted rehospitalization. It appears that mainly such crises in the illness process precipitated the return to hospital of 32 percent of the expatient cohort, while many low level patients could avoid readmission indefinitely.

If the result of speedy release of our short term patients is repeated readmission, such a pattern may be viewed pessimistically as representing treatment failures. But it should be recalled that not too many years ago, the opportunity for mental patients to "fail" was denied by indefinite hospitalization. The long term custodial mental hospital was the dominant model. For mental patients, institutionalization became a way of life, the thought of discharge, a faint hope. Since the mid-1950's, there has been progressive reduction of the in-patient population, a sharp shortening of hospitalization, and a concomitant increase in discharge rates. All this is reflected in the pattern of readmission for our study patients. *More important, the pattern of rehospitalization appears to be an objective manifestation of mental illness as a continuum of chronic-episodic disease.*

By analogy to descriptions of persons with physical problems, one could suggest that the early returnees are "disabled" mental patients, whose pattern of behavior evolved from a long term chronic disease process which shows frequent peaks of active pathology. These peaks of pathology prompt frequent readmission. The later returnees represent those whose residual impairments are typically stable and minimal with only rare activation of the disease. For such expatients, family pressures and social events can aid in triggering readmission. A third type is reflected by the low level performers in the community, the permanently "disabled" who suffer from "functional limitations" in role performance and daily activities. These are the frequently older and organically damaged persons who are genuinely dependent on familial accommodation to their low level functioning.[12] It is in this light that the discharge-readmission cycle takes on new meaning. Readmission rates may be high; they may or may not reflect inadequacy of treatment, but these rates in themselves signally indicate the course that mental illness may take in different individuals.

IMPLICATIONS FOR TREATMENT

It is the practitioners, after all, who in the face of uncertainties, confusion, and contradictions must somehow grapple with the daily problems of deciding whether individuals are mentally ill, how they became ill, what is really wrong with them, into what diagnostic category they ought to be placed, and what kind of treatment would be best. In a word, practitioners cannot easily afford the luxury of intellectual debate. Decisions must be made; the sheer presence of the problem demands attention.

The results of this study suggest two intricately related but analytically separate themes which may serve to unravel current treatment dilemmas. The first of these themes refers to illness per se and is concerned with the treatment implications of varying degrees of chronicity and symptom severity. The second has to do with the extent to which socioenvironmental factors are relevant conditions in the affairs and experiences of mentally ill persons.

It has been amply documented that one of the most critical needs in the mental health area is for larger numbers of trained personnel, facilities, and services to manage the sizeable numbers who seek care and treatment for diverse psychiatric disorders. It is equally evident, however, that a reduction in the discrepancy between these needs and their realization will be a slow and painful process. Every aspect of mental illness is in question, ranging from etiology, through validation of disease indicators, to choice of treatment alternatives. No wonder

[12] Saad Z. Nagi, *op. cit.* For other conceptual discussions of illness see: Gene G. Kasselbaum and Barbara O. Baumann, "Dimensions of the Sick Role in Chronic Illness," *Journal of Health and Human Behavior,* Vol. 6 (Spring 1965), pp. 16–27; David Mechanic, "The Concept of Illness Behavior," *Journal of Chronic Diseases,* Vol. 15 (February 1962), pp. 184–194; and Edward A. Suchman, *Sociology and the Field of Public Health* (New York, Russell Sage Foundation, 1963), p. 65.

there is a readiness to grasp at the possible panaceas of new ideas and treatment styles promising quick and efficient results.

The introduction and extensive use of the psychoactive drugs were the most significant factors in prompting a reconsideration of notions and practices involving mental illness and its treatment. The key date was 1955 for in that year the long-standing trend toward higher in-patient census rates was abruptly reversed. Professional reaction to these trends was at first extremely optimistic. Some believed the decline would continue irreversably, of its own momentum until the mental hospitals would be emptied. Others argued that the continuation of these patient population trends was not inevitable, but that it was desirable, in view of the unsatisfactory and often unsavory "treatment" services provided by mental hospitals; moreover, the falling off of hospital in-patients ought to be accelerated by the provision of extended community service and psychiatric beds in general hospitals. Thus, a combination of factors presented practitioners with a new image of themselves as therapists, and at the same time, placed them at the apex of an enterprise involving several possible alternatives for treatment when just a short time ago there seemed only the limited possibility of long term hospitalization for most and psychotherapy for a few.

This issue of treatment alternatives concerns us for it is often viewed as a source of intense competition and controversy among clinical and paraclinical specialists. A particularly revealing illustration of current controversy lies in the status of the mental hospital and its role in the treatment of mentally ill persons. Many have been quick to welcome the signs that indicate that the mental hospital is no longer necessary.[13] There are two rather strong motives behind the arguments against the mental hospital—one is psychological and is steeped in traditional views of mental illness and the places where patients were cared for, and the other is relevant specifically to a treatment perspective.

First, mental hospitals are not popular places. They have been perceived with fear and misunderstanding and it may well be that

---

[13] Although hospitalization is almost always an index of illness, it can also reflect availability of care and societal attitudes about mental illness. With few or no beds available, rates of hospitalization would be lower, but this would neither imply low rates of illness incidence and prevalence nor reflect the level of illness in the population.

these sufficiently justify a desire to destroy them. "This may be expressed in jokes about 'looney bins' and 'nut-houses.' It may also be expressed in a calm and superficially rational assumption that the mental hospital belongs to the unenlightened past, and that it is 'progressive' to look forward to its dissolution."[14] The prime reason for such a view is that the mental hospital has yet to prove its acceptability either as treatment center or as a humane refuge from society. Whereas mental institutions *were* once humane paradises, they now appear inhuman by contrast with current community conditions. State hospitals today are neither humane nor aesthetic; they provide neither care nor cure. Personnel and money will be required to improve the state hospitals to the point that institutionalization can be offered in a meaningful way for even the sickest cases.

Second, important changes in treatment practices have been brought about by the success of drug therapies in quickly remitting and controlling acute phases of mental illness. Such dramatic successes, while most directly relevant to pathology, have had equally dramatic impact on the conception of who and what a mental patient is as a person. The "therapeutic community" orientation regarding treatment serves to summarize such events.[15] Of special significance is the continuing effort on the part of clinicians to view interpersonal relations as critical dimensions of the mental disorders. In short, once having ameliorated the management problems such as destructiveness, severe depression, hallucinations, and so on, attention has been increasingly drawn to those behavioral manifestations most relevant to everyday community experiences—role performance, instrumental expectations, and social awareness. These interests imply that the mental hospital—and especially the developing community mental health facilities—can no longer be conceived as separate and distinct from the patient's life cycle. Thus, the therapeutic effectiveness of the hospital is based essentially on its role in facilitating continuity of

[14] Kathleen Jones and Roy Sidebotham, *Mental Hospitals at Work* (New York, The Humanities Press, 1962), pp. 19–20.

[15] Maxwell Jones, *The Therapeutic Community: A New Treatment Method in Psychiatry* (New York, Basic Books, 1953); Alfred Stanton and Morris Schwartz, *The Mental Hospital* (New York, Basic Books, 1954); and Milton Greenblatt, Richard York and Esther L. Brown, *From Custodial To Therapeutic Patient Care in Mental Hospitals: Explorations in Social Treatment* (New York, Russell Sage Foundation, 1955).

community living rather than as a manifest intervention in the experiential world of the patient.[16]

Such thinking has emphasized the critical importance of aftercare services to former mental patients. Current interest in such facilities and services as residential and nonresidential halfway centers, vocational services, and day-night hospitals are reflective not only of basic needs for former patients but of concern with how to get patients to utilize properly what is available. Those who espouse such views appear to be convinced that once extreme symptoms are remitted or effectively controlled, the major therapeutic problem is to maintain adequate levels of interpersonal functioning so that patients may remain intact as total social participants.

We concur with such views—up to a point. Based on this study of short term treatment outcome, we certainly applaud the effort to help former patients to achieve and maintain adequate community performance. But there are serious objections to attempts to promote such therapeutic goals as a *general policy for all mental patients*. Not only have such efforts served to foster conflicts among psychiatric specialists regarding appropriate therapeutic responsibilities, but more importantly, they have tended to tax existing facilities and available personnel beyond their capabilities.

The findings of this study reinforce a very obvious but sometimes neglected consideration—namely, that some mentally ill persons are sicker than others. In fact, the range in terms of chronicity and severity is so great that any attempt to generalize either in terms of categorization or treatment is bound to suffer serious consequences. The women studied revealed a definite pattern of chronicity and severity of illness behavior and inability to perform instrumental roles while at home. The early returnees, the sickest of the subjects, are clearly representative of mentally ill persons who require extended treatment over time and may indeed require permanent institutionalization, at least until such time as community treatment facilities are available to provide the sickest patients and their families with ade-

---

[16] Not only have mental health professionals and lay people abetted the "total institution" nature of mental hospitals. Patients themselves have fostered their own permanent tenure. One study reports that 40 percent of patients in a large veteran's hospital are institutional types, that is, they *do not* want to leave the institution. See Ailon Shiloh, "The Total Institution: Profiles of Mental Patient Perception and Adaptation," Paper presented at the meeting of the American Anthropological Association, Pittsburgh, November, 1966.

quate continuing care and support. Admittedly, such a view runs counter to more "progressive" and popular perspectives which hold that anything is better than long term institutionalization. However, this study provided some evidence of the great efforts individual families exert to adjust their style of life to meet the exigencies prompted by housing very sick persons. The focus of what is good for patients has tended to deflect attention away from what may be negative consequences for their families. In the absence of adequate knowledge of the precise features of these adjustment patterns, it is as meaningful to be cautious for the sake of the family and its members as it is for the presumed well-being of the patient. Extended institutionalization can only be eliminated when realistic replacements become available. The refinement of the short term therapies and the use of multiple though brief hospitalizations should intervene in the progress of the disease. Hopefully, community care programs which incorporate such systematic intervention will prevent the patient deterioration so common during long confinement. Projected treatment modes must, therefore, include provision not merely for the psychotic and organically damaged patients but for their families as well. Education, counseling, and emotional sustenance for these families are the *sine qua non* of community-centered care.

At the other end of the continuum are those former patients who are successful in terms of having remitted those symptoms which prompted initial hospitalization and who are clearly performing as well as their normal neighbors. It is assumed that for many of these women, symptom exacerbation was a very temporary and perhaps a cursory event in their lives. Little or no extra effort would need to be expended in order to maintain them as they are. In fact, unsolicited efforts to guide or counsel such former patients may well promote feelings of anxiety or stigma without cause or genuine justification.

The remainder of the subject population reveals symptom and performance profiles which leave much to be desired although they manage to remain at home; these persons also appear to require much in the way of professional attention and posthospital therapeutic talent. In other words, many former patients are not sick enough to warrant hospitalization but at the same time are clearly not performing adequately—as judged by standard expectations. Moreover, the families of such persons may be in great need of professional help in order to manage successfully with a "coping" person in their midst, to recognize serious signs and symptoms, to know how to manage on their own when need be, and when to seek appropriate aid. In short, this is the low level, chronic former patient who by virtue of staying in the community requires access to community mental health attention and service. It is this patient who clearly stands half way between hospital and community and needs the special push to maintain this rather precarious balance.

All types of psychiatric services, such as the day hospital, sheltered workshop, homemaker help, and weekend hotel care, will need to serve not only the patient but also the family. Family members will require rest, relief, encouragement, and some training in home care of the mentally ill. When to lower or raise role expectations, how to judge the adequacy of each phase of home treatment, how to translate psychiatric goals into a meaningful life for all concerned—these are crucial elements in effective community mental health programs.

In delineating the differences among patients and urging a family focus in community care, it is our hope that patients will receive from present and future facilities the kind of treatment most suitable to their intrinsic needs. It is hoped that the evolving facilities will maximize their contribution by specializing in treatment goals to serve the types of patients who can best profit from each service.

Appendix A
Instruments and Procedures

A NOTE ON INSTRUMENT RELIABILITY

The primary type of instrument reliability by which data were obtained is the stability type of reliability.[1] Reference here is to the consistency of repeated measurement using the same instrument under similar conditions at different time intervals. This was achieved through a repeat administration of the Patient Schedule. Former patients living in the county where the hospital is located were ordered chronologically by the date the patient was interviewed, and every eighth case was designated for a repeat interview. This resulted in nine cases for the check on reproduceability. The repeat interview was carried out by an interviewer of opposite sex from the original one. An average of 48 days elapsed between the original interview and the repeat interview with the nine former patients. While the original interviews had lasted about 36 minutes on the average, the repeat interviews took an average of 39 minutes.

The results of this quasi test-retest indicated the generally high reliability of the Patient Schedule. Since the Patient Schedule contained many diverse measures, it was not relevant to compute a coefficient of reliability

---

[1] Claire Selltiz, Marie Jahoda, Morton Deutsch, and Stuart W. Cook, *Research Methods in Social Relations*, (New York, Holt, revised 1959), pp. 166-172; Bert F. Green, "Attitude Measurement," in Gardner Lindzey, Ed., *Handbook of Social Psychology*, (New York, Addison-Wesley, 1954), pp. 338-340.

as is usually done for retest of single scales. Out of a total of 233 individual items which could be answered on the schedule, discrepancies in responses occurred in 82 items, or 35 percent of the items. Where discrepancies occurred in an item, the average number per item for the nine repeat interviews was two. For only six out of 233 items did as many as four discrepancies between test and retest occur. The median percentage of errors for the nine retests was eight while the average errors per schedule was 7.5 percent.

However, it is not clear to what sources the variation may be attributed in the discrepant responses that occurred. There are three possibilities: the effects of the different interviewers, actual attitude or status changes of the respondent, or inadequacies in those schedule items where the discrepancies occurred. The probability is great that all three sources contributed to unreliability. Nor was it possible to establish the amount of variation each contributed within the scope of this study. It should be stressed, however, that no other patient follow-up studies reported in the literature have provided even this much evidence of instrument reliability.

A second, more subjective estimate of reliability was obtained by comparing family background information from two sources: the hospital record and the follow-up interview with the patient. The following items of information were compared: patient's occupation, age, education, place of birth, marital status, birth order, number of siblings, household residents, religion, husband's occupation, and family income. For such items as age and educational level, up to two years of discrepancy between information sources was considered acceptable. The greatest discrepancy between the two sources of information occurred for family income. Minor variations were found in marital status, patient occupation, and household residents. Since in this comparison *at least* six months had elapsed between the completion of hospital record information and the interview, some discrepancies reflected actual changes in the patient's status over time. Many of these changes were verified at the time of follow-up. For example, some patients employed before hospitalization did not seek work after discharge; others changed from married status to separated or divorced. In most instances, however, this comparison indicated comparatively high agreement between the two sources.

It should be added that aside from their experience as psychiatric social workers, the interviewers were carefully trained in administering schedules, in how to define the follow-up, and in how to identify themselves. The schedules were structured with only one or two open-ended questions to eliminate as much variation as possible from the interview situation. Interview schedules were edited by the study's administrative assistant as soon as possible after completion of the interviews. In this way omitted items or dubious responses could be questioned. Interviewers were asked to return to the patient's home or to telephone respondents in order to clarify such matters.

Concerning the stability aspect of reliability, then, a high degree of agreement was obtained between test-retest responses for the various types of measures on the patient schedule for attitudinal measures, such as patient expectations, and factual ones, such as family background. Somewhat lower agreement was found between hospital record data and follow-up interview information on family background. The latter discrepancies were attributed partly to actual status changes in the elapsed time.

Only the patient interview was repeated because it was felt that if reliability between test-retest for patients could be demonstrated, at least the same kind of reliability could be expected from the significant others who were primarily a nonpatient group. As Freeman and Simmons indicated personally to the writers, they and other follow-up researchers had avoided interviewing former patients for fear of unreliable responses. From the present study, it can be concluded that such fears seem unfounded in fact.

A NOTE ON VALIDITY: THE PSYCHIATRIC ASSESSMENT OF COMMUNITY PATIENTS

Of the 246 former patients in the community six months after hospitalization, 65 women, or about one third, came for the psychiatric interview with one of two hospital psychiatrists. For each woman thus assessed, the psychiatrists provided an impairment rating, a diagnosis, and a detailed symptom evaluation using the Lorr Psychiatric Rating Scale, Part 1. The 65 psychiatrically assessed patients were found to be similar to the 54 who refused to participate when contacted in almost every respect in which available data permitted comparison. These included 16 hospital variables, *e.g.,* diagnosis, previous admission, an impairment rating at admission and one at discharge, hospital treatment, and out-patient treatment. The two groups were also similar in their social background characteristics including age, social class standing, education, religion, and size of community in which they resided. They differed only in their marital status. The reevaluation cases included a significantly greater percentage of married women (70 percent) than did the refusal cases (41 percent). In addition, on none of the variables—pre and posthospital and social background—did the reevaluated subjects differ from the 127 cases who were not selected to participate in the psychiatric assessments. This would lead to the conclusion that no appreciable selectivity characterized the psychiatric assessment cases or differentiated them from the refusals or those not involved in this aspect of the outcome study.

Two hospital psychiatrists carried out the assessments. Minimal differences existed in their orientations towards diagnosis and treatment of mental patients and in their orientations towards the etiology of mental disorders. One of the psychiatrists saw 39, the other 26 former patients. This difference was due wholly to scheduling and time factors since patients were assigned randomly to them. As had been the case for the follow-up interviewers, the two psychiatrists were free to recommend rehospitalization or other further treatment for the patients whom they assessed when they deemed it necessary. This occurred for two cases in which the patient and her family were given such advice and gratefully complied.

Prior to their psychiatric evaluations, each of the community patients had been rated by her significant other (usually the husband) on the 32 item scale of psychological functioning. Of these items, 17 were directly comparable with Lorr Scale Items, since they were, in fact, simpler or modified versions of these items; this allowed item-by-item comparison between the psychiatrist's and the significant other's evaluations of the woman's mental status.[1]

The ratings on symptoms given by each psychiatrist and the relevant significant others were found to be highly and significantly correlated: for the 40 item Lorr Scale Score and the psychological functioning score, posi-

---

[1] Although patients had been randomly assigned to the two psychiatrists and their respective patients did not differ significantly in illness or treatment history or in background characteristics, the two sets of patients still were evaluated differently by the two psychiatrists. Physician *A* rated his patients as significantly more ill than Physician *B* rated his on the Lorr Scale. But it is noteworthy that the two groups of former patients were similar in all the 17 symptom areas as viewed by their significant others. The two psychiatrists had been selected because they were only minimally discrepant in orientation; despite this, the differential evaluations emerged. The importance of these differential perceptions of the two psychiatrists is discussed in "Differential Assessment of Posthospital Psychological Functioning: Evaluations by Psychiatrists and Relatives," by Benjamin Pasamanick and Leonard Ristine, *American Journal of Psychiatry*, 117 (July, 1961), pp. 40-46.

tive correlations of 0.71 and 0.50 were obtained for the patients of psychiatrists A and B, respectively.[1]

For four of 17 symptoms, psychiatrist A specified a significantly higher prevalence than did the patient's significant other. Somatic complaints, preoccupation with health, fears about the future, and worries about bodily organs were found with greater frequency by this physician. Psychiatrist B also found four symptoms significantly more often than did the significant others; preoccupation with health was one of these, but this time three symptoms differed from those found by the first physician: these were tension, suicidal thoughts, and paranoia. For ten symptoms in each physician's patients, significant others and psychiatrists agreed on the degree of disability. It appeared that the psychiatrists were greatly concerned with the somatic condition of the patient, while relatives might not consider somatic ailments to be pertinent to mental illness. On the major symptoms associated with mental illness, only minor and random discrepancies existed between physicians and relatives.

Correlations of the impairment rating (ranging from 1 to 100, that is, no impairment to severe impairment) given after the psychiatric assessment, confirmed the general agreement between psychiatrists and relatives on the patient's condition. High and significant correlations were found between each physician and his respective significant other: for psychiatrist A's patients, $r = 0.74$ and for psychiatrist B's patients $r = 0.52$.[2]

The several performance measures—domestic, social, and psychological—were significantly intercorrelated, except for the correlation between social participation and domestic performance which was not significant. All three measures were of course highly related to the index of total performance. For all these measures, high scores in one area of performance were associated with high scores in the other performance area. The psychiatrists' impairment rating, as well as the diagnosis given following the psychiatric interview, was generally found to support the findings obtained by using the significant other's report of posthospital performance. Thus the degree of psychiatric impairment correlated highly with domestic performance, so that higher performers tended to be characterized by no or only minimal impairment; low performers in the domestic

---

[1] For this analysis, Lorr Scale Scores were converted so that high scores signify the patient's good health. Thus we obtained positive r's.
[2] For ease of interpreting these r's, the minus signs are omitted. In these analyses, higher Lorr Scale Scores signified greater disturbance.

area were rated as having *at least* mild impairment. Only seven percent of the low performers were minimally impaired, while half of the high domestic performers were either minimally or not at all impaired.

The psychiatrist's impairment rating at six months after discharge was not significantly related to social participation, psychological functioning or total performance, but the trends were the same as for domestic performance. In total performance, minimal impairment characterized 21 percent of low performers, 36 percent of moderate performers, and 55 percent of high performers. The psychiatrist's diagnosis established at the six month psychiatric interview yielded a similar pattern of results. Patients high and moderate in total performance were primarily diagnosed as having neurotic or characterological disorders, while more than half of the low performers fell in the functional psychosis category.

To summarize, then, both the psychiatric assessment and the measures of performance distributed patients similarly on a continuum of performance. This points first to the desirability of using relatives of patients as raters of the illness and performance level of their significant others. Second, the fact that the physicians' ratings of patient functioning tended to validate the significant others' reports of performance increases confidence in the importance of the findings.

The judgments of significant others seemed to be most reliable when they concerned the actual day-to-day functioning of the patients. Relatives appeared competent to judge overt and meaningful deviations in functioning; perhaps the continuing contact with the patient gave the relative some perspective over time as well. In the division of labor in the mental health area, it is frequently the lot of the social worker to obtain case histories from relatives. The physician or therapist is often, therefore, denied the salutary effort of tempering or modifying or affirming his own judgments by getting these materials either already interpreted for him or possibly not getting them at all except for some social background data. If, as we have tried to indicate, the relatives and significant others are capable of making critical judgments of patient functioning, then these ought to become available, undiluted and uninterpreted by others, to the clinician. These observations seem to point to the necessity for thorough training of psychiatric residents in the securing of reliable anamneses from the relatives of patients. This appears to be an area badly neglected in present day psychiatric training.

As suggested elsewhere, the two psychiatrists in this study were selected because they were only minimally discrepant in their orientation.

Despite this, differences in their evaluations did occur. The extent to which differences between psychiatrists A and B could have been removed had they interviewed relatives as well as patients is a moot point which remains to be tested empirically.

July 14, 1959

NOTICE TO ALL RESIDENTS

Since June 1st, 1959, a follow-up study of all female patients has been going on at Columbus Psychiatric Institute and Hospital. Former patients and their relatives are contacted for interviews six months after the patient leaves CPIH. Each former patient and one significant relative are interviewed at home by a psychiatric social worker. Following this interview, the former patient is asked to come back to the hospital for a psychiatric assessment (which lasts about one hour).

The follow-up has been described to former patients as an official hospital program. We have been receiving excellent cooperation from most of our former patients and their families in this project. But, from time to time, patients fear the interview and hasten to contact their therapist to ask about the follow-up. It is for this reason that we ask the cooperation and support of all psychiatric residents.

The importance of such a study cannot be overrated. We need to know how patients get along in the community once they leave the hospital. We need to know how effective hospital treatment and facilities have been for patients. And we hope to learn what social factors lead to readmission to a psychiatric hospital, as well as what factors are related to successful post-hospital functioning in the community.

We ask help in explaining the importance of these interviews to former patients or relatives who inquire about the follow-up. They will appreciate your clarification; and that will make it easier for us to obtain the information which could eventually lead to more effective care of psychiatric patients.

LETTER TO PATIENT'S FAMILY DOCTOR

Dear Dr.

As part of our hospital program, we are contacting our former patients and their relatives to find out how they are doing. We plan to write to your patient, Mrs._____, so that a member of our hospital staff may see and talk with her and a close family member.

We feel that the importance of this program cannot be overstated. We need to know a great deal more than we now do about the posthospital situation to which patients return, including the problems faced by the patient and by the family. We want to know how a patient is functioning after leaving the hospital, so that we can better assess the value of the treatment received during hospitalization. For these reasons, we hope our interviews with former patients and their relatives will yield information from which we can eventually improve our treatment and facilities.

We are writing you about this follow-up program so that you will be aware of our plans. If for any reason you think that such an interview would be detrimental to the above-mentioned patient, we would appreciate hearing from you about this.

LETTER TO FORMER PATIENT

Dear

As part of our program, the staff of the Columbus Psychiatric Institute and Hospital is seeing former patients in order to find out how they are doing. The information we hope to get from you will also be of use to us in helping those who are in the hospital now and those who will come in the future. We are visiting people who were in the hospital and their relatives for this purpose.

A social worker on our hospital staff plans to visit you on _____. At that time, the social worker would like to interview you and your husband; or if you are not married, the social worker wants to talk with you and a close relative who lives with you, possibly your mother, daughter, or sister. The interview lasts about an hour with each person.

Please indicate on the enclosed reply card the times which are most convenient for both of you and send the card back to us or call for an appointment.

SUGGESTED INTRODUCTION FOR INTERVIEWERS

I am a social worker on the staff of the Columbus Psychiatric Institute and Hospital. The hospital has a program designed to keep in touch with its former patients to find out how they are doing since leaving the hospital.

I have the specific job of talking with former patients and their relatives in the community. We feel that by talking to people who were in our hospital and their relatives, we can learn what happens to our patients once they leave the hospital. With the information you give us, the hospital hopes eventually to expand its program so that we may better help other people who come to the hospital.

If we are to be really useful to people who want help, our program will have to be based on information obtained from the people who know most about these things from their own experience.

In the questions we want to ask you, there are no right or wrong answers. I simply want you to tell me your honest opinions on the matters we discuss.

(Deck 01, 02 and 03)   Schedule No. ____

HOSPITAL RECORD DATA: FORM I

1. Hospital case no. _____   (01:10-13)

2. Patient's name _____ , _____
                  (last)   (first)   (m. init.)

3. Address patient
   released to _____ (01:14)
   (write in alternative
   if not sure of address) _____

4. Telephone number _____

5. Patient's usual occupation _____ (01:15)
   (note if housewife)

6. Name of closest _____ (01:16)
   adult female rela-   __0 only males in household
   tive at address   __1 mother   __6 grandmother
   patient released   __2 sister   __7 aunt
   to (note if step   __3 daughter   __8 female cousin
   parent)   __4 sister-in-law __x not available
                        __5 daughter-in-law

7. Name of closest _____ (01:17)
   adult male rela-   __0 only females in housenold
   tive at address   __1 father   __6 son-in-law
   patient released   __2 husband   __7 grandfather
   to (note if step   __3 brother   __8 uncle
   parent)   __4 son   __9 male cousin
                        __5 brother-in-law __x not available

8. Type of family   __1 parental   __5 nonkin   (01:18)
   patient re-   __2 conjugal   __6 lives alone
   leased to   __3 sibling   __x not available
                        __4 child

NOTE: Each item requires some category filled in. Unless otherwise specified, "x" is used for information not available. Items with asterisks (*) can have multiple punches.

FORM 91   4-7-59

APPENDIX A

9. Established diagnosis last hosp'n (note if alcoholism is included) _____ (use state code) (01:19-22)

10. Patient's birth date _____ (year) (01:23&24)

11. Patient's place of birth
    __ 1 Ohio
    __ 2 other U.S.
    __ x not available
    (01:25)

12. Marital status at discharge from last hosp'n
    __ 1 married   __ 4 widowed
    __ 2 single   __ 5 separated
    __ 3 divorced   __ x not available
    (01:26)

13. Type of family patient lived with before last hosp'n
    __ 1 parental   __ 4 child
    __ 2 conjugal   __ 5 lived alone
    __ 3 sibling   __ x not available
    (01:27)

14. Religion
    __ 1 Protestant
    __ 2 Catholic
    __ 3 Jewish
    __ 4 other _____ (specify)
    __ x not available
    (01:28)

15. Parents (biological) at discharge from last hosp'n
    __ 1 both living
    __ 2 mother living
    __ 3 father living
    __ 4 both deceased
    __ x not available
    (01:29)

16. No. of living brothers at discharge from last hosp'n (count only those of same biological mother) _____ (01:30)

17. No. of living sisters at discharge from last hosp'n (count only those of same biological mother) _____ (01:31)

18. Total number of   _____   (01:32&33)
    living siblings

19. Birth order of   _____ (if oldest, code 1) (01:34&35)
    patient (count
    living siblings
    only)

20. Was patient's   __ 1 yes   (01:36)
    father born   __ 2 no
    in U.S.   __ x not available

21. Was patient's   __ 1 yes   (01:37)
    mother born   __ 2 no
    in U.S.   __ x not available

22. Father's usual   _____ (01:38&39)
    occupation   (code xx if not available)

23. If married, hus-   _____ (01:40&41)
    band's usual   (code 00 if not married, xx if not available)
    occupation

24. Education of   __ 1 some grammar school   (01:42)
    patient   __ 2 completed grammar school (8 yrs)
                       __ 3 some high school
                       __ 4 completed high school (12 yrs)
                       __ 5 some college
                       __ 6 completed college (16 yrs)
                       __ 7 post-grad or professional
                       __ x not available

25. If married, no.   ____ (code 00 if not married, (01:43&44)
    of years (at dis-   xx if not available)
    charge from
    last hosp'n)

26. If married, age   ____   (01:45&46)
    of husband (at
    discharge from
    last hosp'n)

27. If married, no.   ____ (code 8 if 8 or more,   (01:47)
    of children   9 if not married)

APPENDIX A

28.	Total number of household residents (at time of discharge)	____ (excl. patient; code xx if not available)	(01:48&49)
29.	Total number of female residents	____	(01:50)
30.	Total number of male residents	____	(01:51)
31.	No. of male residents under 18	____ (at time of discharge; excl. patient; code x if not available)	(01:52)
32.	No. of female residents under 18	____	(01:53)
33.	Total number of residents under 18	____	(01:54)
34.	Place of residence in past ten years	__1 rural farm __2 rural nonfarm __3 urban __x not available	(01:55)
35.	Estimated intelligence level during last hosp'n	__1 low __2 borderline __3 dull normal __4 normal __5 superior __x not available	(01:56)
36.	Race of patient	__1 white __2 Negro __3 Oriental __x not available	(01:57)
37.	Family relations before last hosp'n	__1 was solely responsible for care of house and children, if any Took considerable responsibility for maintaining family affairs or acted as head of the house	(01:58)

___2 participated in above responsibilities but not solely responsible for them
___3 sporadic responsibility for them
___4 no responsibilities
___x not available

38. Work performance before last hosp'n

___1 worked regularly during 3 years (01:59) prior to last hospitalization, gainfully employed at time of hospitalization
___2 worked some of the time during 3 years prior to last hospitalization and worked in last 6 months prior to last hospitalization more than half the time; gainfully employed at time of last hosp'n
___3 worked some of the time during 3 years prior to last hosp'n and worked in last 6 months prior to hosp'n but less than half the time; gainfully employed at time of last hosp'n
___4 worked some of the time during 3 years prior to last hosp'n and worked in last 6 months prior to last hosp'n but less than half the time; not gainfully employed at time of last hosp'n
___5 worked some of the time during 3 years prior to last hosp'n but not gainfully employed at time of last hosp'n
___6 not gainfully employed during 3 years prior to last hosp'n
___x not available

APPENDIX A

39. Psychiatric symptoms during three years prior to last hosp'n
    — 1 manifested psychiatric symptoms regularly which prevented interpersonal performance (01:60)
    — 2 manifested psychiatric symptom regularly but these did not prevent interpersonal performance
    — 3 manifested psychiatric symptom intermittently which prevented interpersonal performance
    — 4 manifested psychiatric symptom intermittently which did not prevent interpersonal performance
    — 5 illness was of sudden onset
    — x not available

40. Family members' stability (excl. patient)
    — 1 evidence of sexual promiscuity, frequent drunkenness, or violence during last year prior to last hosp'n of patient (01:61)
    — 2 evidence of sexual promiscuity, frequent drunkenness, or violence but more than one year prior to hosp'n
    — 3 evidence against above
    — x not available

41. Patient's stability as family member
    — 1 evidence of sexual promiscuity, frequent drunkenness, or violence during last year prior to hosp'n (01:62)
    — 2 evidence of sexual promiscuity, frequent drunkenness, or violence but more than one year prior to last hosp'n
    — 3 evidence against above
    — x not available

42. Patient's age at time of first hosp'n
    _____ (01:63&64)

43. *Who brought patient to hospital last time (01:65)
    __1 husband
    __2 mother
    __3 father
    __4 child
    __5 sibling or sibling-in-law
    __6 police
    __7 hospital or physician or social welfare
    __8 came in herself
    __9 other _____ (specify)
    __x not available

44. *Who instigated last hospitalization (01:66)
    __1 husband
    __2 mother
    __3 father
    __4 child
    __5 sibling or sibling-in-law
    __6 police
    __7 hospital or physician or social welfare
    __8 self (check only if patient was active in decision)
    __9 other _____ (specify)
    __x not available

45. *Behavior resulting in last admission (01:67)
    __1 threatened or attempted suicide
    __2 abusive toward others—verbal
    __3 assaulted others
    __4 psychosomatic symptoms
    __5 self-abusive
    __6 hallucinations
    __7 delusions
    __8 destructive
    __9 depressed
    __0 other
    __x no information

46. Time spent in hospital residence last hosp'n (in bed) (01:68)
    __1 less than ten days
    __2 ten days to one month
    __3 one to two months
    __4 two to four months
    __5 four to six months
    __6 six months to one year

		__7 over one year __x not available	
47.	Total time hospitalized (time on books excl. last hosp'n)	__1 less than ten days __2 ten days to one month __3 one to two months __4 two to four months __5 four to six months __6 six months to one year __7 one to three years __8 three to six years __9 over six years __0 never previously hospitalized __x not available	(01:69)
48.	No. of times hospitalized over 5 days (in mental institution)	_____	(01:70)
49.	Out-patient or private treatment prior to last hosp'n (on regular basis)	__1 was receiving it regularly at time of last hosp'n but for less than 1 year __2 was receiving it regularly at time of last hosp'n for over 1 year __3 received some prior to last hosp'n but for less than 1 year __4 received some prior to last hosp'n for over 1 year __5 never __x not available	(01:71)
50.	Type of admission (at discharge) last hosp'n	__1 voluntary __2 court __3 emergency __4 transfer __x not available	(02:10)
51.	Therapist during last hosp'n (If more than 1, use	_____	(02:11&12)

therapist of last third of last hosp'n

52. Type of release last hosp'n
    - __1 trial visit
    - __2 extended leave of absence
    - __3 discharged outright or MHB
    - __4 AWOL
    - __5 AMA
    - __6 transfer to another hospital
    - __7 other
    - __x not available

    (02:13)

53. Frequency of patient's home visits during last third of last hosp'n
    - __1 weekly
    - __2 twice a month
    - __3 once a month
    - __4 less than once a month
    - __5 never
    - __x not available

    (02:14)

54. Average no. of visitors to hospital during last third of hosp'n
    - __1 more than one per week
    - __2 one per week
    - __3 less than one per week but one per month
    - __4 rare or none
    - __x not available

    (02:15)

55. Ward changes last hosp'n
    - __1 no ward changes
    - __2 one ward change
    - __3 two or more ward changes
    - __x not available

    (02:16)

56. Outcome of mental condition at release from last hosp'n
    - __1 favorable, recovered, or maximum hospital benefit
    - __2 guarded or improved
    - __3 unfavorable or unimproved
    - __x not available

    (02:17)

57. *Did patient receive organic therapy during last hosp'n
    - __1 electro-shock therapy
    - __2 lobotomies
    - __3 other
    - __4 no
    - __x not available

    (02:18)

APPENDIX A

58. Did patient receive individual psychotherapy during last hosp'n
    - __1 analytic psychotherapy
    - __2 directive therapy
    - __3 other
    - __4 no
    - __x not available
    (02:19)

59. Did patient receive occupational therapy and occupational counseling during last hosp'n
    - __1 both o.t. and counseling
    - __2 occupational therapy
    - __3 occupational counseling
    - __4 neither
    - __x not available
    (02:20)

60. Did patient receive group therapy during last hosp'n
    - __1 while in hospital and prescribed for after release
    - __2 while in hospital only
    - __3 after release
    - __4 no
    - __x not available
    (02:21)

61. Did patient receive drug therapy during last hosp'n
    - __1 while in hospital and prescribed for after release
    - __2 while in hospital only
    - __3 after release
    - __4 no
    - __x not available
    (02:22)

62. Extended family relationships before last hosp'n
    - __1 considerable responsibility, took part in family activities
    - __2 some
    - __3 little
    - __4 none
    - __x not available
    (02:23)

63. Serious physical illness resulting in handicap
    - __1 yes_____(specify)
    - __2 no
    - __x not available
    (02:24)

64. Has patient been in hospital over 2 months for nonpsychiatric reasons
    - __1 yes
    - __2 no
    - __x not available
    (02:25)

65. Has patient ever been imprisoned for over 60 days in a single conviction
- __ 1 yes (how long and for what) (02:26) _____
- __ 2 no
- __ x not available

66. Relations with hospital staff during last hosp'n (02:27)
- __ 1 only positive reports of cooperation
- __ 2 no consistent pattern but several negative reports
- __ 3 pattern of negative reports
- __ 4 destructive and fought with staff
- __ x not available

67. Relations with patients during last hosp'n (02:28)
- __ 1 only positive reports of cooperation
- __ 2 no consistent pattern but several negative reports
- __ 3 pattern of negative reports
- __ 4 destructive or fighting with patients
- __ x not available

68. Behavior while in hospital last time (02:29)
- __ 1 interacted often with one or more persons while in hospital and showed emotions such as tears, laughter, etc.
- __ 2 interacted often with one or more persons but only rarely showed emotions such as tears, laughter, etc.
- __ 3 usually quiet but sometimes interacted with others
- __ 4 almost completely withdrawn
- __ x not available

69. Prognosis at time of discharge from last hosp'n (02:30)
- __ 1 favorable
- __ 2 guarded or fair
- __ 3 unfavorable
- __ x not available

APPENDIX A

70. Ward during most or all of last hosp'n
    - __1 1W
    - __2 2W
    - __3 3W

    (02:31)

71. What was primary therapy during last hosp'n (reported by therapist)
    - __1 EST
    - __2 drug
    - __3 milieu
    - __4 psychotherapy

    (02:32)

72. Suicidal or homicidal attempts during last hosp'n (reported by therapist)
    - __1 attempted both suicide and homicide
    - __2 suicide
    - __3 homicide
    - __4 neither
    - __x not available

    (02:33)

73. Family reaction to patient's release
    - __1 pressured for release strongly
    - __2 mild pressure for release
    - __3 no pressure but concerned
    - __4 no concern at all
    - __x not available

    (02:34)

74. Family reaction to patient's transfer to another hospital
    - __1 general acceptance
    - __2 not concerned at all
    - __3 against transfer
    - __x not available

    (02:35)

75. Degree of remaining psychiatric impairment at discharge % disability) (rating by therapist)
    - __1 none
    - __2 minimal
    - __3 mild
    - __4 moderate
    - __5 severe
    - __x not available

    (02:36)

76. Amount of change during
    - __1 became worse
    - __2 no change

    (02:37)

last hosp'n   __ 3 slightly improved
(rating by   __ 4 moderately improved
therapist)   __ 5 markedly improved
     __ x not available

77. *Symptoms noted during hosp'n by therapist   (02:38-62)
    - __ 1 anxiety
    - __ 2 depression
    - __ 3 manic excitement
    - __ 4 compulsive behavior
    - __ 5 obsessive thoughts
    - __ 6 phobias
    - __ 7 dissociative episodes
    - __ 8 lability in mood
    - __ 9 antisocial behavior
    - __10 paranoid ideation
    - __11 bizarre ideas and behavior
    - __12 hallucinations
    - __13 inappropriate affect
    - __14 poor contact with reality
    - __15 social withdrawal
    - __16 somatic preoccupations
    - __17 impairment of motor control
    - __18 disturbed sensorium
    - __19 memory disturbance
    - __20 disorientation
    - __21 conversion symptoms
    - __22 physiologic reaction
    - __23 convulsions
    - __24 alcoholism
    - __ x no symptom information available

78. Therapist's image of patient at start of last hosp'n (predictive)   (02:63-73)
    - __ 1 patient will be reasonably cooperative in treatment
    - __ 2 patient sees her problems as primarily physical
    - __ 3 attributes her difficulties to alcohol
    - __ 4 is likely to be combative and/or destructive
    - __ 5 is likely to require placement in special care
    - __ 6 is likely to sign out AMA
    - __ 7 is likely to go AWOL
    - __ 8 will be a definite suicidal risk
    - __ 9 will be a definite homicidal risk
    - __10 is likely to be recommended for commitment to the state hospital
    - __ x none of the above available

79. Degree of psychiatric impairment at start of last hosp'n (reported by therapist)   (03:10)
    - __ 1 none
    - __ 2 minimal
    - __ 3 mild
    - __ 4 moderate
    - __ 5 severe
    - __ x not available

APPENDIX A

80. Degree of external precipitating stress (rated by therapist)
    - __ 1 none
    - __ 2 mild
    - __ 3 moderate
    - __ 4 severe
    - __ x not available

    (03:11)

81. Anticipated change while hospitalized (as reported by therapist)
    - __ 1 will become worse
    - __ 2 no change
    - __ 3 slight improvement
    - __ 4 moderate improvement
    - __ 5 marked improvement
    - __ x not available

    (03:12)

82. Hospitalization financial benefits (last hosp'n)
    - __ 1 veteran or other federal aid and health insurance
    - __ 2 veteran or federal aid
    - __ 3 health insurance
    - __ 4 neither of the above
    - __ x not available

    (03:13)

83. Rent per month (as reported last hosp'n) (03:14)
    - __ 1 under $30
    - __ 2 $31-$40
    - __ 3 $41-$50
    - __ 4 $51-$60
    - __ 5 $61-$70
    - __ 6 $71-$80
    - __ 7 $81-$100
    - __ 8 $101-$120
    - __ 9 $121-$150
    - __ 10 over $150
    - __ x not available

84. Family income (03:15)

Weekly	Monthly	Yearly
__ 1 under $20	under $85	under $1040
__ 2 $20-$40	$85-$173	$1041-$2080
__ 3 $41-$60	$174-$260	$2081-$3120
__ 4 $61-$80	$261-$346	$3121-$4160
__ 5 $81-$100	$347-$433	$4161-$5200
__ 6 $101-$125	$434-$540	$5201-$6500
__ 7 $126-$150	$541-$650	$6501-$7800
__ 8 $151-$170	$651-$735	$7801-$8840
__ 9 $171-$200	$736-$866	$8841-$10,500
__ 10 over $200	over $866	over $10,500
__ x not available		

85. Date admitted last hosp'n _____ _____ _____ (03:16-21)
    (month) (day) (year)

86. Date left bed last hosp'n _____ _____ _____ (03:22-27)
    (month) (day) (year)

87. Date patient interviewed with follow-up schedule _____ _____ _____ (03:28-33)
    (month) (day) (year)

88. Number of days between left bed and interview _____ (03:34-36)
    (difference between items 86 and 87)

ADDITIONAL COMMENTS:

Initials of person completing this form

APPENDIX A

(Deck 04)   Schedule No. _____

HOSPITAL RECORD DATA: FORM II (RETURNEES)

1. Hospital returned to
   - ___ 1 Cols. Psychiatric Inst. & Hospital   (04:10)
   - ___ 2 Cols. State Hospital
   - ___ 3 Harding Sanitarium
   - ___ 4 McMillen Sanitarium
   - ___ 5 White Cross Hospital
   - ___ 6 V.A. Hospital, Chillicothe
   - ___ 7 other Ohio hospital
   - ___ 8 other out-of-state hospital
   - ___ x not available

2. Old case no. (CPIH) _____   (04:11-14)

3. New case no. _____

4. Patient's name _____ , _____ _____
                      (last)   (first)   (m. init.)

5. Address patient _____ (04:15)
   returned from
   (write in _____
   alternative if
   not sure of address)

6. Telephone number _____

7. Patient's occupation _____ (04:16)
   at time of return
   (note if housewife)

8. Name of closest adult   _____ (04:17)
   female relative at   ___ 0 only males in household
   address patient returned ___ 1 mother   ___ 6 grandmother
   from (note if step   ___ 2 sister   ___ 7 aunt
   parent)   ___ 3 daughter   ___ 8 female cousin

NOTE: Each item requires some category filled in. Unless otherwise specified "x" is used for information not available. Items with asterisks (*) can have multiple punches.

FORM 92   4-7-59

___ 4 sister-in-law   ___ x not available
___ 5 daughter-in-law

9. Name of closest adult male relative at address patient returned from (note if step parent) _____ (04:18)
   - ___ 0 only females in household
   - ___ 1 father
   - ___ 2 husband
   - ___ 3 brother
   - ___ 4 son
   - ___ 5 brother-in-law
   - ___ 6 son-in-law
   - ___ 7 grandfather
   - ___ 8 uncle
   - ___ 9 male cousin
   - ___ x not available

10. Type of family patient returned from _____ (04:19)
    - ___ 1 parental
    - ___ 2 conjugal
    - ___ 3 sibling
    - ___ 4 child
    - ___ 5 nonkin family
    - ___ 6 lived alone
    - ___ x not available

11. Readmission diagnosis _____ (04:20-23)
    (note if alcoholism is included) (use state code)

12. Ward of patient this hosp'n (if CPIH) (04:24)
    - ___ 1 1W
    - ___ 2 2W
    - ___ 3 3W
    - ___ 4 not in CPIH
    - ___ x not available

13. Therapist this hosp'n (if CPIH) _____ (04:25&26)
    (code 00 if not CPIH; xx if not available)

14. Marital status on return (04:27)
    - ___ 1 married
    - ___ 2 single
    - ___ 3 divorced
    - ___ 4 widowed
    - ___ 5 separated
    - ___ x not available

15. *Type of family patient lived with while in community (04:28)
    - ___ 1 parental
    - ___ 2 conjugal
    - ___ 3 sibling
    - ___ 4 child
    - ___ 5 nonkin
    - ___ 6 lived alone
    - ___ x not available

16. Parents on return (biological) (04:29)
    - ___ 1 both living
    - ___ 2 mother living
    - ___ 3 father living
    - ___ 4 both deceased
    - ___ x not available

17. Total number of household residents _____ (At time of return, excl. patient, code xx if not available) (04:30&31)

APPENDIX A 213

18.	Total number of female residents	____	(04:32)
19.	Total number of male residents	____	(04:33)
20.	Number male residents under 18	____ (At time of return, excl. pt, code x if not available)	(04:34)
21.	Number female residents under 18	____	(04:35)
22.	Total number of residents under 18	____	(04:36)

23. Family relations while in community between last hosp'n and this hosp'n

   __ 1 was solely responsible for care of house and children, if any Took considerable responsibility for maintaining family affairs or acted as head of the house
   __ 2 participated in above responsibilities but not solely responsible for them
   __ 3 sporadic responsibility for them
   __ 4 no responsibilities
   __ x not available

(04:37)

24. Work performance while in community between last hosp'n and this hosp'n

   __ 1 worked regularly prior to this hosp'n; gainfully employed at time of hosp'n
   __ 2 worked some of the time prior to this hosp'n and worked in last month prior to this hosp'n more than half the time; gainfully employed at time of this hosp'n
   __ 3 worked some of the time prior to this hosp'n and worked in last month prior to hosp'n but less than half the time; gainfully employed at time of hosp'n

(04:38)

        ___ 4 worked some of the time prior to this hosp'n and worked in last month prior to hosp'n but less than half the time; not gainfully employed at time of hosp'n
        ___ 5 worked some of the time prior to this hosp'n but not gainfully employed at time of hosp'n
        ___ 6 not gainfully employed while in community
        ___ x not available

25. Psychiatric symptoms during period prior to this hosp'n
        ___ 1 manifested psychiatric symptoms regularly which prevented interpersonal performance   (04:39)
        ___ 2 manifested psychiatric symptoms regularly but these did not prevent interpersonal performance
        ___ 3 manifested psychiatric symptoms intermittently which prevented interpersonal performance
        ___ 4 manifested psychiatric symptoms intermittently which did not prevent interpersonal performance
        ___ 5 present illness was of sudden onset
        ___ x not available

26. Family stability (excl. patient) during period patient was in community
        ___ 1 evidence of sexual promiscuity, frequent drunkenness, or violence   (04:40)
        ___ 2 evidence against above
        ___ x not available

27. Patient's stability as family member while in community
        ___ 1 evidence of sexual promiscuity, frequent drunkenness, or violence   (04:41)

APPENDIX A

___ 2 evidence against above
___ x not available

28. *Who brought patient to hospital this time
    ___ 1 husband (04:42)
    ___ 2 mother
    ___ 3 father
    ___ 4 child
    ___ 5 sibling or sibling-in-law
    ___ 6 police
    ___ 7 hospital or physician or social welfare
    ___ 8 came in herself
    ___ 9 other _____ (specify)
    ___ x not available

29. *Who instigated this hosp'n
    ___ 1 husband (04:43)
    ___ 2 mother
    ___ 3 father
    ___ 4 child
    ___ 5 sibling or sibling-in-law
    ___ 6 police
    ___ 7 hospital or physician or social welfare
    ___ 8 self (check only if patient was active in decision)
    ___ 9 other _____ (specify)
    ___ x not available

30. *Behavior resulting in this admission
    ___ 1 threatened or attempted suicide (04:44)
    ___ 2 abusive toward others—verbal
    ___ 3 assaulted others
    ___ 4 psychosomatic symptoms
    ___ 5 self-abusive
    ___ 6 hallucinations
    ___ 7 delusions
    ___ 8 destructive
    ___ 9 depressed
    ___ 0 other
    ___ x not available

31. Out-patient or private treatment prior to this hosp'n (on regular basis)
    ___ 1 was receiving it regularly while in community and at time of this hosp'n (04:45)

                    ___ 2 was receiving regularly while in community but not at time of this hosp'n
                    ___ 3 did not receive while in community
                    ___ x not available

32. Type of readmission
    ___ 1 voluntary   (04:46)
    ___ 2 court
    ___ 3 emergency
    ___ 4 transfer
    ___ x not available

33. Conditions of readmission
    ___ 1 returned from trial visit   (04:47)
    ___ 2 returned from extended leave of absence
    ___ 3 returned from AWOL or AMA
    ___ 4 new admission to present hospital
    ___ 5 other _____ (specify)
    ___ x not available

34. *Is patient receiving organic therapy during this hosp'n
    ___ 1 electro-shock therapy   (04:48)
    ___ 2 insulin shock treatment
    ___ 3 lobotomies
    ___ 4 other
    ___ 5 no
    ___ x not available

35. *Is patient receiving individual psychotherapy during this hosp'n
    ___ 1 analytic psychotherapy   (04:49)
    ___ 2 directive therapy
    ___ 3 other
    ___ 4 no
    ___ x not available

36. Is patient receiving occupational therapy and counseling during this hosp'n
    ___ 1 both O.T. and counseling   (04:50)
    ___ 2 O.T. only
    ___ 3 occupational counseling
    ___ 4 neither
    ___ x not available

37. Is patient receiving group therapy during this hosp'n
    ___ 1 yes   (04:51)
    ___ 2 no
    ___ x not available

APPENDIX A

38. Did patient receive drug therapy while in the community and during this hosp'n
    — 1 while in community and pre- (04:52)
    scribed for this hosp'n
    — 2 while in hospital only
    — 3 while in community only
    — 4 no
    — x not available

39. Extended family relationships while in community
    — 1 considerable responsibility, (04:53)
    took part in family activities
    — 2 some
    — 3 little
    — 4 none
    — x not available

40. Serious physical illness resulting in handicap
    — 1 yes _____ (specify) (04:54)
    — 2 no
    — x not available

41. *Use of community resources and treatment while in community
    — 1 financial assistance (04:55)
    — 2 hospital out-patient or social service depts.
    — 3 private therapy or counseling with professional individual
    — 4 counseling from clergymen or welfare workers
    — 5 counseling or therapy with groups like the A.A.
    — 6 other _____ (specify)
    — x not available

42. Relations with hospital staff during this hosp'n
    — 1 only positive reports of cooperation (04:56)
    — 2 no consistent pattern but several negative reports
    — 3 pattern of negative reports
    — 4 destructive and fighting with staff
    — x not available

43. Relations with patients during this hosp'n
    — 1 only positive report of cooperation (04:57)

___2 no consistent pattern but several negative reports
___3 pattern of negative reports
___4 destructive and fighting with patients
___x not available

44. Behavior since rehospitalized
___1 interacts frequently with one or more persons while in hospital and shows emotions such as tears, laughter, etc. (04:58)
___2 interacts frequently with one or more persons but only rarely shows emotions such as tears, laughter, etc.
___3 usually quiet but sometimes interacts with others
___4 almost completely withdrawn
___x not available

45. Prognosis (this hosp'n)
___1 favorable (04:59)
___2 guarded or fair
___3 unfavorable
___x not available

46. Date readmitted, this hosp'n _____ _____ _____ (04:60-65)
(month) (day) (year)

47. No. of days between left bed last hosp'n and readmission _____ (04:66-68)

48. Date interviewed with follow-up schedule (relative of patient) _____ _____ _____ (04:69-74)
(month) (day) (year)

49. Number of days between readmission and follow-up interview with relative (difference between items 46 and 48) _____ (04:75-77)

APPENDIX A 219

ANY ADDITIONAL COMMENTS:

Initials of person completing this form

Schedule No. _____

INTERVIEWER RATINGS

1) *House Type* (Check one):

_____ 1. Excellent houses. This includes only houses which are very large single-family dwellings in good repair and surrounded by large lawns and yards which are landscaped and well cared for. These houses have an element of ostentation with respect to size, architectural style, and general condition of yards and lawns.

_____ 2. Very good houses. Roughly, this includes all houses which do not quite measure up to the first category. The primary difference is one of size. They are slightly smaller, but still larger than utility demands for the average family.

_____ 3. Good houses. In many cases they are only slightly larger than utility demands. They are more conventional and less ostentatious than the two higher categories.

_____ 4. Average houses. One-and-a-half- to two-story wood frame and brick single-family dwellings. Conventional style, with lawns well cared for but not landscaped.

_____ 5. Fair houses. In general, this includes houses whose condition is not quite as good as those houses given a 4 rating. It also includes smaller houses in excellent condition.

_____ 6. Poor houses. In this, and the category below, size is less important than condition in determining evaluation. Houses in this category are badly run-down but have not deteriorated sufficiently that they cannot be repaired. They suffer from lack of care but do not have the profusion of debris which surrounds houses in the lowest category.

APPENDIX A

_____ 7. Very poor houses. All houses which have deteriorated so far that they cannot be repaired. They are considered unhealthy and unsafe to live in. All buildings not originally intended for dwellings, shacks and over-crowded buildings. The halls and yards are littered with junk, and many have an extremely bad odor.

_____ x. Did not see house.

2) *Dwelling Area* (Check one:)

_____ 1. Very high. The best houses in town are located in such an area. The streets are wide and clean and have many trees.

_____ 2. High. Dwelling areas felt to be superior and well above average but a little below the top. There are fewer mansions and pretentious houses in such districts than in the first. However, the chief difference is one of reputation.

_____ 3. Above average. A little above average in social reputation and to the eye of the scientific observer. This is an area of nice but not pretentious houses. The streets are kept clean and the houses are well cared for.

_____ 4. Average. These are areas of workingmen's homes which are small and unpretentious but neat in appearance.

_____ 5. Below average. All the areas in this group are undesirable because they are close to factories, or because they include the business section of town, or are close to the railroad. This is a more congested and heterogeneous area than those above.

_____ 6. Low. These areas are run-down and semi-slums. The houses are set close together. The streets and yards are often filled with debris, and in some of the smaller towns, some of the streets are not paved.

_____ 7. Very low. Slum districts, the areas with the poorest reputation in town, not only because of unpleasant and unhealthy geographical positions—for example, being near a garbage dump or a swamp—but also because of the social stigma attached to those who live there.

_____ x. Did not see dwelling area.

4) Rate the respondent on each characteristic, even though you don't know (her) (him) very well. Circle the diagonal mark at the point that best describes the subject.

Definitely does not describe subject / · · · / · · · / · · · / · · · / · · · / · · · / Definitely describes subject well

1. Is very active   / · · · / · · · / · · · / · · · / · · · / · · · / · · · /
2. Shows friendliness   / · · · / · · · / · · · / · · · / · · · / · · · / · · · /
3. Is intelligent   / · · · / · · · / · · · / · · · / · · · / · · · / · · · /
4. Is very tense   / · · · / · · · / · · · / · · · / · · · / · · · / · · · /
5. Shows initiative   / · · · / · · · / · · · / · · · / · · · / · · · / · · · /
6. Makes others feel (he) (she) understands them   / · · · / · · · / · · · / · · · / · · · / · · · / · · · /
7. Shows rationality and logic   / · · · / · · · / · · · / · · · / · · · / · · · / · · · /
8. Gets upset easily   / · · · / · · · / · · · / · · · / · · · / · · · / · · · /
9. Makes many suggestions   / · · · / · · · / · · · / · · · / · · · / · · · / · · · /
10. Is likable   / · · · / · · · / · · · / · · · / · · · / · · · / · · · /
11. Gets confused easily / · · · / · · · / · · · / · · · / · · · / · · · / · · · /
12. Tends to be nervous   / · · · / · · · / · · · / · · · / · · · / · · · / · · · /
13. Is assertive   / · · · / · · · / · · · / · · · / · · · / · · · / · · · /
14. Tends to be emotional / · · · / · · · / · · · / · · · / · · · / · · · / · · · /
15. Is very verbal   / · · · / · · · / · · · / · · · / · · · / · · · / · · · /

APPENDIX A

3) *Appearance of House Interior* (Check one:)

_____ 1. Messy, dusty, dirty, or untidy; papers, clothes, toys, etc.; strewn about; almost no unlittered place to sit.

_____ 2. Somewhat messy; a few things scattered; some dust or dirt evident.

_____ 3. Orderly, casual, clean, neat; things seem to be in place; house appears tidy and cared for.

_____ 4. Extremely orderly; fastidiously neat; house appears almost stiff and untouchable with care.

_____ x. Did not see house interior.

4) (See p. 222.)

5) *Respondent's feeling toward significant other* (Check one:)

_____ 1. Positive

_____ 2. Generally positive, some hostility shown in remarks or attitudes

_____ 3. Neutral, or no clear impression obtainable

_____ 4. Generally negative, expresses clear criticism and some hostility

_____ 5. Negative

6) *Attitude toward the hospital* (Check one:)

_____ 1. Resents hospital, including personnel and hospital policy, sees no value in hospitalization and tends to give such institutions negative connotation

_____ 2. Not impressed with hospital, but accepts its potential usefulness; criticizes one or two specific aspects, *e.g.,* unavailability of doctors, visiting hours at bad time, etc.

_____ 3. Respects hospital and personnel in general, but has some specific criticisms

_____ 4. Respects and appreciates the hospital function; is especially grateful for hospital help

_____ x. Don't know

7) *Respondent's interest in interview*

    At start
- __ 1. Lack of interest
- __ 2. Mild interest
- __ 3. High interest
- __ x. Don't know

    At close
- __ 1. Lack of interest
- __ 2. Mild interest
- __ 3. High interest
- __ x. Don't know

8) *Respondent's tension level*

    At start
- __ 1. Nervous, fidgety
- __ 2. Sporadic nervousness
- __ 3. Mostly relaxed
- __ x. Don't know

    At close
- __ 1. Nervous, fidgety
- __ 2. Sporadic nervousness
- __ 3. Mostly relaxed
- __ x. Don't know

9) *Distractions during interview*
- __ 1. Much distraction (other people, TV)
- __ 2. Some or occasional distraction
- __ 3. No distractions (ideal interview situation)
- __ x. Don't know

10) *Attitude toward interview*
- __ 1. Hostile
- __ 2. Suspicious, guarded
- __ 3. Friendly
- __ 4. Solicitous
- __ x. Don't know

11) *Alertness and estimated intelligence*
- __ 1. Dull, uncomprehending
- __ 2. Slow, needs explaining
- __ 3. Average intelligence
- __ 4. Above average intelligence and quick
- __ x. Don't know

12) *Appearance and habits*
- __ 1. Inappropriate, sloppy
- __ 2. Somewhat untidy
- __ 3. Casual, neat
- __ 4. Overly neat, fastidious
- __ x. Don't know

APPENDIX A

FORM 12 (4-7-59)
SCHEDULE NO._____

PATIENT INTERVIEW SCHEDULE

1. THE FIRST THINGS I WANT TO KNOW ARE SOME FACTS, LIKE AGES, ABOUT YOUR FAMILY. I KNOW THAT IT IS SOMETIMES DIFFICULT TO REMEMBER THINGS LIKE EXACT DATES. IF YOU ARE NOT SURE ABOUT ANY OF THE THINGS I WOULD LIKE TO KNOW, JUST GIVE ME ESTIMATES.

	(1) Living or dead	(2) Marital status	(3) Present age or at death	(4) Residence — In household	(4) Residence — If not in household, where?	(5) Birthplace	(6) Education	(7) Usual occupation	(8) Now employed full or part time
(a) ****									
(b) Husband									
(c) Mother									
(d) Father									
(e) Mother-in-law									
(f) Father-in-law									
(g) Sister									
(h) Sister									
(i) Sister									
(j) Brother									
(k) Brother									
(l) Brother									
(m) Daughter									
(n) Daughter									
(o) Daughter									
(p) Son									
(q) Son									
(r) Son									
other household residents (s)									
(t)									

Fill in only if household resident

NEXT, WE WOULD LIKE TO KNOW SOMETHING ABOUT WHERE YOU HAVE LIVED.

2. Did you spend most of your time before you were 16 in a
   - 1 farm
   - 2 village
   - 3 town (1000-10,000)
   - 4 small city (10,000-100,000)
   - 5 medium city (100,000-500,000)
   - 6 large city (500,000 and over)

   (__ X NR)

3. How many years have you lived in the Columbus area? _____

4. How long have you lived at your present address? _____

5. In general, how well do you like the people who live around you? Would you say you like them ___1 a lot ___2 so-so ___3 not at all (___ X NR)

6. How many women who live around you do you know well enough to say "hello" to? ___1 none ___2 few (one to three) ___3 many (4 or more) (___ X NR)

7. How many women around your neighborhood do you visit back and forth with in the daytime? ___1 none ___2 few (one to three) ___3 many (4 or more) (___ X NR)

8. What do you usually do: keep house, work full time, work part time, or something else?
   - ___ 1 keep house
   - ___ 2 work full time
   - ___ 3 work part time
   - ___ 4 something else: What?_____

   (___ X NR)

9. (If usually works:) What kind of work do you usually do? _____

10. Since you have been home from the hospital (the last time), do you prefer to
    - ___ 1 be at home
    - ___ 2 work full time
    - ___ 3 work part time
    - ___ 4 something else: What?_____

    (___ X NR)

11. Do you sometimes do anything in your spare time like

	Yes	No	(NR)
a. Take part in any organized groups or clubs	___1	___2	(___X)
b. Knit, sew, crochet, or embroider	___1	___2	(___X)

APPENDIX A

	Yes	No	(NR)
c. Go to movies	__1	__2	(__X)
d. Listen to the radio or watch TV	__1	__2	(__X)
e. Play cards	__1	__2	(__X)
f. Go to plays or concerts	__1	__2	(__X)
g. Read books or magazines	__1	__2	(__X)
h. Go to parties or dances	__1	__2	(__X)
i. Go to watch sports	__1	__2	(__X)
j. Visit with friends or relatives	__1	__2	(__X)

12. How do you usually distribute your time? That is, in the past month, what percent of your time have you spent on each of these things?

	% time	(NR)
a. Job (if any)	____	(__X)
b. Household chores like cleaning, laundry, mending, preparing meals	____	(__X)
c. Care of children (if any)	____	(__X)
d. Going to visit friends or relatives and having people over to your house	____	(__X)
e. Doing the family shopping (grocery and clothes)	____	(__X)
f. Going to club meetings, religious services, or other group activities	____	(__X)
g. Hobbies and other leisure activities (*e.g.*, TV, movies, reading, knitting)	____	(__X)

STUDIES SHOW THAT VERY OFTEN FAMILIES AND PATIENTS DON'T AGREE ON WHERE THE PATIENT SHOULD LIVE AFTER LEAVING THE HOSPITAL.

13. When you left the hospital (the last time), was this the only place you could come to live? ____ 1 yes ____ 2 no (____ X NR)

14. Did you want to come here to live? ____ 1 definitely wanted to ____ 2 had mixed feelings ____ 3 did not want to (____ X NR)

15. Did your (husband, mother, etc.) want you to come here to live? ____ 1 definitely wanted me to ____ 2 had mixed feelings ____ 3 did not want me to (____ X NR)

16. (If others, besides husband, mother, etc., live in household:) Did the other people living in this household want you to come here to live? ____ 1 definitely wanted me to ____ 2 some of them wanted me to ____ 3 none of them wanted me to (____ X NR)

17. Do you know if the hospital wanted you to come here to live?
____ 1 definitely approved ____ 2 felt it was acceptable
____ 3 did not approve (____ X DK)

18. Did someone in the family first suggest that you go to the hospital for your mental condition? ____ 1 yes: Who? _____
____ 2 no: Who did? _____ (____ X NR)

19. Since you have been home from the hospital (the last time), have you ever considered living elsewhere than here in this household?
____ 1 yes ____ 2 no (____ X NR)
If yes: Where? _____
With whom? _____
(Relationship to respondent)

20. At what age did you first become ill with this mental condition?
_____

NOW WE WOULD LIKE TO KNOW . . .

Skip if respondent is not married

21. During your marriage (this marriage), did you at any time consider divorce or separation? ____ 1 yes ____ 2 no (____ X NR)

22. Have you considered divorce or separation since you have been home from the hospital (the last time)? ____ 1 yes
____ 2 no (____ X NR)
If yes: Are you considering it now more than before you went to the hospital (the last time)?
____ 1 more than before ____ 3 less than before
____ 2 same as before (____ X NR)

23. In general, how do you think you and your husband get along compared to most other couples you know of?
____ 1 better than most other couples
____ 2 as well as most other couples
____ 3 not as well as other couples
(____ X DK)

APPENDIX A

24. Are there ever any arguments between you and your (husband, mother, daughter, etc.) about such things as

	Yes	No	(NR)
a. Money	__1	__2	(__X)
b. Staying out late	__1	__2	(__X)
c. Being noisy	__1	__2	(__X)
d. Not helping out around the house	__1	__2	(__X)
e. Drinking	__1	__2	(__X)

25. (Ask only if respondent is not married:)
Everything considered, how well do you think you get along with your (mother, daughter, etc.)? ____ 1 well ____ 2 average
____ 3 not well (____ X NR)

26. NEXT, I WANT TO ASK YOU WHAT YOU THINK YOU *SHOULD BE DOING NOW,* SINCE BEING HOME FROM THE HOSPITAL. DO YOU FEEL YOU SHOULD BE DOING THESE THINGS NOW?

	Yes	No	(NR)
a. Dust, sweep, and do other usual cleaning	__1	__2	(__X)
b. Help with the family shopping	__1	__2	(__X)
c. Entertain people at home	__1	__2	(__X)
d. Dress and take care of yourself	__1	__2	(__X)
e. Handle the grocery money	__1	__2	(__X)
f. Prepare the morning and evening meals	__1	__2	(__X)
g. Take care of laundry and mending	__1	__2	(__X)
h. (Ask only if preschool children in house) Dress and bathe the children	__1	__2	(__X)
i. (Ask only if school children in house) Make sure the children get to school on time	__1	__2	(__X)
j. Go visit your friends or relatives	__1	__2	(__X)

		Yes	No	(NR)
k.	Get along with family members	__1	__2	(__X)
l.	Get along with the neighbors	__1	__2	(__X)
m.	Go to parties and other social activities	__1	__2	(__X)
n.	Hold a job full time or part time	__1	__2	(__X)

27. LET ME READ YOU THE LIST ONE MORE TIME. THIS TIME I WOULD LIKE YOU TO TELL ME WHICH OF THESE THINGS YOU EXPECT TO BE DOING *SIX MONTHS* FROM NOW.

		Yes	No	(NR)
a.	Dust, sweep, and do other usual cleaning	__1	__2	(__X)
b.	Help with the family shopping	__1	__2	(__X)
c.	Entertain people at home	__1	__2	(__X)
d.	Dress and take care of yourself	__1	__2	(__X)
e.	Handle the grocery money	__1	__2	(__X)
f.	Prepare morning and evening meals	__1	__2	(__X)
g.	Take care of laundry and mending	__1	__2	(__X)
h.	(Ask only if preschool children in house) Dress and bathe the children	__1	__2	(__X)
i.	(Ask only if school children in house) Make sure the children get to school on time	__1	__2	(__X)
j.	Go visit your friends or relatives	__1	__2	(__X)
k.	Get along with family members	__1	__2	(__X)
l.	Get along with the neighbors	__1	__2	(__X)
m.	Go to parties and other social activities	__1	__2	(__X)
n.	Hold a job full or part time	__1	__2	(__X)

28. Now, since you have been home from the hospital (the last time), do you think your (husband, mother, daughter, etc.) wants you to do too much, wants you to do very little, wants you to do about the right amount, of the household chores? ____ 1 too much ____ 2 very little ____ 3 right amount   (____ X NR)

APPENDIX A

29. How about in the way of general activities, do you think your (husband, mother, daughter, etc.) wants you to do too much, very little, or just the right amount? ____1 too much ____2 very little ____3 right amount (____X NR)

THERE ARE JUST ONE OR TWO MORE THINGS WE WOULD LIKE YOUR OPINION ON, AND THEN I WILL HAVE ALL THE INFORMATION I NEED. FIRST,

30. I AM GOING TO READ YOU A LIST OF STATEMENTS DESCRIBING WHAT MEN AND WOMEN SHOULD DO IN THEIR EVERYDAY ACTIVITIES. PLEASE TELL ME FOR EACH STATEMENT WHETHER YOU AGREE OR DISAGREE WITH IT. THERE MAY BE ONE OR TWO YOU ARE NOT SURE ABOUT.

	Agree	*Disagree*	*(NR)*
a. A husband should help with the housework.	__1	__2	(__X)
b. A woman who does not have to take a job should not.	__1	__2	(__X)
c. If a husband insists, the wife should quit a job which she enjoys.	__1	__2	(__X)
d. Women are too independent these days.	__1	__2	(__X)
e. Husbands should be more strict with their wives.	__1	__2	(__X)
f. A Woman's place is in the home.	__1	__2	(__X)
g. Marriage is the best career for a woman.	__1	__2	(__X)
h. The man should wear the pants in the family.	__1	__2	(__X)
i. A woman's interests should be mainly in children, recipes, clothes, and housekeeping.	__1	__2	(__X)

31. What is your idea of the best way, the ideal way, for a young married woman (with children) to distribute her time? What percent of her time should she spend on each of these things?

% time *(NR)*

a. Job ____ (__X)

                                                             % time   (NR)

   b. Household chores like cleaning, laundry,
      mending, preparing meals   ___   (__X)

   c. Care of children   ___   (__X)

   d. Going to visit friends or relatives and having
      people over to the house   ___   (__X)

   e. Doing the family shopping (grocery
      and clothes)   ___   (__X)

   f. Going to club meetings, religious
      services or other group activities   ___   (__X)

   g. Hobbies and other leisure activities,
      (*e.g.,* TV, movies, reading, knitting)   ___   (__X)

NOW, ABOUT THE HOSPITAL,

32. From your experience with the hospital, on what ward do you think patients get the best care? _____ (___ X NR)

33. If you ever needed help for a mental condition again, where would you be most likely to go for such help?

   ___ 1 to CPIH   ___ 4 private psychiatrist
   ___ 2 to another hospital   ___ 5 community agency
   ___ 3 to mental hygiene clinic ___ 6 other: What? _____
                               ___(X NR)

34. Now, I would like to ask whether you have any comments or ideas about improving the hospital program? (*e.g.* open door policy)
_____
_____
_____

(CHECK COMPLETENESS OF SCHEDULE. GO BACK TO THE BEGINNING AND INSPECT EACH QUESTION. IF ANY QUESTION HAS BEEN OMITTED THAT SHOULD HAVE BEEN ASKED, ASK IT BEFORE TERMINATING THE INTERVIEW.)

ITEMS ADDED TO PATIENT SCHEDULE FOR SECOND FOLLOW-UP

35. Have you been a patient in any hospital since leaving CPIH?

   _____ 1 yes _____ 2 no   (_____ X NR)

   If yes: Which one? _____
   When and how long? (get dates) _____
   Why? _____

36. Have you seen any professional person for medical, psychiatric, or other advice since leaving CPIH?

   _____ 1 yes _____ 2 no   (_____ X NR)

   If yes: Who? _____ 1 psychiatrist   _____ 3 social worker
              _____ 2 medical physician _____ 4 other: Who? _____
   If yes: Why? _____
   When? _____
   How often? (if makes regular visits) _____

FORM 22 (4-7-59)
S.O. SCHEDULE NO.

SIGNIFICANT OTHER'S INTERVIEW SCHEDULE

WE WOULD LIKE TO KNOW SOMETHING ABOUT WHERE YOU HAVE LIVED. IF YOU CANNOT REMEMBER EXACTLY, TRY TO MAKE AS CLOSE AN ESTIMATE AS POSSIBLE.

1. Did you spend most of your time before you were 16 in a
   ____ 1 farm
   ____ 2 village
   ____ 3 town (1000-10,000)
   ____ 4 small city (10,000-100,000)
   ____ 5 medium city (100,000-500,000)
   ____ 6 large city (500,000 and over)
   (____ X NR)

2. How many years have you lived in the Columbus area? _____

3. How long have you lived at your present address? _____

4. Where did you live before? _____
   (Address) (City) (State)

5. For how long? _____ years.

6. All together, how many different addresses have you lived at in the past five years? (Include college and military service) _____

7. Where and with whom has **** lived in the past five years? (include college and military service)

Place (city and state)	With whom?	How long?	When?

8. Do you own or rent your home? ____ 1 own ____ 2 rent
   (____ X NR)

9. How much does your rent (or monthly payments, taxes, etc.) come to each month? (Hand respondent Card #1) _____

APPENDIX A

10. (If house is rented:)
    Does the house come furnished or unfurnished?
    ___ 1 furnished   ___ 2 unfurnished   (___ X NR)

11. (If house is rented:)
    How good do you think the chances are of you owning your own home some day? Would you say your chances are
    ___ 1 very good   ___ 4 not at all good
    ___ 2 fairly good   ___ 5 don't want to own home, don't care
    ___ 3 not very good   ___ 6 is buying home   (___ X NR)

12. How many rooms do you have? _____

13. How many bedrooms do you have? _____

14. Which neighborhood—this one or any other place, do you think of as your real home—that is, where do you feel you really belong?
    ___ 1 this neighborhood
    ___ 2 other neighborhood in Franklin County (Columbus area)
    ___ 3 other neighborhood outside Franklin County (Columbus area)
    ___ 4 no special place   (___ X NR)

15. Have you ever thought of moving from your neighborhood altogether: Would you say you have thought of it ___ 1 often
    ___ 2 occasionally ___ 3 never   (___ X NR)

16. In general, would you say this neighborhood is
    ___ 1 very good as a place to live
    ___ 2 fairly good
    ___ 3 not good at all as a place to live?   (___ X NR)

17. In general, how do you like your house? ___ 1 a lot
    ___ 2 a little ___ 3 not at all   (___ X NR)

18. Is anyone in the family (in the household) ever bothered because there is not enough space in the house?   ___ 1 yes ___ 2 no
    (___ X NR)

19. Do you generally like or dislike the people who live on your block?
    ___ 1 like ___ 2 dislike   (___ X NR)

20. Does **** generally like or dislike the people who live on the block?
    ___ 1 like ___ 2 dislike   (___ X NR)

21. During this past month (last four weeks), how often did **** visit with the neighbors? ____ 1 often (once a week) ____ 2 sometimes (at least once a month) ____ 3 rarely (less than once a month) (____ X DK)

22. About how often in the past month (last four weeks), did neighbors drop in to see ****? ____ 1 often (once a week) ____ 2 sometimes (at least once a month) ____ 3 rarely (less than once a month) (____ X DK)

23. To which of these three groups do you feel closest? ____ 1 working class ____ 2 middle class ____ 3 upper class (____ X NR)

24. How about most of the people who live around you, where would you say they belong? ____ 1 working class ____ 2 middle class ____ 3 upper class (____ X NR)

NEXT, WE WOULD LIKE TO KNOW ABOUT WHERE **** HAS WORKED

25. Before **** went to the hospital (the last time), did she usually ____ 1 have a job ____ 2 keep house ____ 3 other: What? ____

> Skip if never worked before hosp'n

26. (If **** usually worked:) At what age did **** first start working? _____

27. What type of work did she usually do? _____

28. What type of job did she prefer to have? _____

29. What would you say were the main reasons she worked then? _____

30. Between the age when she started working and (the last time) when she was in the hospital, do you remember the number of different places she worked? _____
(____ X DK)

31. Before **** was in the hospital (the last time), what was the last place she worked, job she held, and for how long?

Type of industry or business	Job	Dates
		From: To:

APPENDIX A

Skip if never worked before hosp'n

32. Before **** was in the hospital (the last time), what was the place she worked the longest, job held, and for how long?

Type of industry or business	Job	Dates
		From: To:

33. Before **** went to the hospital (the last time), what was the longest period she did not work? _____ years.

34. Has **** held any jobs since returning home from the hospital (the last time)? _____ 1 yes _____ 2 no (_____ X NR)

    If yes: Is she working now? _____ 1 yes, full time
    _____ 2 yes, part time or irregularly _____ 3 no (_____ X NR)

Skip if has not worked since last hospitalization

35. Since **** left the hospital, what different jobs has she had?

Description	How long employed	Salary	Full or part time	Why did she leave?

36. What would you say are the main reasons that she works? _____
    _____

37. What type of job does she prefer to have now? _____

38. How does **** get along with people at work? _____ 1 very well _____ 2 average _____ 3 poorly (_____ X DK)

39. How would you say she gets along with people at work now compared to before she went to the hospital (the last time)?
    _____ 1 better _____ 2 same _____ 3 worse (_____ X DK)

40. Does she prefer _____ 1 to be at home or _____ 2 to take a job?
    (_____ X DK)

41. NOW, SINCE **** LEFT THE HOSPITAL (THE LAST TIME), IS SHE THE PERSON WHO USUALLY DOES THESE THINGS, OR DOES SOMEONE ELSE DO THEM?

	Usually only by herself	Usually others help	Usually only by others	If ans. 2 or 3 who? (relationship to patient)	(NR)
a. Prepares morning and evening meals	___1	___2	___3	_____	(__X)
b. Does the grocery shopping	___1	___2	___3	_____	(__X)
c. Handles the grocery money	___1	___2	___3	_____	(__X)
d. Dusts, sweeps, and does other usual cleaning	___1	___2	___3	_____	(__X)
e. Take care of laundry and mending	___1	___2	___3	_____	(__X)
f. (Ask only if preschool children in house) Dresses and bathes the children	___1	___2	___3	_____	(__X)
g. (Ask only if school age children in house) Makes sure the children get to school on time	___1	___2	___3	_____	(__X)

42. How does **** do in the housework now compared to before she went to the hospital (the last time)? ____ 1 better ____ 2 same ____ 3 worse (____ X NR)

43. (If children school age or younger are in household:)
How does **** do in caring for the children now compared to before she went to the hospital (the last time)? ____ 1 better ____ 2 same ____ 3 worse (____ X NR)

APPENDIX A

44. Whom do you consider the chief breadwinner in the family?
    ____ 0 ****
    ____ 1 ****'s husband
    ____ 2 ****'s mother
    ____ 3 ****'s father
    ____ 4 ****'s brother (or brother-in-law)
    ____ 5 ****'s sister (or sister-in-law)
    ____ 6 ****'s son (or son-in-law)
    ____ 7 ****'s daughter (or daughter-in-law)
    ____ 8 other (specify) _____
    ____ 9 no one
    (____ X NR)

45. If the person you consider as the chief breadwinner became unemployed for some reason, who would you then count on as the chief breadwinner?
    ____ 0 ****
    ____ 1 ****'s husband
    ____ 2 ****'s mother
    ____ 3 ****'s father
    ____ 4 ****'s brother (or brother-in-law)
    ____ 5 ****'s sister (or sister-in-law)
    ____ 6 ****'s son (or son-in-law)
    ____ 7 ****'s daughter (or daughter-in-law)
    ____ 8 other (specify) _____
    ____ 9 no one
    (____ X NR)

NEXT, WE WOULD LIKE SOME INFORMATION ON YOUR FAMILY'S EVERYDAY LIFE AND SPARE TIME ACTIVITIES. FIRST,

46. Does your family belong to any church or religious group?
    ____ 1 yes ____ 2 no

If yes: Which one? ____ 1 Protestant ____ 2 Catholic ____ 3 Jewish
____ 4 other: What? _____ (____ X NR)

If no: Is there any religious faith which you put down when you are filling out a form? ____ 1 Protestant ____ 2 Catholic ____ 3 Jewish
____ 4 other: What? _____ (____ X NR)

47. How often have you attended religious services in the past month (last four weeks)?
    ____ 1 not at all
    ____ 2 one or two times
    ____ 3 once a week
    ____ 4 several times a week
    (____ X NR)

48. How often has **** attended religious services in the past month (last four weeks)?
    ____ 1 not at all   ____ 3 once a week
    ____ 2 one or two times ____ 4 several times a week
    (____ X NR)

49. Do you belong to or take part in any organized clubs or groups like card clubs, lodges, bowling leagues, unions? ____ 1 yes
    ____ 2 no   (____ X NR)

    If yes: Which ones? _____
    If yes: Do you attend their meetings? ____ 1 regularly
    ____ 2 sometimes ____ 3 rarely (____ X NR)

50. Does **** belong to or take part in any organized clubs or groups like card clubs, lodges, bowling leagues, unions? ____ 1 yes
    ____ 2 no   (____ X NR)

    If yes: Which ones? _____
    If yes: Does she attend their meetings? ____ 1 regularly
    ____ 2 sometimes ____ 3 rarely (____ X NR)

51. Since **** has been home from the hospital (the last time), have you felt she should take part in a religious or other social group?
    ____ 1 yes ____ 2 no   (____ X NR)

52. Why? _____

53. About how many magazines would you say you have read in the past month (last four weeks)? ____

54. How about ****, how many magazines has she read in the past month (last four weeks)? ____

55. Aside from magazines, about how many books or novels have you read for pleasure in the past month (last four weeks)? ____

56. How about ****? ____

57. About how often have you been reading a daily paper in the past month (last four weeks)? ____ 1 every day ____ 2 few times a week
    ____ 3 once a week ____ 4 rarely   (____ X NR)

58. How about ****? ____ 1 every day ____ 2 few times a week
    ____ 3 once a week ____ 4 rarely   (____ X NR)

APPENDIX A 241

59. About how many hours have you spent listening to the radio and watching TV on an average weekday evening this past month? _____

60. How about ****? _____

61. How many times during the past month have you gone to the movies? _____

62. How about ****? _____

63. Do you have any hobbies (or regular spare time activities)?
    ____ 1 yes ____ 2 no   (____ X NR)

    If yes: What? _____
    If yes: How much time each week do you now spend on this? ____

64. How about ****, does she have any hobbies (like sewing, knitting, embroidery, etc.)? ____ 1 yes ____ 2 no   (____ X NR)

    If yes: What? _____
    If yes: How much time each week does she now spend on this? ___

65. How many families who are relatives of yours (respondent's) live in or around Columbus, say in about a half-hour's drive from your house? _____

66. How many of these families did you see during the past month (last four weeks)? _____

67. How many of these families did **** see during the past month (last four weeks)? _____

68. About how often do you have friends (not relatives) over to the house each month? _____

69. Does **** usually join you and your friends when they visit your home? ____ 1 yes ____ 2 no   (____ X NR)

70. About how often do you visit with friends at their homes each month? _____

71. Does **** usually go with you? ____ 1 yes ____ 2 no
    (____ X NR)

72. Does **** have any friends who are not also friends of yours?
    ____ 1 many (over 6) ____ 2 some (3-6) ____ 3 few (1-2)
    ____ 4 none   (____ X NR)

73. (Skip if "none")
    Does **** have people over to the house who are not friends of yours? ____ 1 often (once a week) ____ 2 sometimes (once a month) ____ 3 rarely (less than once a month)   (____ X NR)

74. In the past month, how often did you go to parties or social get-togethers? ____ 1 often (once a week) ____ 2 sometimes (once a month) ____ 3 rarely (less than once a month)   (____ X NR)

75. (If often or sometimes:)
    How often did **** go with you to these parties or social get-togethers? ____ 1 often (once a week) ____ 2 sometimes (once a month) ____ 3 rarely (less than once a month)   (____ X NR)

76. I asked you some questions about the visiting that you and **** have been doing. Would you say that in the past month you and **** have been ____ 1 visiting and being visited more than usual, ____ 2 about the same as usual, ____ 3 less than usual?
    (____ X NR)

77. Does **** get any special consideration from family members now compared to before she went to the hospital (the last time)? Would you say she gets ____ 1 more than before ____ 2 same as before ____ 3 less than before   (____ X NR)

78. Do you think she should get special consideration from family members now? ____ 1 yes definitely ____ 2 yes when necessary ____ 3 no   (____ X NR)

79. If **** needs special consideration from family members, would you feel that she ____ 1 definitely needs further treatment ____ 2 might need further treatment ____ 3 does not need further treatment?   (____ X NR)

80. Sometimes a person wants to be alone somewhere in the house without being bothered by other people in the house. How easy would it be for you to do this if you wanted to? Would you say ____ 1 very easy ____ 2 fairly easy ____ 3 fairly hard ____ 4 very hard
    (____ X NR)

APPENDIX A

81. | DURING THE *MONTH BEFORE **** WENT TO THE HOSPITAL* (LAST TIME), WHICH OF THESE THINGS DID SHE USUALLY DO, OR DID SOMEONE ELSE DO THEM? | BEFORE **** WENT TO THE HOSPITAL, *HOW WELL* DID SHE DO THESE THINGS? (Ask only for things she did, ans. 1 or 3) |

	Herself	Others	Both	(NR)	Well	Average	Poorly	(NR)
a. Dust, sweep, and do other usual cleaning	__1	__2	__3	(_X)	__1	__2	__3	(_X)
b. Help with the family shopping	__1	__2	__3	(_X)	__1	__2	__3	(_X)
c. Entertain people at home	__1	__2	__3	(_X)	__1	__2	__3	(_X)
d. Dress and take care of herself	__1	__2	__3	(_X)	__1	__2	__3	(_X)
e. Handle the grocery money	__1	__2	__3	(_X)	__1	__2	__3	(_X)
f. Prepare morning and evening meals	__1	__2	__3	(_X)	__1	__2	__3	(_X)
g. Take care of laundry and mending	__1	__2	__3	(_X)	__1	__2	__3	(_X)
h. (Ask only if preschool children in house) Dress and bathe the children	__1	__2	__3	(_X)	__1	__2	__3	(_X)

	Her-self	Others	Both	(NR)	Well	Aver-age	Poorly	(NR)
i. (Ask only if school children in house) Make sure the children get to school on time	__1	__2	__3	(_X)	__1	__2	__3	(_X)

82. HOW ABOUT THESE THINGS, THE *MONTH BEFORE* **** *WENT TO THE HOSPITAL,* DID SHE GENERALLY DO THEM?

	Yes	No	(NR)
a. Go visit her friends or relatives	__1	__2	(_X)
b. Get along with family members	__1	__2	(_X)
c. Do what's expected of her without coaxing	__1	__2	(_X)
d. Get along with the neighbors	__1	__2	(_X)
e. Go to parties and other social activities	__1	__2	(_X)
f. Hold a job full time or part time	__1	__2	(_X)
g. Attend religious services	__1	__2	(_X)
h. Take part in clubs or organized groups	__1	__2	(_X)

83. INCLUDING THE WHOLE TIME YOU KNOW ****, WHEN SHE WAS *AT HER BEST,* WHICH OF THESE THINGS DID SHE USUALLY DO, OR DID SOMEONE ELSE DO THEM? | AT HER BEST, *HOW WELL* DID SHE DO THEM? (Ask only for things she usually did, ans. 1 or 3)

APPENDIX A

	Herself	Others	Both	(NR)	Well	Average	Poorly	(NR)
a. Dust, sweep, and do other usual cleaning	__1	__2	__3	(_X)	__1	__2	__3	(_X)
b. Help with the family shopping	__1	__2	__3	(_X)	__1	__2	__3	(_X)
c. Entertain people at home	__1	__2	__3	(_X)	__1	__2	__3	(_X)
d. Dress and take care of herself	__1	__2	__3	(_X)	__1	__2	__3	(_X)
e. Handle the grocery money	__1	__2	__3	(_X)	__1	__2	__3	(_X)
f. Prepare morning and evening meals	__1	__2	__3	(_X)	__1	__2	__3	(_X)
g. Take care of laundry and mending	__1	__2	__3	(_X)	__1	__2	__3	(_X)
h. (Ask only if preschool children in house) Dress and bathe the children	__1	__2	__3	(_X)	__1	__2	__3	(_X)
i. (Ask only if school children in house) Make sure the children get to school on time	__1	__2	__3	(_X)	__1	__2	__3	(_X)

84. HOW ABOUT THESE THINGS, *AT HER BEST*, DID **** GENERALLY DO THEM?

	Yes	*No*	*(NR)*
a. Go visit her friends or relatives	__1	__2	(__X)
b. Get along with family members	__1	__2	(__X)
c. Do what's expected of her without coaxing	__1	__2	(__X)
d. Get along with the neighbors	__1	__2	(__X)
e. Go to parties and other social activities	__1	__2	(__X)
f. Hold a job full time or part time	__1	__2	(__X)
g. Attend religious services	__1	__2	(__X)
h. Take part in clubs or organized groups	__1	__2	(__X)

NEXT, WE ARE INTERESTED IN ANY TREATMENT **** HAS GOTTEN SINCE SHE LEFT THE HOSPITAL (THE LAST TIME).

85. Has she seen any of the hospital staff since she left the hospital (the last time)? ____ 1 yes ____ 2 no (____ X NR)

   If yes: Who? ____ 1 psychiatrist ____ 3 social worker
   ____ 2 medical ____ 4 other: Who? _____
   physician (____ X NR)

   If yes: Why? _____

   If yes: How often? _____

86. Has she been to see anyone else who is *not connected with the hospital* for advice or care? ____ 1 yes ____ 2 no (____ X NR)

   If yes: Who? ____ 1 psychiatrist ____ 3 social worker
   ____ 2 medical ____ 4 other: Who? _____
   physician (____ X NR)

APPENDIX A

87. Does she take any medicine to make her feel better? ____ 1 yes
____ 2 no   (____ X DK)

If yes: Do you happen to know their names? _____
_____

If yes: Do you think the drugs help her?
____ 1 definitely help   ____ 3 probably not helping
____ 2 not sure   ____ 4 makes her worse   (____ X NR)

If yes: Was she told to take them by the hospital or a physician?
____ 1 hospital ____ 2 physician ____ 3 not prescribed
____ 4 other: Who? _____ (____ X NR)

88. Often, relatives of patients receive or want help and advice about their (wife's, daughter's, mother's etc.) problems. Have you or another family member (in the household) received any advice?
____ 1 yes ____ 2 no   (____ X NR)

If yes:

	Problems	Who gave?	When?	Was it useful?
Before hospitalization				
During hospitalization				
Since hospitalization				

89. Have you or another family member (in the household) wanted any advice which for some reason could not be obtained? ____ 1 yes
____ 2 no   (____ X NR)

If yes:

	Problems	Why did not receive?
Before hospitalization		
During hospitalization		
Since hospitalization		

90. What other family members (in this household) have ever gone to a hospital, professional person, or community agency about emotional problems? ____ None

Family member	Why?	To whom?	When?

NOW, WE WOULD LIKE TO KNOW ABOUT ****'S HEALTH.

91. What were ****'s specific complaints when she was brought to the hospital (the last time?) _____

_____

_____

92. Has she had any of these complaints since she has been home from the hospital?
    ____ 1 yes, all of them   ____ 3 no, none of them
    ____ 2 yes, some of them   (____ X NR)

93. In general, how is ****'s mental condition *now* compared to when she *left* the hospital (the last time)? ____ 1 better ____ 2 same ____ 3 worse   (____ X NR)

94. In general, how is ****'s mental condition *now* compared to *before* she went to the hospital (last time)?   ____ 1 better ____ 2 same ____ 3 worse   (____ X NR)

95. LET ME READ YOU SOME STATEMENTS WHICH FAMILIES OF PATIENTS HAVE USED TO DESCRIBE THE BEHAVIOR OF THEIR RELATIVES. HOW OFTEN DOES **** ACT THIS WAY, *SINCE SHE LEFT THE HOSPITAL (THE LAST TIME)*?

	Often	*Sometimes*	*Never*	*(NR)*
a. Makes no sense when talking	__1	__2	__3	(__X)
b. Walks, sits, or stands awkwardly	__1	__2	__3	(__X)

APPENDIX A

	Often	Sometimes	Never	(NR)
c. Moves around restlessly	__1	__2	__3	(__X)
d. Swears, curses often compared to other women	__1	__2	__3	(__X)
e. Always seems worn out or tired	__1	__2	__3	(__X)
f. Tries to hit or hurt someone	__1	__2	__3	(__X)
g. Lacks control of toilet habits	__1	__2	__3	(__X)
h. Says she hears voices	__1	__2	__3	(__X)
i. Does not want to see people	__1	__2	__3	(__X)
j. Just hangs around the house doing nothing	__1	__2	__3	(__X)
k. Tries to hurt or kill herself	__1	__2	__3	(__X)
l. Gets drunk often	__1	__2	__3	(__X)
m. Gets grouchy or bad-tempered	__1	__2	__3	(__X)
n. Misbehaves sexually	__1	__2	__3	(__X)
o. Needs coaxing to do what is expected of her	__1	__2	__3	(__X)
p. Has trouble going to sleep	__1	__2	__3	(__X)
q. Takes many pills	__1	__2	__3	(__X)
r. Needs help dressing, bathing, or going to the toilet	__1	__2	__3	(__X)
s. Does not know what goes on around her	__1	__2	__3	(__X)
t. Acts tense or nervous	__1	__2	__3	(__X)

		Often	*Some- times*	*Never*	*(NR)*
u.	Thinks she is sinful or evil compared to other people	__1	__2	__3	(__X)
v.	Thinks people want to control or harm her	__1	__2	__3	(__X)
w.	Worries about her bodily organs	__1	__2	__3	(__X)
x.	Mumbles or talks to herself	__1	__2	__3	(__X)
y.	Tries to get her way by saying she has pains	__1	__2	__3	(__X)
z.	Gets depressed suddenly	__1	__2	__3	(__X)
aa.	Says she sees people who are not there	__1	__2	__3	(__X)
bb.	Worries about her health	__1	__2	__3	(__X)
cc.	Teases and picks on people	__1	__2	__3	(__X)
dd.	Thinks people are watching her or talking about her	__1	__2	__3	(__X)
ee.	Expects bad things to happen in the future without good reason	__1	__2	__3	(__X)
ff.	Does not eat well	__1	__2	__3	(__X)

96. (If **** gets no psychiatric care now:)
    With **** feeling as she does now, what do you think it would be best for her to do?
    _____ 1 return to the hospital
    _____ 2 get out-patient care
    _____ 3 see a private doctor
    _____ 4 live somewhere else: Where? _____

APPENDIX A   251

_____ 5 stay at home
_____ 6 other: What?
(_____ X NR)

STUDIES SHOW THAT VERY OFTEN PATIENTS AND FAMILIES DON'T AGREE ON WHERE THE PATIENT SHOULD LIVE AFTER LEAVING THE HOSPITAL.

97. When **** left the hospital (the last time), was this the only place she could come to live? _____ 1 yes _____ 2 no (_____ X NR)

98. Did **** want to come here to live? _____ 1 definitely wanted to _____ 2 had mixed feelings _____ 3 did not want to (_____ X NR)

99. Did you want her to come here to live? _____ 1 definitely wanted her to _____ 2 had mixed feelings _____ 3 did not want her to
(_____ X NR)

100. (If there are persons in household other than **** and respondent:) Did the other people who live in this household want her to come here to live? _____ 1 definitely wanted her to _____ 2 some of them wanted her to _____ 3 none of them wanted her to
(_____ X NR)

101. Do you know if the hospital wanted her to come here to live?
_____ 1 definitely approved _____ 2 felt it was acceptable
_____ 3 did not approve (_____ X DK)

102. Did someone in the family first suggest that **** go to the hospital for her mental condition? _____ 1 yes: Who? _____
_____ 2 No: Who did? _____ (_____ X NR)

103. Do you think it would have been better for **** to have remained in the hospital for a longer period of time? _____ 1 yes
_____ 2 no (_____ X DK)

   If yes: How much longer? _____
   If no: Do you think it would have been better for **** to have left the hospital sooner than she did?
   _____ 1 yes _____ 2 no   (_____ X DK)
   If yes: When? _____

104. Have you ever considered having **** live elsewhere other than with you? ____ 1 yes ____ 2 no (____ X NR)
    If yes: Where? _____
    With whom? (relationship to ****) _____

CAN YOU TELL ME

> 105. (If respondent is husband of ****:)
> How long have you been married to ****? ____ years
>
> 106. Was **** ever married before this time? ____ 1 yes ____ 2 no (____ X NR)
> *If yes:* When and for how long?
>
> | Dates previous marriages | Reason for termination |
> |---|---|
> | From: To: | |
> | From: To: | |
>
> 107. During your marriage (this marriage), have you at any time considered divorce or separation? ____ 1 yes ____ 2 no (____ X NR)
>
> 108. Have you considered divorce or separation since **** has been home from the hospital (the last time)? ____ 1 yes ____ 2 no (____ X NR)
> *If yes:* Are you considering it now more than before **** went to the hospital (the last time)?
> ____ 1 more than before   ____ 3 less than before
> ____ 2 same as before   (____ X NR)
>
> 109. In general, how do you think you and your wife get along compared to most other couples you know of?
> ____ 1 better than most other couples
> ____ 2 as well as most other couples
> ____ 3 not as well as other couples (____ X NR)

*Skip if respondent is not ****'s husband*

110. Are there ever any arguments between you and **** about such things as . . .

	Yes	No	(NR)
a. Money	____1	____2	(____X)
b. Staying out late	____1	____2	(____X)
c. Being noisy	____1	____2	(____X)
d. Not helping out around the house	____1	____2	(____X)
e. Drinking	____1	____2	(____X)

APPENDIX A

111. (If respondent is *not* ****'s husband:)
Everything considered, how well do you get along with ****?
Would you say ____ 1 well ____ 2 average ____ 3 not well
(____ X NR)

112. HAVING A FAMILY MEMBER WHO HAS BEEN IN A MENTAL HOSPITAL MAY RAISE PROBLEMS FOR THE FAMILY. HERE ARE SOME STATEMENTS THAT HAVE BEEN MADE BY RELATIVES BECAUSE A FORMER PATIENT IS LIVING IN THE HOUSE. WE WOULD LIKE TO KNOW WHICH ONES HAVE BEEN *PROBLEMS* SINCE **** HAS BEEN HOME.

	Problem	Not a problem	(NR)
a. Because she lives here, I sometimes have to neglect my responsibilities to other family members	___1	___2	(___X)
b. It is a financial burden	___1	___2	(___X)
c. Having her home makes family members less willing to invite people to the house	___1	___2	(___X)
d. Once a person has been mentally ill, she needs more supervision and advice from her family than would otherwise be necessary	___1	___2	(___X)
e. A mental patient finds it difficult to make everyday decisions	___1	___2	(___X)
f. Having her home makes other family members nervous	___1	___2	(___X)
g. It affects the family's normal ways of life, like eating times and sleeping times	___1	___2	(___X)
h. It is like having a ten-year-old child around	___1	___2	(___X)

	Problem	Not a problem	(NR)

i. Having her home may cause some neighbors to make remarks about the family ___1 ___2 (___X)

j. Family members sometimes avoid their friends because they are embarrassed ___1 ___2 (___X)

k. If one wants the respect of his fellow workers, it is much better not to let people know a member of the family has been in a mental hospital ___1 ___2 (___X)

l. I see less of my relatives because I am ashamed ___1 ___2 (___X)

113. NEXT, I WOULD LIKE YOU TO TELL ME WHETHER YOU *EXPECT* **** TO BE DOING THESE THINGS *NOW*.

	Yes	No	(NR)

a. Dust, sweep, and do other usual cleaning ___1 ___2 (___X)

b. Help with the family shopping ___1 ___2 (___X)

c. Entertain people at home ___1 ___2 (___X)

d. Dress and take care of herself ___1 ___2 (___X)

e. Handle the grocery money ___1 ___2 (___X)

f. Prepare the morning and evening meals ___1 ___2 (___X)

g. Take care of laundry and mending ___1 ___2 (___X)

h. (Ask only if preschool children in house) Dress and bathe the children ___1 ___2 (___X)

APPENDIX A

	Yes	No	(NR)
i. (Ask only if school children in house) Make sure the children get to school on time	___1	___2	(___X)
j. Go visit her friends or relatives	___1	___2	(___X)
k. Get along with family members	___1	___2	(___X)
l. Do what's expected of her without coaxing	___1	___2	(___X)
m. Get along with the neighbors	___1	___2	(___X)
n. Go to parties and other social activities	___1	___2	(___X)
o. Hold a job full time or part time	___1	___2	(___X)

114. LET ME READ YOU THE LIST ONE MORE TIME. THIS TIME I WOULD LIKE YOU TO TELL ME WHICH OF THESE THINGS YOU WILL DEFINITELY *INSIST* THAT **** BE DOING *SIX MONTHS* FROM NOW.

	Definitely would insist	Would not insist	(NR)
a. Dust, sweep and do other usual cleaning	___1	___2	(___X)
b. Help with the family shopping	___1	___2	(___X)
c. Entertain people at home	___1	___2	(___X)
d. Dress and take care of herself	___1	___2	(___X)
e. Handle the grocery money	___1	___2	(___X)
f. Prepare morning and evening meals	___1	___2	(___X)

		Definitely would insist	Would not insist	(NR)
g.	Take care of laundry and mending	___1	___2	(___X)
h.	(Ask only if preschool children in house) Dress and bathe the children	___1	___2	(___X)
i.	(Ask only if school children in house) Make sure the children get to school on time	___1	___2	(___X)
j.	Go visit her friends or relatives	___1	___2	(___X)
k.	Get along with family members	___1	___2	(___X)
l.	Do what is expected of her without coaxing	___1	___2	(___X)
m.	Get along with the neighbors	___1	___2	(___X)
n.	Go to parties and other social activities	___1	___2	(___X)
o.	Hold a job full time or part time	___1	___2	(___X)

115. I HAVE HERE A LIST OF REASONS FAMILIES HAVE GIVEN FOR CONTACTING THE HOSPITAL OR OTHER PROFESSIONAL PEOPLE *TO ASK IF THEIR (WIFE, MOTHER, DAUGHTER, ETC.) NEEDS TO GO BACK TO THE HOSPITAL.* WOULD YOU CONTACT THE HOSPITAL:

		Would contact hospital	Would not contact hospital	(NR)
a.	If **** made no sense when talking	___1	___2	(___X)

APPENDIX A

	Would contact hospital	Would not contact hospital	(NR)
b. If **** always seemed worn out or tired	___1	___2	(___X)
c. If **** tried to hit or hurt someone	___1	___2	(___X)
d. If **** just hung around the house doing nothing	___1	___2	(___X)
e. If **** tried to kill herself	___1	___2	(___X)
f. If **** got grouchy or bad-tempered	___1	___2	(___X)
g. If **** needed coaxing to do what's expected of her	___1	___2	(___X)
h. If **** acted tense or nervous	___1	___2	(___X)
i. If **** did not eat well	___1	___2	(___X)
j. If **** was hearing things or seeing things	___1	___2	(___X)
k. If **** could not control her toilet habits	___1	___2	(___X)
l. If **** got drunk often	___1	___2	(___X)
m. If **** took many pills	___1	___2	(___X)
n. If **** stayed away from people	___1	___2	(___X)
o. If **** misbehaved sexually	___1	___2	(___X)
p. If **** got depressed suddenly	___1	___2	(___X)
q. If **** mumbled or talked to herself	___1	___2	(___X)
r. If **** neglected household chores	___1	___2	(___X)

| | Would contact hospital | Would not contact hospital | (NR) |

    s. If **** did not know what went on around her   ___ 1   ___ 2 (___ X)

116. As things look now, do you think your (wife, mother, daughter, etc.) will have to go back to the hospital at some time in the future?
 ___ 1 yes, definitely   ___ 4 no, not likely
 ___ 2 yes, quite likely   ___ 5 no, definitely not
 ___ 3 cannot say now   (___ X NR)

NOW LET'S GO ON TO SOMETHING ELSE.

(Skip if no school age or younger children in household.)

117. (If respondent has one or more children of school age or younger:)
 Through what grade in school do you hope to be able to send your (child) (children)?
 ___ 1 through grade school or less (any grade, 1 to 6)
 ___ 2 through junior high school (grade 7, 8, or 9)
 ___ 3 through high school (grade 10, 11, or 12)
 ___ 4 through college (1 or more years)
 (___ X DK)

118. How good do you think the chances are of sending your (child) (children) as far through school as you hope to: Would you say the chances are
 ___ 1 very good   ___ 2 fifty-fifty
 ___ 3 not at all good   (___ X NR)

(Skip if 117 and 118 were answered.)

119. (If respondent has *no* children of school age or younger:)
 If you now had children of school age or younger, through what grade in school would you hope to be able to send your children?
 ___ 1 through grade school or less (any grade, 1 to 6)
 ___ 2 through junior high school (grade 7, 8, or 9)
 ___ 3 through high school (grade 10, 11, or 12)
 ___ 4 through college (1 or more years)
 (___ X DK)

APPENDIX A

Skip if 117 and 118 were answered.

120. How good do you think the chances would be now of sending your children as far through school as you hoped to: Would the chances be
   ___ 1 very good   ___ 2 fifty-fifty
   ___ 3 not at all good   (___ X NR)

121. When you left school, what particular kind of occupation or life work was it your ambition to achieve some day? _____

122. What about ****, at the time she left school, do you know what occupation or life work she wanted to achieve? _____

123. NEXT, I'M GOING TO READ A LIST OF STATEMENTS DESCRIBING WHAT MEN AND WOMEN SHOULD DO IN THEIR EVERYDAY ACTIVITIES. PLEASE TELL ME FOR EACH STATEMENT WHETHER YOU AGREE OR DISAGREE WITH IT. THERE MAY BE ONE OR TWO YOU'RE NOT SURE ABOUT.

	Agree	Disagree	(NR)
a. A husband should help with the housework	___1	___2	(___ X)
b. A woman who does not have to take a job should not	___1	___2	(___ X)
c. If a husband insists, the wife should quit a job which she enjoys	___1	___2	(___ X)
d. Women are too independent these days	___1	___2	(___ X)
e. Husbands should be more strict with their wives	___1	___2	(___ X)
f. A Woman's place is in the home	___1	___2	(___ X)

	Agree	Disagree	(NR)

g. Marriage is the best career for a woman ___1 ___2 (___ X)

h. The man should wear the pants in the family ___1 ___2 (___ X)

i. A woman's interests should be mainly in children, recipes, clothes, and housekeeping ___1 ___2 (___ X)

NEXT, I WOULD LIKE TO KNOW ABOUT THE EXPENSES INVOLVED IN ****'S LAST HOSPITALIZATION.

124. Have you received a bill from the hospital? ___ 1 yes ___ 2 no (___ X NR)
   If yes: Have you paid all of it or part of it? ___ 1 paid all ___ 2 paid part ___ 3 not paid (___ X NR)

125. (If partly paid or not paid:) Why has it not been paid (paid in full)? _____

126. (If partly paid or paid in full:) Here is a list of ways families meet the costs of hospitalization. Were any of the costs of ****'s last hospitalization met in these ways?

	All of it	Part of it	None of it	(NR)
a. Current income	___1	___2	___3	(___ X)
b. Savings	___1	___2	___3	(___ X)
c. Health insurance	___1	___2	___3	(___ X)
d. Loans from banks or finance companies	___1	___2	___3	(___ X)
e. Loans or help from relatives	___1	___2	___3	(___ X)
f. Employer or union	___1	___2	___3	(___ X)

APPENDIX A

	All of it	Part of it	None of it	(NR)
g. V.A. or other federal help	___1	___2	___3	(___X)
h. Private charities and church organizations	___1	___2	___3	(___X)
i. State or city welfare	___1	___2	___3	(___X)
j. Other: What?_____	___1	___2	___3	(___X)

127. In addition to hospital bills, did ****'s last hospitalization impose other financial problems on the household such as loss of income or having to hire someone to help around the house? ____ 1 yes
____ 2 no   (____ X NR)
If yes: What? _____
If yes: How did you meet these financial problems? _____

NOW WE NEED A FEW FACTS ABOUT INCOME AND THEN I'LL HAVE JUST ONE MORE QUESTION ABOUT THE HOSPITAL.

128. How much money does the person who is the chief breadwinner of the family earn? (Before taxes) (Hand respondent Card #2)
_____

129. Is he paid ____ 1 weekly ____ 2 twice a month
____ 3 monthly ____ 4 fees or commissions
____ 5 other?   (____ X NR)

130. Do you receive any pension or welfare money? ____ 1 yes
____ 2 no   (____ X NR)
(If yes, insert number from Card #2) _____

131. What is the total family income? (Insert number from Card #2) _____

132. Now I's like to ask whether you have any comments or ideas about improving the hospital program? (*e.g.* open door policy)
_____
_____
_____

(CHECK COMPLETENESS OF SCHEDULE. GO BACK TO THE BEGINNING AND INSPECT EACH QUESTION. IF ANY QUESTION HAS BEEN OMITTED THAT SHOULD HAVE BEEN ASKED, ASK IT BEFORE TERMINATING THE INTERVIEW.)

ITEMS ADDED TO S.O. SCHEDULE FOR SECOND FOLLOW-UP

133. Has **** been a patient in any hospital since leaving CPIH?
____ 1 yes ____ 2 no   (____ X NR)
If yes: Which one? _____
When and how long? (get dates) _____
Why? _____

134. Has **** seen any professional person for medical, psychiatric, or other advice?
____ 1 yes ____ 2 no   (____ X NR)
If yes: Who? ____ 1 psychiatrist   ____ 3 social worker
____ 2 medical physician ____ 4 other: Who? ____
If yes: Why? _____
When? _____
How often? (if makes regular visits) _____

APPENDIX A

SCHEDULE No._____

CARD #1

RENT PER MONTH

____ 1 Under $30
____ 2 $31-$40
____ 3 $41-$50
____ 4 $51-$60
____ 5 $61-$70
____ 6 $71-$80
____ 7 $81-$100
____ 8 $101-$120
____ 9 $121-$150
____ 10 Over $150

- -

SCHEDULE No._____

CARD #2

INCOME

Weekly	*Monthly*	*Yearly*
____ 1 Under $20	Under $85	Under $1040
____ 2 $20-$40	$85-$173	$1041-$2080
____ 3 $41-$60	$174-$260	$2081-$3120
____ 4 $61-$80	$261-$346	$3121-$4160
____ 5 $81-$100	$347-$433	$4161-$5200
____ 6 $101-$125	$434-$540	$5201-$6500
____ 7 $126-$150	$541-$650	$6501-$7800
____ 8 $151-$170	$651-$735	$7801-$8840
____ 9 $171-$200	$736-$866	$8841-$10,500
____ 10 Over $200	Over $866	Over $10,500

FORM 31 (4-7-59)
S.O.R. SCHEDULE NO. _____

INTERVIEW SCHEDULE FOR SIGNIFICANT OTHER OF RETURNEE

1. FIRST, I WOULD LIKE TO KNOW ON WHAT DATE **** WENT BACK TO THE HOSPITAL (THIS TIME) _____

2. Did **** go back to Columbus Psychiatric Institute and Hospital?
   ____ 1 yes ____ 2 no   (____ X DK)
   If no: To what hospital did she go? _____

3. NEXT, I WOULD LIKE TO KNOW WHERE **** LIVED WHEN SHE WAS HOME FROM THE HOSPITAL BETWEEN
   _____ and _____
   (insert dates here)

4. At what address did she live after leaving the hospital? _____

5. Did she live at this address the whole time she was out of the hospital? (between dates in No. 3)
   ____ 1 yes ____ 2 no   (____ X NR)

APPENDIX A

Ask only if **** moved while out of the hospital

6. *If no:*
   When **** left this address did:
   ____ 1 the whole household including **** move?
   ____ 2 **** leave and the rest of the household remain at this address?
   ____ 3 the household members separate and not live at the same address?
   ____ 4 other_____
   (____ X NR)

7. Including the first address, how many different places did **** live while out of the hospital (between the above dates)? _____

   For each place, including the first address, tell me:

Address	Time **** lived there	Why she moved

CAN YOU TELL ME

8. Did **** spend most of her time before she was 16 in a
   ____ 1 farm   ____ 4 small city (10,000-100,000)
   ____ 2 village   ____ 5 medium city (100,000-500,000)
   ____ 3 town (1,000-10,000) ____ 6 large city (500,000 and over)
   (____ X NR)

9. Did you spend most of your time before you were 16 in a
   ____ 1 farm   ____ 4 small city (10,000-100,000)
   ____ 2 village   ____ 5 medium city (100,000-500,000)
   ____ 3 town (1,000-10,000) ____ 6 large city (500,000 and over)
   (____ X NR)

10. NOW, I WOULD LIKE TO GET SOME FACTS, LIKE AGES, ABOUT **** AND HER FAMILY. I KNOW THAT IT IS SOMETIMES HARD TO REMEMBER THINGS LIKE EXACT DATES. IF YOU'RE NOT SURE ABOUT ANY OF THE THINGS, JUST GIVE ME ESTIMATES.

	(1) Living or dead	(2) Marital status	(3) Age now or at death	(4) Residence (City/State)	(5) Birthplace	(6) Education	(7) Usual occupation	(8) Now employed full or part time
a. ****								
b. Husband								
c. Mother								
d. Father								
e. Mother-in-law								
f. Father-in-law								
g. Sister								
h. Sister								
i. Sister								
j. Brother								
k. Brother								
l. Brother								
m. Daughter								
n. Daughter								
o. Daughter								
p. Son								
q. Son								
r. Son								

11. WHICH OF THESE RELATIVES WAS **** LIVING WITH *AT THE TIME SHE RETURNED TO THE HOSPITAL*?

If not in household now

Relationship to ****	Marital status	Age	Where	When moved	Why moved

APPENDIX A

12. NOW, I WOULD LIKE TO KNOW WHO *ELSE* (*e.g.* friends, roomers, visiting relatives, etc.) LIVED WITH **** DURING THE PERIOD SHE WAS HOME?

Relationship to ****	Marital status	Age	Birthplace	Education	Present occupation	Full or pt	How long lived w/ ****	In HH at time of rehosp.

13. Was the place **** lived at the time she returned to the hospital _____ 1 owned or _____ 2 rented? (_____ X NR)

14. How much did the rent come to each month (or taxes, mortgage payments, etc.)? (Hand respondent Card #1) _____

15. How many rooms were there? _____

16. How many bedrooms were there? _____

17. Was **** or anyone else in the household bothered because there was not enough space in the house (while **** was home)?
    _____ 1 yes _____ 2 no (_____ X NR)

18. During the time **** was home from the hospital (between dates on page 1) how often did she visit with the neighbors?
    _____ 1 often (once a week) _____ 3 rarely (less than once a month)
    _____ 2 sometimes (at least once a month) (_____ X NR)

19. About how often, during the time **** was home from the hospital, did neighbors drop in to see her? _____ 1 often (once a week)
    _____ 2 sometimes (at least once a month)
    _____ 3 rarely (less than once a month) (_____ X NR)

20. To which of these three groups do you feel closest?
    _____ 1 working class _____ 2 middle class
    _____ 3 upper class (_____ X NR)

21. How about most of the people who live around you, where would you say they belong? _____ 1 working class
    _____ 2 middle class _____ 3 upper class (_____ X NR)

22. (If **** lived in residence other than respondent's:) How about the people who lived around **** when she was home from the hospital, where would you say they belong? ____ 1 working class ____ 2 middle class ____ 3 upper class (____ X DK)

NEXT, WE WOULD LIKE TO KNOW ABOUT WHERE **** HAS WORKED.

23. Before **** went to the hospital (before very first hospitalization), did she usually ____ 1 have a job ____ 2 keep house ____ 3 other: What? _____

24. (If **** usually worked:) At what age did **** first start working? _____

25. What type of work did she usually do? _____

26. What type of work did she prefer to have? _____

27. What would you say were the main reasons she worked then? _____

28. Between the age when **** started working and the hospitalization six months ago at CPIH, do you remember the number of different places she worked? _____ (____ X NR)

29. Before **** was in the hospital six months ago at CPIH, what was the place she worked at last, job she held, and for how long?

Type of business or industry	Job	Dates
		From: To:

30. Before **** was in the hospital six months ago at CPIH, what was the place she worked the longest, job held, and for how long?

Type of business or industry	Job	Dates
		From: To:

31. Before **** went to the hospital six months ago at CPIH, what was the longest period she did not work? _____ years.

Skip if never worked before last hosp'n. Reference is to last *hosp'n,* not *to present hosp'n.*

APPENDIX A

32. Did **** work during the time she was home from the hospital (between dates on page 1)? ____ 1 yes ____ 2 no (____ X NR)
    If yes:

Description	How long employed	Salary	Full or pt	Why did she leave
	From: To:			
	From: To:			

33. (Skip if not worked)
    During this (last) period when **** was out of the hospital (between dates on page 1), how did people **** worked with get along with her? ____ 1 very well ____ 2 well ____ 3 fair ____ 4 poorly
    (____ X NR)

34. Do you know if, during this time, she preferred ____ 1 to take a job or ____ 2 to be at home? (____ X DK)

35. DURING THE TIME **** WAS HOME FROM THE HOSPITAL (BETWEEN DATES ON PAGE 1), DID SHE USUALLY DO THESE THINGS, OR DID SOMEONE ELSE DO THEM?

	Usually only by herself	Usually others helped	Usually only by others	If ans. 2 or 3, who? (relationship to patient)	(NR)
a. Prepared morning and evening meals	____ 1	____ 2	____ 3	_____	(____ X)
b. Did the grocery shopping	____ 1	____ 2	____ 3	_____	(____ X)
c. Handled the grocery money	____ 1	____ 2	____ 3	_____	(____ X)
d. Dusted, swept, and did other usual cleaning	____ 1	____ 2	____ 3	_____	(____ X)

	Usually only by herself	Usually others helped	Usually only by others	If ans. 2 or 3, who? (relationship to patient)	(NR)
e. Took care of laundry and mending	___1	___2	___3	_____	(___X)
f. (Ask only if preschool children in house) Dressed and bathed the children	___1	___2	___3	_____	(___X)
g. (Ask only if school children in house) Made sure the children got to school on time	___1	___2	___3	_____	(___X)

36. How did **** do in the housework during the time **** was home from the hospital? ____ 1 well ____ 2 fair ____ 3 poorly
(____ X NR)

37. (If school age or younger children were in household:) How did she do in caring for the children during the time she was home from the hospital? ____ 1 well ____ 2 fair ____ 3 poorly (____ X NR)

38. During the period **** was out of the hospital (between dates on page 1), was she considered
____ 1 the chief breadwinner
____ 2 the person counted on as chief breadwinner if the breadwinner became unemployed
____ 3 neither
(____ X NR)

39. Whom do you now consider the chief breadwinner in the family?
    - ____ 1 ****'s husband
    - ____ 2 ****'s mother
    - ____ 3 ****'s father
    - ____ 4 ****'s brother
      (or brother-in-law)
    - ____ 5 ****'s sister
      (or sister-in-law)
    - ____ 6 ****'s son
      (or son-in-law)
    - ____ 7 ****'s daughter
      (or daughter-in-law)
    - ____ 8 other (specify) _____
    - ____ 9 no one
    - (____ X NR)

40. If the person you now consider the chief breadwinner became unemployed for some reason, who would you then count on as the chief breadwinner?
    - ____ 1 ****'s husband
    - ____ 2 ****'s mother
    - ____ 3 ****'s father
    - ____ 4 ****'s brother
      (or brother-in-law)
    - ____ 5 ****'s sister
      (or sister-in-law)
    - ____ 6 ****'s son
      (or son-in-law)
    - ____ 7 ****'s daughter
      (or daughter-in-law)
    - ____ 8 other (specify) _____
    - ____ 9 no one
    - (____ X NR)

41. Does your family belong to any church or religious group? ____ 1 yes ____ 2 no
    If yes: Which one? ____ 1 Protestant ____ 2 Catholic ____ 3 Jewish ____ 4 other: What? _____
    (____ X NR)
    If no: Is there any religious faith you put down when you are filling out a form? ____ 1 Protestant ____ 2 Catholic ____ 3 Jewish ____ 4 other: What? _____
    (____ X NR)

42. How often did you attend religious services during the last month before **** returned to the hospital? ____ 1 not at all ____ 2 one or two times ____ 3 once a week ____ 4 several times a week (____ X NR)

43. How often did **** attend religious services during the last month before she returned to the hospital? ____ 1 not at all ____ 2 one or two times ____ 3 once a week ____ 4 several times a week (____ X NR)

44. Do you belong to or take part in any organized clubs or groups like card clubs, lodges, bowling leagues, unions? ____ 1 yes ____ 2 no (____ X NR)
    If yes: Which ones? _____
    If yes: Generally, while **** was home (between dates on page 1), did you attend their meetings ____ 1 regularly ____ 2 sometimes ____ 3 rarely (____ X NR)

45. Does **** belong to or take part in any organized clubs or groups like card clubs, lodges, bowling leagues, unions? ____ 1 yes ____ 2 no (____ X NR)
    If yes: Which ones? _____
    If yes: During the period **** was home (between dates on page 1), did she attend their meetings ____ 1 regularly ____ 2 sometimes ____ 3 rarely? (____ X NR)

46. During the time **** was home (between dates on page 1), about how often did she do any of these things?

	Often	Sometimes	Never	(NR)
a. Read magazines	___ 1	___ 2	___ 3	(___ X)
b. Read books	___ 1	___ 2	___ 3	(___ X)
c. Read a daily paper	___ 1	___ 2	___ 3	(___ X)
d. Go to movies	___ 1	___ 2	___ 3	(___ X)
e. Watch TV or listen to radio	___ 1	___ 2	___ 3	(___ X)

47. During the time she was home, about how often did you do any of these things?

	Often	Sometimes	Never	(NR)
a. Read magazines	___ 1	___ 2	___ 3	(___ X)
b. Read books	___ 1	___ 2	___ 3	(___ X)
c. Read a daily paper	___ 1	___ 2	___ 3	(___ X)
d. Go to movies	___ 1	___ 2	___ 3	(___ X)
e. Watch TV or listen to radio	___ 1	___ 2	___ 3	(___ X)

APPENDIX A

48. Did you feel that **** should take part in a religious or social group during the time she was home (between dates on page 1)?
    ____ 1 yes ____ 2 no   (____ X NR)

49. Why? _____

50. Does **** have any hobbies (or regular spare time activities) (like sewing, knitting, embroidery, etc.)? ____ 1 yes ____ 2 no   (____ X NR)
    If yes: What? _____
    If yes: During the period **** was home (between dates on page 1), how much time each week did she spend on them? _____

51. How about you, do you have any hobbies (or regular spare time activities)? ____ 1 yes ____ 2 no   (____ X NR)
    If yes: What? _____
    If yes: On the average, during the period **** was home (between dates on page 1), how much time each week did you spend on them? _____

52. During the last month **** was home from the hospital, about how often did you have friends (not relatives) over to the house? _____
    _____

53. Did **** usually join you and your friends when they visited your home? ____ 1 yes ____ 2 no   (____ X NR)

54. About how often did you visit with friends at their homes the month before **** went back to the hospital? _____

55. Did **** usually go with you? ____ 1 yes ____ 2 no   (____ X NR)

56. Does **** have any friends who are not also friends of yours?
    ____ 1 many (over 6) ____ 2 some (3-6) ____ 3 few (1-2)
    ____ 4 none   (____ X NR)

57. During the period **** was home, did she have people over to the house who are not friends of yours? ____ 1 often (once a week)
    ____ 2 sometimes (once a month) ____ 3 rarely (less than once a month)   (____ X NR)

58. Did **** visit friends without other family members being along?
    ____ 1 often (once a week) ____ 2 sometimes (once a month)
    ____ 3 rarely (less than once a month)   (____ X NR)

59. During the time **** was home, how many families who are related to you did you see, say once a month? _____

60. During the time **** was home, how many of these families did she see, say once a month? _____

61. During the period **** was home, did she require any special consideration from family members? ____ 1 all the time ____ 2 sometimes ____ 3 rarely (____ X NR)

62. Sometimes a person wants to be alone somewhere in the house without being bothered by other people in the house. During the period **** was home, how easy was it for you to do this if you wanted to?
    ____ 1 very easy   ____ 3 fairly hard
    ____ 2 fairly easy   ____ 4 very hard   (____ X NR)

63. INCLUDING THE WHOLE TIME YOU KNEW **** WHEN SHE WAS *AT HER BEST*, WHICH OF THESE THINGS DID SHE USUALLY DO, OR DID SOMEONE ELSE DO THEM? | AT HER BEST, *HOW WELL* DID SHE DO THEM? (Ask only for the things she usually did, ans. 1 or 3)

	Herself	Others	Both	(NR)	Well	Average	Poorly	(NR)
a. Dust, sweep, and do other usual cleaning	__1	__2	__3	(_X)	__1	__2	__3	(_X)
b. Help with the family shopping	__1	__2	__3	(_X)	__1	__2	__3	(_X)
c. Entertain people at home	__1	__2	__3	(_X)	__1	__2	__3	(_X)
d. Dress and take care of herself	__1	__2	__3	(_X)	__1	__2	__3	(_X)
e. Handle the grocery money	__1	__2	__3	(_X)	__1	__2	__3	(_X)
f. Prepare morning and evening meals	__1	__2	__3	(_X)	__1	__2	__3	(_X)

APPENDIX A   275

		Her-self	Others	Both	(NR)	Well	Aver-age	Poorly	(NR)
g.	Take care of laundry and mending	__1	__2	__3	(__X)	__1	__2	__3	(__X)
h.	(Ask only if pre-school children in house) Dress and bathe the children	__1	__2	__3	(__X)	__1	__2	__3	(__X)
i.	(Ask only if school children in house) Make sure the children get to school on time	__1	__2	__3	(__X)	__1	__2	__3	(__X)

64. HOW ABOUT THESE THINGS, *AT HER BEST*, DID SHE GENERALLY DO THEM?

		Yes	*No*	*(NR)*
a.	Go visit her friends or relatives	__1	__2	(__X)
b.	Get along with family members	__1	__2	(__X)
c.	Do what's expected of her without coaxing	__1	__2	(__X)
d.	Get along with the neighbors	__1	__2	(__X)
e.	Go to parties and other social activities	__1	__2	(__X)
f.	Hold a job full time or part time	__1	__2	(__X)
g.	Attend religious services	__1	__2	(__X)
h.	Take part in clubs or organized groups	__1	__2	(__X)

NEXT, WE ARE INTERESTED IN PROFESSIONAL TREATMENT **** RECEIVED WHILE SHE WAS OUT OF THE HOSPITAL.

65. Did **** see any of the hospital staff after she left CPIH six months ago? ____ 1 yes ____ 2 no (____ X NR)
    If yes: Who? ____ 1 psychiatrist   ____ 4 other: Who? _____
              ____ 2 medical physician
              ____ 3 social worker   (____ X NR)
    If yes: Why? _____
    If yes: How often? _____

66. Did **** see anyone *not connected* with the hospital for advice or care? ____ 1 yes ____ 2 no (____ X NR)
    If yes: Who? ____ 1 psychiatrist   ____ 4 other: Who? _____
              ____ 2 medical physician
              ____ 3 social worker   (____ X NR)

67. Did she take any medicine to make her feel better?
    ____ 1 yes ____ 2 no (____ X NR)
    If yes: Do you happen to know their names? _____
    If yes: Do you think the drugs helped her? ____ 1 definitely helped ____ 2 not sure ____ 3 probably did not help ____ 4 made her worse (____ X NR)
    If yes: Was she told to take them by the hospital or a physician?
    ____ 1 hospital ____ 2 physician ____ 3 not prescribed
    ____ 4 other: Who? _____ (____ X NR)

68. Often, relatives of patients receive or want help and advice about their (wife's, mother's, daughter's, etc.) problems. Have you or another family member received any advice? ____ 1 yes
    ____ 2 no (____ X NR)

    If yes:

	Problems	Who gave?	When?	Was it useful?
During last hospitalization				
While she was home				
Since rehospitalization				

APPENDIX A 277

69. Have you or another family member wanted any advice which for some reason could not be obtained? ____ 1 yes ____ 2 no
(____ X NR)

If yes:

	Problems	Why did not receive
During last hospitalization		
While she was home		
Since rehospitalization		

70. During the period **** was home, did any other family members (in this household) go to a hospital, professional person, or community agency about emotional problems?

____ 1 yes ____ 2 no (____ X NR)

If yes:

Family member	Why?	To whom?

71. While **** was home (this last time), did she have any contacts with the police or other legal authorities? ____ 1 yes ____ 2 no
(____ X NR)

If yes: Who and why? _____

72. LET ME READ YOU SOME STATEMENTS WHICH FAMILIES OF PATIENTS HAVE USED TO DESCRIBE THE BEHAVIOR OF THEIR RELATIVES. HOW OFTEN DID **** ACT THIS WAY *DURING THE TIME SHE WAS HOME* FROM THE HOSPITAL (between dates on page 1)?

	Often	*Sometimes*	*Never*	*(NR)*
a. Made no sense when talking	____1	____2	____3	(____X)
b. Walked, sat, or stood awkwardly	____1	____2	____3	(____X)

		Often	Sometimes	Never	(NR)
c.	Moved around restlessly	___1	___2	___3	(___X)
d.	Swore, cursed often compared to other women	___1	___2	___3	(___X)
e.	Always seemed worn out or tired	___1	___2	___3	(___X)
f.	Tried to hit or hurt someone	___1	___2	___3	(___X)
g.	Lacked control of toilet habits	___1	___2	___3	(___X)
h.	Said she heard voices	___1	___2	___3	(___X)
i.	Didn't want to see people	___1	___2	___3	(___X)
j.	Just hung around the house doing nothing	___1	___2	___3	(___X)
k.	Tried to hurt or kill herself	___1	___2	___3	(___X)
l.	Got drunk often	___1	___2	___3	(___X)
m.	Got grouchy or bad-tempered	___1	___2	___3	(___X)
n.	Misbehaved sexually	___1	___2	___3	(___X)
o.	Needed coaxing to do what was expected of her	___1	___2	___3	(___X)
p.	Had trouble going to sleep	___1	___2	___3	(___X)
q.	Took many pills	___1	___2	___3	(___X)
r.	Needed help dressing, bathing, or going to the toilet	___1	___2	___3	(___X)
s.	Didn't know what went on around her	___1	___2	___3	(___X)

APPENDIX A

	Often	Sometimes	Never	(NR)
t. Acted tense or nervous	__1	__2	__3	(__X)
u. Thought she was sinful or evil compared to other people	__1	__2	__3	(__X)
v. Thought people wanted to control or harm her	__1	__2	__3	(__X)
w. Worried about her bodily organs	__1	__2	__3	(__X)
x. Mumbled or talked to herself	__1	__2	__3	(__X)
y. Tried to get her way by saying she had pains	__1	__2	__3	(__X)
z. Got depressed suddenly	__1	__2	__3	(__X)
aa. Said she saw people who were not there	__1	__2	__3	(__X)
bb. Worried about her health	__1	__2	__3	(__X)
cc. Teased and picked on people	__1	__2	__3	(__X)
dd. Thought people were watching her or talking about her	__1	__2	__3	(__X)
ee. Expected bad things to happen in the future without good reason	__1	__2	__3	(__X)
ff. Did not eat well	__1	__2	__3	(__X)

STUDIES SHOW THAT VERY OFTEN PATIENTS AND FAMILIES DON'T AGREE ON WHERE THE PATIENT SHOULD LIVE AFTER LEAVING THE HOSPITAL.

73. When **** left CPIH six months ago, was this the only place she could come to live? ____ 1 yes ____ 2 no (____ X NR)

74. Did **** want to come here to live? ____ 1 definitely wanted to ____ 2 had mixed feelings ____ 3 did not want to (____ X NR)

75. Did you want her to come here to live? ____ 1 definitely wanted her to ____ 2 had mixed feelings ____ 3 did not want her to
(____ X NR)

76. Did the other people who live in this household want her to come here to live? ____ 1 definitely wanted her to ____ 2 some of them wanted her to ____ 3 none of them wanted her to ____ 4 no others in household (____ X NR)

77. Do you know if the hospital wanted her to come here to live?
____ 1 definitely approved ____ 2 felt it was acceptable
____ 3 did not approve (____ X NR)

78. The *first* time **** went to a hospital, did someone in the family first suggest that she go to the hospital for her mental condition?
____ 1 yes: Who?_____
____ 2 no: Who did?_____ (____ X NR)

79. Have you ever considered having **** live elsewhere other than with you? ____ 1 yes ____ 2 no (____ X NR)
If yes: Where?_____
With whom? (Relationship to ****) _____

CAN YOU TELL ME

> 80. (If respondent is husband to ****:)
> How long have you been married to ****? _____ years
>
> 81. Was **** ever married before this time? ____ 1 yes
> ____ 2 no (____ X NR)
> *If yes:* When and for how long?
>
> | Dates previous marriages | Reason for termination |
> |---|---|
> | From: To: | |
> | From: To: | |
>
> 82. During your marriage (this marriage), did you at any time consider divorce or separation? ____ 1 yes ____ 2 no
> (____ X NR)

Skip if respondent is *not* ****'s husband

APPENDIX A

Skip if respondent is *not* ****'s husband

83. During the time that **** was home from the hospital (between dates on page 1), did you consider divorce or separation?
    ____ 1 yes ____ 2 no (____ X NR)
    If yes: Are you considering it now? ____ 1 yes ____ 2 no
    (____ X NR)

84. Did **** consider divorce or separation during the time she was home from the hospital (between dates on page 1)?
    ____ 1 yes ____ 2 no (____ X DK)

85. In general, how do you think you and your wife get along compared to most other couples you know of?
    ____ 1 better than most other couples
    ____ 2 as well as most other couples
    ____ 3 not as well as other couples
    (____ X NR)

86. During the period **** was home from the hospital, were there ever any arguments between you and **** about such things as

	Yes	No	(NR)
a. Money	___1	___2	(___X)
b. Staying out late	___1	___2	(___X)
c. Being noisy	___1	___2	(___X)
d. Not helping out around the house	___1	___2	(___X)
e. Drinking	___1	___2	(___X)

Ask only if respondent is *not* ****'s husband

87. Everything considered, how well do you get along with ****? Would you say ____ 1 well ____ 2 average
    ____ 3 not well (____ X NR)

88. How about during the time **** was home from the hospital?
    ____ 1 well ____ 2 average ____ 3 not well
    (____ X NR)

HAVING A FORMER MENTAL PATIENT IN THE HOME MAY RAISE PROBLEMS FOR THE FAMILY. HERE ARE SOME STATEMENTS THAT HAVE BEEN MADE BY RELATIVES BECAUSE A FORMER PATIENT WAS IN THE HOME. WE WOULD LIKE TO KNOW WHICH ONES WERE *PROBLEMS* WHILE **** WAS HOME (between dates on page 1).

89.

	Problem	Not a problem	(NR)
a. Because she lived here, it was sometimes necessary to neglect responsibilities to other family members	___1	___2	(___X)
b. It was a financial burden	___1	___2	(___X)
c. Having her home made family members less willing to invite people to the house	___1	___2	(___X)
d. Because she had been mentally ill, she needed more supervision and advice from her family than would otherwise be necessary	___1	___2	(___X)
e. She found it difficult to make even everyday decisions	___1	___2	(___X)
f. Having her home made other family members nervous	___1	___2	(___X)
g. It affected the family's normal ways of life, like eating times and sleeping times	___1	___2	(___X)
h. It was like having a ten-year-old child around	___1	___2	(___X)
i. Having her home made some neighbors talk about the family	___1	___2	(___X)

APPENDIX A

	Problem	Not a problem	(NR)
j. Family members sometimes avoided their friends because they were embarrassed	___1	___2	(___X)
k. To keep the respect of fellow workers, it was necessary not to let people know a member of the family had been in a mental hospital	___1	___2	(___X)
l. I saw less of my relatives because I was ashamed	___1	___2	(___X)

90. FAMILIES VARY IN WHAT THEY THINK THEIR RELATIVES SHOULD DO AFTER THEY COME HOME FROM THE HOSPITAL. I WOULD LIKE YOU TO TELL ME WHICH OF THESE THINGS YOU EXPECTED **** TO DO WHILE SHE WAS OUT OF THE HOSPITAL (between dates on page 1).

	Expected	Did not expect	(NR)
a. Dust, sweep, and do other usual cleaning	___1	___2	(___X)
b. Help with the family shopping	___1	___2	(___X)
c. Entertain people at home	___1	___2	(___X)
d. Dress and take care of herself	___1	___2	(___X)
e. Handle the grocery money	___1	___2	(___X)
f. Prepare morning and evening meals	___1	___2	(___X)
g. Take care of laundry and mending	___1	___2	(___X)

	Expected	Did not expect	(NR)
h. (Ask only if preschool children in house) Dress and bathe the children	___ 1	___ 2	(___ X)
i. (Ask only if school children in house) Make sure the children get to school on time	___ 1	___ 2	(___ X)
j. Go visit her friends or relatives	___ 1	___ 2	(___ X)
k. Get along with family members	___ 1	___ 2	(___ X)
l. Do what's expected of her without coaxing	___ 1	___ 2	(___ X)
m. Get along with the neighbors	___ 1	___ 2	(___ X)
n. Go to parties and other social activities	___ 1	___ 2	(___ X)
o. Hold a job full time or part time	___ 1	___ 2	(___ X)

91. NOW LET'S GO BACK OVER THE LIST. THIS TIME I'D LIKE YOU TO TELL ME WHICH OF THESE THINGS YOU *INSISTED* **** DO WHILE OUT OF THE HOSPITAL (between dates on page 1).

	Insisted	Did not insist	(NR)
a. Dust, sweep, and do other usual cleaning	___ 1	___ 2	(___ X)
b. Help with the family shopping	___ 1	___ 2	(___ X)
c. Entertain people at home	___ 1	___ 2	(___ X)

APPENDIX A

	Insisted	Did not insist	(NR)
d. Dress and take care of herself	___1	___2	(___X)
e. Handle the grocery money	___1	___2	(___X)
f. Prepare morning and evening meals	___1	___2	(___X)
g. Take care of laundry and mending	___1	___2	(___X)
h. (Ask only if preschool children in house) Dress and bathe the children	___1	___2	(___X)
i. (Ask only if school children in house) Make sure the children get to school on time	___1	___2	(___X)
j. Go to visit her friends or relatives	___1	___2	(___X)
k. Get along with family members	___1	___2	(___X)
l. Do what's expected of her without coaxing	___1	___2	(___X)
m. Get along with the neighbors	___1	___2	(___X)
n. Go to parties and other social activities	___1	___2	(___X)
o. Hold a job full time or part time	___1	___2	(___X)

NEXT, WE WANT TO KNOW ABOUT THE EVENTS LEADING TO ****'S RETURN TO THE HOSPITAL.

92. Was it a family member or someone outside the family who first suggested that **** go back to the hospital?
    ____ 1 family   ____ 3 both
    ____ 2 outside family   ____ 4 patient
                            (____ X NR)

93. (Ask if family only or both:)
    Which family members first suggested that **** return to the hospital?
    ____ 1 ****'s husband   ____ 6 ****'s son
    ____ 2 ****'s mother   (or son-in-law)
    ____ 3 ****'s father   ____ 7 ****'s daughter
    ____ 4 ****'s brother   (or daughter-in-law)
         (or brother-in-law)   ____ 8 other (specify) _____
    ____ 5 ****'s sister   (____ X NR)
         (or sister-in-law)

94. (Ask if outside family or both:)
    Who outside the family first suggested it?
    ____ 1 hospital personnel   ____ 6 employer
    ____ 2 private physician   ____ 7 mental hygiene clinic
    ____ 3 social worker   ____ 8 other (specify) _____
    ____ 4 friend   (____ X NR)
    ____ 5 police

95. How long before **** went back to the hospital did someone first suggest it? _____ wks/mos.

96. How long after it had been suggested was going back to the hospital first mentioned to ****? _____ wks/mos.
    ____ 0 not mentioned to ****   ____ 1 mentioned to **** when it was first suggested

97. Who first talked to **** about going back to the hospital?
    ____ 1 family member: Who? _____
    ____ 2 professional person: Who? _____
    ____ 3 other: Who? _____
    ____ 4 no one
    (____ X NR)

APPENDIX A

98. How did **** feel about going back to the hospital when it was first mentioned to her?
    ____ 1 was in favor of it right away
    ____ 2 did not seem to care one way or another
    ____ 3 agreed to it but only after talking it over
    ____ 4 against it even after talking it over
    ____ 5 other: What? _____
    (____ X NR)

99. How long before going back did **** know that rehospitalization was being considered? _____ wks/mos.
    ____ 0 **** did not know

100. Did **** have anything to do with deciding whether she should go back to the hospital? ____ 1 yes ____ 2 no   (____ X NR)

101. Did **** know where she was going when being taken back to the hospital? ____ 1 yes ____ 2 no   (____ X NR)
    If no: What was she told? _____

102. Do you think **** now feels it was necessary for her to go back to the hospital?
    ____ 1 **** now feels it was necessary
    ____ 2 **** now is uncertain
    ____ 3 **** now feels it was unnecessary
    (____ X NR)

103. Do you think **** now feels being in the hospital again is helping her?
    ____ 1 **** feels it is helping her
    ____ 2 **** feels it has not helped so far but will probably help after a longer time in the hospital
    ____ 3 **** feels it is not helping her and is not going to help her even after a longer time in the hospital
    ____ 4 **** is uncertain whether it is helping her or going to help her
    (____ X NR)

104. When **** was *first returned* to the hospital, did you feel the decision to send her back was the right one?
    ____ 1 felt it was the right decision
    ____ 2 was not sure
    ____ 3 did not feel it was the right decision
    (____ X NR)

105. Everything considered, do you now feel the decision to send **** to the hospital again was the right one?
    ____ 1 now feel it was the right decision
    ____ 2 not sure now
    ____ 3 do not feel it was the right decision
    (____ X NR)

106. Do you think the (other) persons living with **** at the time she was hospitalized agree with you? ____ 1 yes ____ 2 no: Why?
    _____
    ____ 3 no others lived with **** then   (____ X DK)

107. NOW, HERE IS A LIST OF REASONS FOR WHICH PATIENTS ARE OFTEN REHOSPITALIZED. WHICH ONES WERE REASONS FOR ****'S RETURN TO THE HOSPITAL?

	Was a reason	Was not reason	(NR)
a. Made no sense when talking	____1	____2	(____X)
b. Always seemed worn out or tired	____1	____2	(____X)
c. Tried to hit or hurt someone	____1	____2	(____X)
d. Just hung around the house doing nothing	____1	____2	(____X)
e. Tried to kill herself	____1	____2	(____X)
f. Got grouchy or bad-tempered	____1	____2	(____X)
g. Needed coaxing to do what was expected of her	____1	____2	(____X)
h. Acted tense or nervous	____1	____2	(____X)
i. Did not eat well	____1	____2	(____X)
j. Was hearing or seeing things	____1	____2	(____X)

APPENDIX A

	Was a reason	Was not reason	(NR)
k. Could not control her toilet habits	___1	___2	(___X)
l. Got drunk often	___1	___2	(___X)
m. Took many pills	___1	___2	(___X)
n. Stayed away from people	___1	___2	(___X)
o. Misbehaved sexually	___1	___2	(___X)
p. Got depressed suddenly	___1	___2	(___X)
q. Mumbled or talked to herself	___1	___2	(___X)
r. Neglected household chores	___1	___2	(___X)
s. Didn't know what went on around her	___1	___2	(___X)

108. Were there any other reasons that led to ****'s return to the hospital? ____ 1 yes ____ 2 no   (____ X NR)
   If yes: What? _____

109. (If more than one reason given above:)
   Of the things you told me, was there any one particular reason that was most important in ****'s rehospitalization? ____ 1 yes ____ 2 no   (____ X NR)
   If yes: What? _____

110. Do you think **** was returned home too soon from CPIH six months ago? ____ 1 yes ____ 2 no   (____ X NR)
   If no: Do you think **** stayed in the hospital too long (last time)? ____ 1 yes ____ 2 no   (____ X NR)

111. Do you think **** would have been hospitalized again if she had gone to a *different hospital* the time before?
   ____ 1 yes ____ 2 no   (____ X DK)
   If no: Which one or what kind? _____

112. Do you think **** would have been hospitalized again if she had been given *different treatment* while in CPIH six months ago?
  ____ 1 yes ____ 2 no (____ X DK)
  If no: In what ways? _____

113. (If **** now *out* of hospital, ask:) Do you think **** received as good treatment in her rehospitalization as in CPIH six months ago?
  ____ 1 yes ____ 2 no: Why? _____
  (If **** now *in* hospital, ask:) Do you think **** is receiving as good treatment as last time? ____ 1 yes ____ 2 no: Why? ____
  _____

114. Are there any other things CPIH could have done for **** when she was there six months ago? ____ 1 yes ____ 2 no
  (____ X NR)
  If yes: What? _____

115. (If **** now *in* hospital ask:) Is there anything the hospital could be doing for her now that they are not doing? ____ 1 yes
  ____ 2 no (____ X DK)
  If yes: What? _____
  (If **** now *out* of hospital ask:) Is there anything the hospital to which she returned could have done that they did not do?
  ____ 1 yes ____ 2 no (____ X DK)
  If yes: What? _____

116. (Ask only if **** is *now* in hospital:)
  Compared with the last time, do you think **** will be in the hospital ____ 1 a longer time ____ 2 about the same time ____ 3 a shorter time? (____ X NR)

117. Did ****'s condition become worse suddenly, or did it happen gradually (between dates on page 1)? ____ 1 suddenly
  ____ 2 gradually ____ 3 no change while home (____ X NR)

118. (If suddenly or gradually)
  How long after she was home did she begin to get worse? ____

119. (If suddenly or gradually:)
  What do you think caused this to happen? _____
  _____

APPENDIX A

120. Looking back, do you think there is some other way ****'s condition could have been helped besides returning her to the hospital?
____ 1 yes ____ 2 no   (____ X NR)
If yes: What might have been done? _____

121. (Ask only if **** is *now* in hospital:)
In general, how has ****'s mental condition been during this hospitalization compared with her mental condition while she was in CPIH six months ago?
____ 1 better ____ 2 same ____ 3 worse   (____ X NR)

122. (Ask only if **** now *out* of hospital:)
In general, how is her mental condition now compared with her mental condition after she left CPIH six months ago?
____ 1 better ____ 2 same ____ 3 worse   (____ X NR)

123. SOMETIMES PATIENTS FACE PROBLEMS WHEN THEY LEAVE THE HOSPITAL BECAUSE OF THE WAY SOME PEOPLE IN THE COMMUNITY FEEL ABOUT FORMER MENTAL PATIENTS. WHILE **** WAS IN THE COMMUNITY (between dates on page 1), DID SHE HAVE ANY OF THE FOLLOWING PROBLEMS?

	Problem	*Not a problem*	*(NR)*
a. Having been a mental patient prevented **** from finding or holding a job	____ 1	____ 2	(____ X)
b. Having been a mental patient made some of ****'s friends avoid her	____ 1	____ 2	(____ X)
c. Having been a mental patient prevented **** from being able to buy something on credit	____ 1	____ 2	(____ X)
d. Having been a mental patient made some of ****'s relatives look down on her	____ 1	____ 2	(____ X)

	Problem	Not a problem	(NR)

e. Having been a mental patient caused some of the neighbors to make remarks ___1 ___2 (___X)

f. Having been a mental patient caused the police to check up on **** ___1 ___2 (___X)

124. SOMETIMES THINGS MIGHT HAVE TURNED OUT BETTER FOR A MENTAL PATIENT IF CONDITIONS FACED BY PEOPLE IN THE HOUSEHOLD WERE DIFFERENT. WOULD IT HAVE TURNED OUT BETTER FOR **** IF THESE THINGS HAD BEEN DIFFERENT? (between dates on page 1)?

	Turned out better	If better how	Made no difference	(NR)

a. If the neighborhood had been different ___1 _____ ___2 (___X)

b. If the house lived in had been different ___1 _____ ___2 (___X)

c. If the work household members did had been different ___1 _____ ___2 (___X)

d. If the friends household members had had been different ___1 _____ ___2 (___X)

e. If there had been no emotional problems in other household members ___1 _____ ___2 (___X)

f. If household members had not had debts and other financial problems ___1 _____ ___2 (___X)

g. If certain persons had not lived in household ___1 _____ ___2 (___X)

APPENDIX A

125. LIKE EVERYTHING ELSE, WHEN FAMILIES LOOK BACK OVER THE TIME A RELATIVE WAS HOME FROM THE HOSPITAL (between dates on page 1), THEY OFTEN THINK THAT THEY WOULD DO SOME THINGS DIFFERENTLY, IF THEY HAD IT TO DO OVER AGAIN. DO YOU THINK IT WOULD HAVE BEEN BETTER FOR **** IF FAMILY MEMBERS HAD DEMANDED MORE OR LESS OF HER IN THE WAY OF:

	Better if demanded more	*Better if demanded less*	*Would have made no difference*	*(NR)*
a. Dusting, sweeping, and other usual cleaning	___1	___2	___3	(___X)
b. Helping with the family shopping	___1	___2	___3	(___X)
c. Entertaining people at home	___1	___2	___3	(___X)
d. Dressing and taking care of herself	___1	___2	___3	(___X)
e. Handling the grocery money	___1	___2	___3	(___X)
f. Preparing morning and evening meals	___1	___2	___3	(___X)
g. Taking care of laundry and mending	___1	___2	___3	(___X)
h. (Ask only if preschool children in house) Dressing and bathing the children	___1	___2	___3	(___X)

	Better if demanded more	*Better if demanded less*	*Would have made no difference*	*(NR)*
i. (Ask only if school children in house) Making sure the children get to school on time	___1	___2	___3	(___X)
j. Going to visit her friends or relatives	___1	___2	___3	(___X)
k. Getting along with family members	___1	___2	___3	(___X)
l. Doing what's expected of her without coaxing	___1	___2	___3	(___X)
m. Getting along with the neighbors	___1	___2	___3	(___X)
n. Going to parties and other social activities	___1	___2	___3	(___X)
o. Holding a job full time or part time	___1	___2	___3	(___X)

NOW LET'S GO ON TO SOMETHING ELSE.

Skip if no school age or younger children in household {

126. (If respondent has one or more children of school age or younger)
Through what grade in school do you hope to be able to send your (child) (children)?
____ 1 through grade school or less (any grade 1 to 6)
____ 2 through junior high school (grade 7, 8, or 9)
____ 3 through high school (grade 10, 11, or 12)
____ 4 through college (1 or more years)
(____ X NR)

127. How good do you think are the chances of sending your (child) (children) as far through school as you hope to: Would you say the chances are ____ 1 very good ____ 2 fifty-fifty ____ 3 not at all good? (____ X NR)

APPENDIX A 295

Skip if respondent answered 126 and 127

128. (If respondent has *no* children of school age or younger:)
    If you now had children of school age or younger, through what grade in school would you hope to be able to send your children?
    ____ 1 through grade school or less (any grade 1 to 6)
    ____ 2 through junior high school (grade 7, 8, or 9)
    ____ 3 through high school (grade 10, 11, or 12)
    ____ 4 through college (1 or more years)
    (____ X NR)

129. (If respondent has *no* children of school age or younger:)
How good do you think the chances would be now of sending your children as far through school as you hoped to: Would the chance be ____ 1 very good ____ 2 fifty-fifty
____ 3 not at all good?   (____ X NR)

130. When you left school what particular kind of occupation or life work was it your ambition to achieve some day? _____

131. What about ****, at the time she left school, do you know what occupation or life work she wanted to achieve? _____

THERE ARE JUST A FEW MORE THINGS I WANT TO ASK AND THEN WE WILL BE THROUGH.

132. I'M GOING TO READ A LIST OF STATEMENTS DESCRIBING WHAT MEN AND WOMEN SHOULD DO IN THEIR EVERYDAY ACTIVITIES. PLEASE TELL ME FOR EACH STATEMENT WHETHER YOU AGREE OR DISAGREE WITH IT. THERE MAY BE ONE OR TWO YOU'RE NOT SURE ABOUT.

	Agree	*Disagree*	*(NR)*
a. A husband should help with the housework	___1	___2	(___X)
b. A woman who does not have to take a job should not	___1	___2	(___X)
c. If a husband insists, the wife should quit a job which she enjoys	___1	___2	(___X)

	Agree	Disagree	(NR)

d. Women are too independent these days ___1 ___2 (___X)

e. Husbands should be more strict with their wives ___1 ___2 (___X)

f. A Woman's place is in the home ___1 ___2 (___X)

g. Marriage is the best career for a woman ___1 ___2 (___X)

h. The man should wear the pants in the family ___1 ___2 (___X)

i. A woman's interests should be mainly in children, recipes, clothes and housekeeping ___1 ___2 (___X)

NEXT, I WOULD LIKE TO KNOW ABOUT THE EXPENSES INVOLVED IN ****'S HOSPITALIZATION AT CPIH SIX MONTHS AGO.

133. Have you received a bill from the hospital? ___ 1 yes ___ 2 no (___ X NR)
 If yes: Have you paid all or part of it? ___ 1 paid all ___ 2 paid part ___ 3 not paid (___ X NR)

134. (If partly paid or not paid:) Why has it not been paid (paid in full)? _____

135. (If partly paid or paid in full:) Here is a list of ways families meet the costs of hospitalization. Were any of the costs of ****'s last hospitalization met in these ways?

	All of it	Part of it	None of it	(NR)
a. Current income	___1	___2	___3	(___X)
b. Savings	___1	___2	___3	(___X)
c. Health insurance	___1	___2	___3	(___X)
d. Loans from banks or finance companies	___1	___2	___3	(___X)

APPENDIX A

	All of it	Part of it	None of it	(NR)
e. Loans or help from relatives	__1	__2	__3	(__X)
f. Employer or union	__1	__2	__3	(__X)
g. V.A. or other federal help	__1	__2	__3	(__X)
h. Private charities and church organizations	__1	__2	__3	(__X)
i. State or city welfare	__1	__2	__3	(__X)
j. Other: What?_____	__1	__2	__3	(__X)

136. In addition to hospital bills, did ****'s last hospitalization impose other financial problems on the household, such as loss of income or having to hire someone to help around the house?
 ____ 1 yes ____ 2 no   (____ X NR)
 If yes: What? _____
 If yes: How did you meet these financial problems? _____
 _____

NOW, WE NEED A FEW FACTS ABOUT INCOME AND THEN I'LL HAVE ALL THE INFORMATION I NEED.

137. How much money does the person who is the chief breadwinner of the family earn? (Before taxes) (Hand respondent Card #2)

 _____

138. Is he paid ____ 1 weekly ____ 2 twice a month ____ 3 monthly
 ____ 4 fees or commissions ____ 5 other?   (____X NR)

139. Do you receive any pension or welfare money? ____ 1 yes
 ____ 2 no (____X NR)
 (If yes, insert number from card #2) _____

140. What is the total family income? (Insert number from Card #2)

 _____

(CHECK COMPLETENESS OF QUESTIONNAIRE. GO BACK TO THE BEGINNING AND INSPECT EACH QUESTION. IF ANY QUESTION HAS BEEN OMITTED THAT SHOULD HAVE BEEN ASKED, ASK IT BEFORE TERMINATING THE INTERVIEW.)

LETTER TO NEIGHBOR

FAMILY HEALTH SURVEY

A health survey is now being carried out in the Greater Columbus area. This Family Health Survey is supported by the United States Public Health Service. We are doing this survey because of the necessity to learn more about the health needs and problems of families. One special reason for the study is to learn more about the health and activities of women in the community.

The survey will ask questions about health and its relation to other aspects of life such as recreation, activities in the home, and work outside the home of family members. Persons chosen from a selected number of households from each area in the community have been asked to participate in the survey. We sincerely hope you will cooperate with us in this important task.

A trained interviewer on our staff plans to contact you within the next two weeks to discuss the arrangement of an appointment. The interviewer would like to interview you and your husband; or, if you are not married, our interviewer wants to talk with you and a close relative who lives with you, possibly your mother, daughter, or sister. The interview lasts about half an hour with each person.

In order for us to arrange an interview at the time best suited to you, please indicate on the enclosed reply card the items most convenient for both of you and send the card back to us.

APPENDIX A

INTERVIEWERS' PROCEDURE FOR SELECTING CONTROL CASES

We have selected the address ten numbers higher than the patient's address, or the next existing address above ten numbers from the patient's address.

The following rules apply when the assigned respondents don't work out, and substitute respondents are necessary.

1. If the assigned address turns out to be in the building next door to the patient, choose the dwelling in the third building (higher in address) from the patient's building. *(Never select a control case in the building next door to the patient.)*

2. If the assigned address does not exist (e.g. because the street doesn't go that far, or because of slum clearance), take the address ten numbers lower than the patient's address.

3. If the dwelling ten numbers higher or lower does not exist on the particular street (*e.g.* as on a short street with only two dwellings), choose the dwelling with the same address as the patient's address, but on the street paralleling the patient's street. Even if the patient's *house number* does not exist on the parallel street, use the same house number as the patient's for your reference point and then apply the above rules in selecting the control dwelling. If the patient's street runs north and south, take the first parallel street to the east. If the patient's street runs east and west, take the first parallel street north. (See diagram)

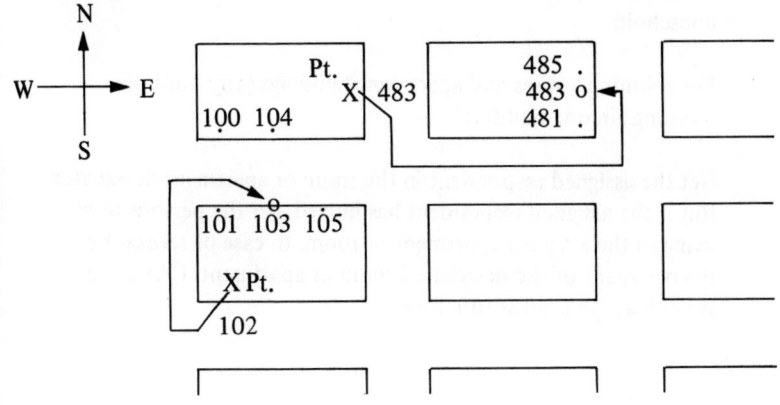

4. When a street or road has dwellings with no house numbers on them, take the fifth dwelling higher (going north or east) from the patient's dwelling.

5. If the dwelling selected is vacant (unoccupied), choose the dwelling with the next higher address.

6. Skip all places of industry or business.

7. Only a dwelling which contains at least one female 18 years old or over in the household is an eligible control case. If household members are all males, this cannot be used as a control case.

8. Always assume there is a female in the household. When, upon visiting or phoning the household, it is found that a man lives alone or there are no women in the household, drop that dwelling and select the next eligible dwelling for the study. If a woman lives alone, include her in the study.

9. If occupants of a selected dwelling are found to have moved when contacted, then interview those people *who now live* in that selected dwelling. Do not follow residents who have moved from the selected address.

10. Do not consider a telephone refusal as final. Always go to see the household members of the selected dwelling at least once. If they refuse to cooperate after such a visit, only then can we drop that household.

11. For rooming houses and apartment buildings (any multiple dwellings in one building):

    Get the assigned respondent in the room or apartment designated. But if the assigned respondent has moved, get the persons now living in the assigned apartment or room. In case of refusal by the occupant of the designated room or apartment, CALL US. We will assign a substitute case.

APPENDIX A

(12-9-59)

SUGGESTED INTRODUCTION FOR INTERVIEWERS

I am an interviewer employed by the Institute Study Center of the Ohio State University Health Center. We are carrying out a Family Health Survey sponsored by the U.S. Public Health Service. The general purpose of the study is to learn about the particular health needs and health problems of families in the Columbus metropolitan area. One particular purpose of the Survey is to find out about the health and functioning of women in the community.

We want to ask you questions about health and its relation to other aspects of life such as recreation, activities in the home, and work outside the home of family members. The interview lasts about half an hour with each person. We are asking a selected number of persons from households chosen at random from each area of the city to participate in the survey. We want to interview two adults in each selected household.

Your cooperation in the survey will help us learn more about health needs and health practices in this area.

In the questions I will ask you, there are no right or wrong answers. Your honest opinions on the matters we discuss would be appreciated.

Appendix B
Tables

Table 1. Description of Performance Measures

Variable	Source of Information	Examples of Items	Scoring	Measure
Domestic Performance	Significant Other Schedule Items 41A-41G SOR Schedule Items 35A-35G	41. NOW, SINCE THE PATIENT LEFT THE HOSPITAL, IS SHE THE ONE WHO USUALLY DOES THESE THINGS, OR DOES SOMEONE ELSE DO THEM? A. Prepares morning and evening meals B. Does the grocery shopping	Each item scored as follows: 1 = only by others 2 = {others help / no response} 3 = does it herself Total score based on addition of 7 item weights. High total score means high performance, *i.e.*, patient does most domestic chores herself without help. Range = 7 to 21	Domestic Performance Level
Psychological Functioning	Significant Other Schedule Items 95A-95FF SOR Schedule Items 72A-72FF	95. LET ME READ YOU SOME STATEMENTS WHICH FAMILIES OF PATIENTS HAVE USED TO DESCRIBE THE BEHAVIOR OF THEIR RELATIVES. HOW OFTEN DOES (THE PATIENT) ACT THIS WAY, SINCE SHE LEFT THE HOSPITAL? A. Makes no sense when talking F. Tries to hit or hurt someone	Each item is scored as follows: 1 = often 2 = sometimes or no response 3 = never Item scores are added to get the total score. High score means high level functioning, *i.e.*, patient never manifests abnormal symptoms. Range = 32 to 96	Psychological Functioning Level

Total Performance	Three measures of performance: domestic, psychological, and social participation		An additive measure based on scores in each of three areas of performance: domestic performance, social participation, psychological functioning. Range = 50 to 216	Index of Total Performance
Social Participation	Significant Other Schedule Items 47-50, 53-64, 65-71, 73 SOR Schedule Items 42-45, 50-55, 57, 46A-46E, 47A-47E	59. About how many hours have you spent listening to the radio and watching TV on the average weekday evening this past month? 60. How about (the patient)?	Each patient and her significant other are scored 0, 1, or 2 according to frequency with which activity is done. 　0 = rarely or not at all 　1 = average* number times in a given time period, or sometimes 　2 = above average* number times in given time period, or often *Average here is derived from distribution of activities of 50 patients and significant others. For each of eleven areas of social participation (including hobbies, reading, visiting, watching TV, etc.), each pair of item weights given to the woman and her significant other were converted to a weighted (cont'd)	Composite Social Participation

Table 1. Description of Performance Measures (Cont'd)

Variable	Source of Information	Examples of Items	Scoring	Measure
			score from 1 to 9, with the high score of 9 representing greater social participation and the lowest score of 1 representing low participation. The conversion key follows: S.O. and Patient Score Weight 2 0 = 1 1 0 = 2 2 1 = 3 0 0 = 4 1 1 = 5 0 1 = 6 2 2 = 7 1 2 = 8 0 2 = 9 High total score means high performance, *i.e.*, patient does as much as or more than her significant other. Range = 11 to 99	

Table 2. Description of Measures of Expectations

Variable	Source of Information	Examples of Items	Scoring	Measure
Self-expectations	Patient Schedule Items 26A-26N	NEXT, I WANT TO ASK YOU WHAT YOU THINK YOU SHOULD BE DOING NOW SINCE BEING HOME FROM THE HOSPITAL. DO YOU FEEL YOU SHOULD BE DOING THESE THINGS NOW? A. Dust, sweep, and do other usual cleaning K. Get along with family members N. Hold a job full time or part time	Each item is scored as follows: 1 = no 2 = no response 3 = yes Item scores are summed to get total score. High total score means high expectations, *i.e.*, patient feels she should do most of the items. Range = 14 to 42	Patient's Self-expectation Level
Significant Other's Expectations	Significant Other Schedule Items 113A-113K, 113M, 113N, 113O SOR Schedule Items 90A-90K, 90M, 90N, 90O	NEXT, I WOULD LIKE YOU TO TELL ME WHETHER YOU EXPECT (THE PATIENT) TO BE DOING THESE THINGS NOW. A. Dust, sweep, and do other usual cleaning K. Get along with family members N. Hold a job full time or part	Each item is scored as follows: 1 = no 2 = no response 3 = yes Item scores are summed to get total score. High score means high expectations, *i.e.*, significant other feels patient Should do most of the items. Range = 14 to 42	Significant Other's Expectation Level

Table 2. Description of Measures of Expectations (Cont'd)

Variable	Source of Information	Examples of Items	Scoring	Measure
Expectation Agreement	Patient and Significant Other (from the above two sets of items)		Patient's self-expectation total score is subtracted from significant other's expectation total score to obtain discrepancy. The larger the discrepancy, the higher the disagreement in expectation level.	Agreement-Disagreement in Expectation Level
Tolerance of Deviance	Significant Other Schedule Items 115A-115S SOR Schedule Items 107A-107S	I HAVE HERE A LIST OF REASONS FAMILIES HAVE GIVEN FOR CONTACTING THE HOSPITAL OR OTHER PROFESSIONAL PEOPLE TO ASK IF THEIR (WIFE, MOTHER, ETC.) NEEDS TO GO BACK TO THE HOSPITAL. WOULD YOU CONTACT THE HOSPITAL? *A.* If (the patient) made no sense when talking *B.* If (the patient) tried to kill herself	Each item is scored as follows: 1 = would contact 2 = no response 3 = would not contact Item scores are added to get total score. High total score means high tolerance of deviant behavior, *i.e.,* significant other would not contact help for most symptoms. Range = 19 to 57	Level of Tolerance of Deviant Behavior

Table 3. Comparison of Nonstudy and Study Patients on Social and Psychiatric Variables Significantly Different for Both Categories (in Percentages)

Variable	Nonstudy Patients	Study Patients	P[1]
Marital Status	(N = 89)	(N = 287)[2]	
Married	43	63	
Single	24	10	0.01
Widowed	11	9	
Separated	22	18	
Diagnosis			
Organic	9	11	
Psychotic	53	35	0.05
Characterological	38	54	
Length of stay (in days)			
1-30	60	31	
31-60	16	41	0.01
61-90	11	16	
90+	13	12	
Type of admission			
Voluntary	87	97	
Other	13	3	0.01
Number of admissions			
One	47	67	
Two or more	53	33	0.01

[1] Based on chi square tests of the differences between study and nonstudy patients.

[2] N's are slightly less than 287 for several variables because of insufficient data.

Table 4. Degree and Type of Change in Domestic Performance Between First and Second Follow-ups for 33 Schizophrenics

Domestic Tasks	Percent No Change	Percent Change "Better"	Percent Change "Worse"
Prepares morning and evening meals	61	27	12
Does the grocery shopping	55	30	15
Handles the grocery money	61	27	12
Dusts, sweeps, and other usual cleaning	67	12	21
Takes care of laundry and mending	58	27	15
Dresses and bathes the children[1]	89	0	11
Makes sure the children get to school on time[2]	88	0	12

[1] The total N is reduced to nine to refer to those patients who had preschool children at both the first and second follow-ups.

[2] The total N is reduced to 16 to refer only to those patients who had school children at both follow-ups.

Table 5. Degree and Type of Change in Social Participation Between First and Second Follow-ups for 33 Schizophrenics

Item	Percent No Change	Percent Change "Better"	"Worse"
Attend religious services	55	9	36
Take part in clubs or groups	52	30	18
Go to visit relatives	49	36	15
Have friends to house	43	30	27
Visit friends at their homes	36	30	33
Read magazines	46	30	24
Read books	46	27	27
Read a daily paper	82	0	18
Listen to radio and watch TV	49	21	30
Go to movies	46	9	45
Spend time on hobbies	33	33	33

Table 6. Degree and Type of Change in Psychological Functioning Between First and Second Follow-ups for 33 Schizophrenics

Symptoms	Percent No Change	Percent Change "Better"	Percent Change "Worse"
Makes no sense when talking	88	12	0
Walks, sits, or stands awkwardly	82	12	6
Moves around restlessly	49	30	21
Swears, curses often compared to other women	91	3	6
Always seems worn out or tired	39	27	34
Tries to hit or hurt someone	97	3	0
Lacks control of toilet habits	97	0	3
Says she hears voices	97	3	0
Does not want to see people	67	21	12
Just hangs around the house doing nothing	58	27	15
Tries to hurt or kill herself	100	0	0
Gets drunk often	97	0	3
Gets grouchy or bad-tempered	58	15	27
Misbehaves sexually	94	3	3
Needs coaxing to do what's expected	67	21	12
Has trouble going to sleep	43	33	24
Takes many pills	73	12	15
Needs help dressing, bathing, or going to the toilet	97	3	0
Does not know what goes on around her	94	0	6
Acts tense or nervous	61	9	30
Thinks she is sinful or evil compared to other people	91	6	3
Thinks people want to control or harm her	85	9	6
Worries about her bodily organs	76	15	9
Mumbles or talks to herself	88	12	0
Tries to get her way by saying she has pains	91	6	3
Gets depressed suddenly	49	21	30
Says she sees people who are not there	97	3	0
Worries about her health	58	15	27
Teases and picks on people	91	6	3
Thinks people are watching her or talking about her	76	15	9
Expects bad things to happen in the future without good reason	73	15	12
Does not eat well	61	24	15

Table 7. Percentage of Returnees and Community Patients Performing Domestic Tasks Unaided

Domestic Tasks	Returnees (N = 38)	Community Patients (N = 230)
Prepared morning and evening meals	55	68
Did the grocery shopping	34	37
Handled the grocery money	47	50
Dusted, swept, and other usual cleaning	61	66
Took care of laundry and mending	58	70
Dressed and bathed the children[1]	78	88
Made sure the children got to school on time[2]	56	91
Mean domestic performance score	16	17

[1] Based on N = 9 returnees and N = 68 community patients with preschool children.

[2] Based on N = 18 returnees and N = 84 community patients with school age children.

Table 8. Percentage of Returnees and Community Patients Whose Social Participation Equaled or Exceeded That of Their Significant Others

Social Activities	Returnees (N = 38)	Community Patients (N = 230)
Attended religious services	40	53
Participated in social groups	21	29
Visited relatives	76	79
Entertained friends at home[1]	42	72
Visited friends	50	49
Read magazines	71	69
Read books	40	36
Read daily newspaper	74	84
Listened to radio or watched TV	79	90
Went to movies	47	32
Spent time on hobbies	37	36
Mean social participation score	53	55

[1] For chi square with 1 df, $p = < 0.01$.

Table 9. Percentage of Patients with Specific Diagnoses by Outcome Categories

Diagnosis	Community Patients[1] Low (N = 78)	Moderate (N = 73)	High (N = 76)	Total (N = 227)	Early Returnees (N = 41)
Organic	23	4	4	11	20
Functional psychotic	28	38	41	36	36
Psychoneurotic	33	43	46	40	34
Personality disturbance and psychophysiological	16	15	9	13	10
Total	100	100	100	100	100
Alcoholism or addiction	13	12	4	10	17

[1] Low, moderate, and high categories are based on level of total performance among community patients.

Table 10. Percentage of Significant Others Who Expected the Community Patient to Perform Specific Items and Percentage of Patients Who Actually Performed Them

Item	Significant Others Expected (N = 231)	Patients Actually Performed (N = 230)
Dust, sweep, and other usual cleaning	86	66
Help with the family shopping	80	37
Handle the grocery money	71	50
Prepare morning and evening meals	84	68
Take care of laundry and mending	83	70
Dress and bathe the children[1]	96	87
Make sure the children get to school on time[2]	93	84
Entertain people at home	75	72
Go visit friends and relatives	89	64
Hold a job full time or part time	33	26

[1] Based on N = 68 of former patients with preschool children in the household.

[2] Based on N = 88 of former patients with school children in the household.

Table 11. Percentage of Significant Others of High and Low Performers Who Expected the Patient to Perform Each Item

Item	High Performers (N = 76)	Low Performers (N = 79)	P[1]
Dust, sweep, and other usual cleaning	92	73	0.01
Help with the family shopping	91	62	0.01
Entertain people at home	93	52	0.01
Dress and take care of herself	100	94	
Handle the grocery money	84	51	0.01
Prepare the morning and evening meals	92	72	0.01
Take care of laundry and mending	91	70	0.01
Dress and bathe the children[2]	88	40	0.01
Make sure the children get to school on time[3]	100	96	
Visit friends or relatives	96	76	0.01
Get along with family members	100	91	0.05
Get along with the neighbors	100	85	0.01
Go to parties and other social activities	76	48	0.01
Hold a job full time or part time	32	27	
Mean significant other expectations score	38	32	0.01

[1] Based on chi square with 1 df.

[2] Based on N = 43 of high and low performers with preschool children in the household.

[3] Based on N = 58 of high and low performers with school children in the household.

Table 12. Psychiatric Variables Associated with Expectations[1]

Psychiatric Variables	Patient Expectations	Significant Other Expectations	Expectation Agreement
Diagnosis	++	++	−
Posthospital drugs	++	+	−
Impairment at discharge	−	++	−
Posthospital treatment	−	−	+
Hospital drug treatment	−	−	−
Hospital EST	−	−	−
Ward assignment	−	−	+
Impairment at admission	−	−	−
Type of discharge	−	−	−
Prognosis at discharge	−	−	−
Number of previous admissions	−	−	−
Illness duration	−	−	−
Length of hospital stay	−	−	−
Alcoholism or drug addiction	−	−	−

[1] Relationships between pairs of variables are indicated with ++ for $p < 0.01$, + for $p < 0.05$, and − for no statistical significance.

Table 13. Social Variables Associated with Expectations[1]

Social Variables	Patient Expectations	Significant Other Expectations	Expectation Agreement
Patient's ISC score	+	++	++
Patient's education	++	++	—
Significant other's education	+	++	—
Patient's house type	—	—	—
Patient's dwelling area	—	—	—
Family type	++	++	+
Marital status	++	++	—
Children in household	++	++	—
Adult females in household	++	++	—
Relationship of significant other to patient	++	++	—
Adult males in household	++	+	—
Significant other in household	—	+	—
Age	++	++	—
Race	—	—	+
Religion	—	—	—
Urban-rural residence	—	—	—

[1] Relationships between pairs of variables are indicated with ++ for $p < 0.01$, + for $p < 0.05$, and — for no statistical significance.

Table 14. Mean Expectation Scores of 62 Patients and Husbands by Middle and Working Class Position

	Middle (N = 21)	Working (N = 41)	P[1]
Patients' Expectations (Total)	33.67	32.12	0.05
Husbands' Expectations (Total)	33.57	32.39	0.05
Patients' Expectations (Social)	13.05	11.83	0.05
Husbands' Expectations (Social)	13.05	11.98	0.01
Patients' Expectations (Domestic)	14.71	14.49	N.S.
Husbands' Expectations (Domestic)	14.52	14.27	N.S.

[1] Based on t-test between means.

Source: From Mark Lefton, Shirley Angrist, Simon Dinitz, and Benjamin Pasamanick, "Social Class, Expectations and Performance of Mental Patients," *American Journal of Sociology, 68* (July, 1962), p. 84. By permission of The University of Chicago Press.

Table 15. Percentage of Low and High Tolerance Significant Others Who Would Rehospitalize the Former Patient for Specific Symptoms[1]

Symptom	Low Tolerance Significant Others (N = 88)	High Tolerance Significant Others (N = 66)
Made no sense when talking	100	73
Always seemed worn out or tired	77	14
Tried to hit or hurt someone	97	80
Just hung around the house doing nothing	93	20
Tried to hurt or kill herself	100	97
Got grouchy or bad-tempered	80	5
Needed coaxing to do what's expected of her	84	6
Acted tense or nervous	84	9
Did not eat well	85	11
Was hearing or seeing things	100	85
Could not control toilet habits	99	62
Got drunk often	97	50
Took many pills	98	50
Stayed away from people	93	30
Misbehaved sexually	99	58
Got depressed suddenly	94	41
Mumbled or talked to herself	98	52
Neglected household chores	88	5
Did not know what went on around her	100	80

[1] Differences between low and high tolerance categories are statistically significant at $p < 0.01$ based on chi square with 1 df for all symptoms except "Tried to hurt or kill herself" which is not significant.

Source: From Mark Lefton, Shirley Angrist, Simon Dinitz, and Benjamin Pasamanick, "Tolerance of Deviant Behavior, Posthospital Performance Levels, and Rehospitalization," *Proceedings of the Third World Congress of Psychiatry* (June, 1961), University of Toronto Press and McGill University Press, Montreal, Vol. 1., p. 238.

Table 16. Self-expectations of 157 Pairs of Former Patients and Their Neighbors

Item	Percent Patients	Percent Neighbors	P
Dust, sweep, and other usual cleaning	92	98	0.05
Help with family shopping	88	91	
Entertain people at home	75	90	0.01
Dress and take care of self	100	100	
Handle the grocery money	74	88	0.01
Prepare morning and evening meals	88	97	0.01
Take care of laundry and mending	90	96	0.05
Dress and bathe the children[1]	94	98	
Make sure the children get to school on time[2]	97	95	
Visit her friends or relatives	86	96	0.01
Get along with family members	94	99	0.05
Get along with the neighbors	96	100	0.05
Go to parties and other social activities	62	70	
Hold a job full time or part time	44	38	
Mean score	36.1	38.1	0.01

[1] N's are reduced to 48 patients and 60 neighbors with preschool children.

[2] N's are reduced to 60 patients and 62 neighbors with school age children.

Table 17. Significant Other's Expectations of 157 Pairs of Former Patients and Their Neighbors

Item	Percent Patients	Percent Neighbors	P
Dust, sweep, and other usual cleaning	87	92	0.01
Help with family shopping	79	87	0.05
Entertain people at home	76	80	
Dress and take care of self	99	100	
Handle the grocery money	69	87	0.01
Prepare morning and evening meals	85	94	0.01
Take care of laundry and mending	83	94	0.01
Dress and bathe the children[1]	96	100	
Make sure the children get to school on time[2]	93	100	
Go visit her friends or relatives	90	92	
Get along with family members	97	100	
Get along with the neighbors	95	92	
Go to parties and other social activities	68	64	
Hold a job full time or part time	35	31	
Mean score	35.8	37.1	0.01

[1] N's are reduced to 48 patients and 60 neighbors with preschool children.

[2] N's are reduced to 60 patients and 62 neighbors with school age children.

Table 18. Tolerance of Deviance of 157 Former Patients and Their Neighbors: Symptoms for Which Significant Others Would Not Seek Treatment

Item	Percent Patients	Percent Neighbors	P
Makes no sense when talking	6	5	
Always seems worn out or tired	52	44	
Tries to hit or hurt someone	7	11	
Just hangs around the house doing nothing	35	43	
Tries to kill herself	1	0	
Gets grouchy or bad-tempered	55	65	
Needs coaxing to do what's expected	55	56	
Acts tense or nervous	51	45	
Eats poorly	51	30	0.01
Hears or sees things	2	1	
Cannot control toilet habits	17	1	0.01
Gets drunk often	18	18	
Takes many pills	15	22	
Stays away from people	29	31	
Misbehaves sexually	17	34	0.01
Gets depressed suddenly	28	19	
Mumbles or talks to herself	13	15	
Neglects household chores	52	55	
Does not know what goes on around her	3	5	
Mean score	29.2	29.0	

NAME INDEX

Adler, Leta, 41, 106
Albee, George W., 2
Albert, Robert S., 49
Angrist, Shirley S., 17, 109, 175

Bauman, B. O., 178
Bell, Norman W., 174
Biddle, Bruce J., 113
Bockoven, J. S., 87
Brown, Esther L., 34, 180
Brown, George W., 43
Buck, C., 63, 80
Burgess, E. W., 120

Carse, Joshua, 12
Carstairs, G. Morris, 43, 126, 176
Clausen, John, 135
Clayton, W. H., 175
Coddington, James W., 40
Colarelli, Nick J., 3
Cook, Stuart, 70
Cornelison, Alice R., 174
Coser, Lewis, 120

Dawson, William, 47, 79, 80
Deutsch, Albert, 17
Deutsch, Morton, 70
Dinitz, Simon, 22, 28, 35, 51, 63, 80, 105, 109
Dix, Dorothea, 18

Eaton, J. W., 126
Eells, K., 58
Ehrlich, H. J., 168

Elinson, Jack, 86
Ellsworth, Robert B., 175

Fairweather, George, 38
Fantz, R. L., 174
Farber, Bernard, 174
Fein, Rashi, 2
Felix, Robert, 24
Fleck, Stephen, 174
Fleming, D. F., 63, 80
Freeman, Howard, 1, 44, 57, 59, 79, 87, 106, 111, 126, 175

Goffman, Erving, 9, 23, 27
Greenblatt, Milton, 34, 49, 87, 180
Gross, Neal, 59, 113, 120
Gurel, Lee, 133

Hobbs, G. E., 63, 80
Hoch, Paul, 133, 166
Hollingshead, August B., 11, 58, 111, 134, 165
Hurvitz, Nathan, 120

Jahoda, Marie, 70, 135
Jones, Kathleen, 180
Jones, Maxwell H., 25, 34, 180

Kasselbaum, G. G., 178
Kennedy, John F., 30
Kreuger, Dean, 134

Langner, Thomas, 111, 134
Lefton, Mark, 35, 105, 109
Leighton, Alexander, 135

Lemert, Edwin, 79, 87, 126
Lemkau, Paul, 134
Lidz, Theodore, 174
Lindesmith, Alfred, 59
Locke, H. J., 120
Lorr, Maurice, 57

Mason, Ward S., 59, 113
McEachern, Alexander, 59, 113
McHale, Julia L., 174
McLaughlin, B. E., 133
Mechanic, David, 9, 172, 178
Meeker, M., 58
Merton, Robert K., 113
Michael, Stanley, 111, 134
Miller, Dorothy, 1, 22, 45, 47, 79, 80
Moore, Robert E., 49

Nagi, Saad Z., 172, 178
Nunnally, Jum, 86

Opler, Marvin, 111, 126, 134, 176

Padilla, Elena, 86
Panton, Nydia E., 12
Pasamanick, Benjamin, 22, 28, 35, 51, 63, 80, 105, 109, 134, 175
Payak, Bertha J., 10
Perkins, Marion, 86
Person, Philip H., Jr., 106
Phillips, Leslie, 166
Pinel, Phillippe, 18
Pollak, Otto, 10
Preiss, Jack J., 168

Rapoport, Robert N., 25
Redlich, Frederick C., 111, 134, 135, 165
Rees, T. P., 87
Rennie, Thomas, 111, 134
Ristine, Leonard, 134
Roberts, Dean, 134
Rogler, Lloyd, 11

Rose, Arnold, 40
Rushing, William A., 59, 113

Sarbin, T. R., 113
Scarpitti, Frank, 22, 28, 51, 63, 80
Scheff, Thomas J., 8, 96, 165, 172
Schwartz, Charlotte, 172
Schwartz, Morris S., 25, 34, 180
Selltiz, Claire, 70
Shiloh, Ailon, 181
Sidebotham, Roy, 180
Siegel, Saul M., 3
Simmons, Ozzie G., 1, 44, 57, 59, 79, 87, 106, 111, 126, 175
Sletto, Raymond, 172
Solomon, Maida H., 49
Srole, Leo, 111, 134
Stanton, Alfred H., 25, 34, 180
Stewart, Donald H., 40
Strauss, Anselm, 59
Suchman, Edward A., 178
Sussman, Marvin B., 172
Szasz, Thomas S., 8

Terry, Dorothy, 174
Thomas, Edwin J., 113
Topping, Gillian T., 43
Tuke, William, 19

Vincent, Clark E., 174
Vogel, Ezra F., 174

Wanklin, J. M., 63, 80
Warner, Loyd W., 58
Watt, Alexander, 12
Weil, R. J., 126
Whittington, H. G., 32
Wilson, Robert, 135
Wootton, Barbara, 175
Wrong, Dennis, 173

York, Richard H., 34, 180

Zubin, Joseph, 133, 166

SUBJECT INDEX

Accommodation, hypothesis, 171–172
  of family, 170–172
    defined, 171–172
    in expectations, 123, 171, 173
    and outcome, 171
    significant other, 173
Arkansas outcome study, 40–41

Brain syndrome, 42, 163
  See also Symptoms.

Characterologic disorders, 162
Class. See Social class.
Columbus Psychiatric Institute and Hospital, admission policies, 61
  history of, 60
  and outcome study, 6, 61, 63, 65–66
  research program, 35–38, 60
  treatment policies, 61, 74–75
Columbus State Hospital, 60
Community mental health centers, cost of services, 2
  expenditures for, 3, 30
  guidelines for, 31
  manpower problems of, 2
  new models of, 28, 29
  nonprofessionals in, 2–3
  professional practitioners in, 20, 29
  Public Law 88–164 and, 30
  shortages of facilities, 28
  trends, 29, 159
Community patients, community services for, 182
  defined, 72
  demographic atypicalities, 164
  employment status, 46, 110
  families of, 182
  role performance of, 112, 161–163, 167, 182
  social attributes, 72–73, 106
  social class and performance of, 111–113
Community residence, drug treatment during, 76
  psychiatric care during, 76
  success in, 80–82, 163, 166
Controls. See Normal neighbors.
Cornell Medical Index, 140

Deviant behavior, female, 11
  See also Tolerance of deviance.
Diagnosis, brain syndrome, 42
  characterological disorders, 162
  as factor in ward behavior of patients, 36
  functional psychoses, 42, 162
  organic, as indicator of readmission, 83, 162
  and posthospital performance levels, 38, 161
  as predicting avoidance of hospitalization, 50

Diagnosis *(Cont.)*
   and results of treatment, 50
   as selective of patient populations, 141
   See also Mental illness *and* Symptoms.
Domestic performance, measure of, 56–57
   of normal neighbors, 147
   patient attitudes related to, 162
   of patients with children, 146
   and psychological functioning, 146
   refined analysis of, 151
   role definitions of, 168
   and social factors, 147
   See also Role theory.
Drugs (in treatment), 20, 23, 52–54, 180
   See also Treatment modes.

Education of patients, 76
   compared with normal neighbors, 143
   and low performance, 112
Epidemiological variables, 163–164
Etiology of mental illness, 178
Expatients. *See* Community patients.
Expectations, agreement in, 120–122, 154–155
   and domestic performance, 120–121
   of normal neighbors, 152, 154–155
   of self and significant other, 155
   trends, 118, 120
   and education, 24
   hypothesis, 102
   and illness, 122
   and marital status, 110, 123
   measures of, 59, 139, 307, 308
   of normal neighbors, 136, 147–148, 154–155
   and patient's age, 123
   and performance, 113–115, 162
   and readmission, 86–90
   and role substitute, 123
   of significant others, 86–90, 118–120, 152–155
      explanations of, 87–89
      importance of, 172–173
      of normal neighbors, 148, 154–155
   and social class, 125

Factor analysis, 156–158
Family accommodation to patient, 182
   and expectations, 45–46
   negative consequences, 182
   and outcome, 44
   understanding of, 174
Family context of patient, nuclear family, 110
   parental versus conjugal, 44
   and performance, 106, 110
   and outcome, 38
Female. *See* Women.
Functional psychosis, 42, 162

Hollingshead Index of Social Position, 58, 112n, 124n
Home care of patients, 50–54, 182
   and deterioration of patients, 54
   improved role performance in, 54
   for schizophrenics, 51–54
   as a treatment alternative, 50–51
Hospital records, 58, 61
Hospitalization, mental. *See* Mental hospitalization.
Hospital, mental. *See* Mental hospitals.

SUBJECT INDEX

Interviewing procedures, 62–66, 67
  with normal neighbors, 137–139
  observer contamination in reporting, 173
  for psychiatric social workers, 64–65
  respondents' reactions to, 65

Lorr Psychiatric Rating Scale, 66–67, 67n
Louisville, Institute Treatment Center study, 51–54

Manic depressive psychosis, 74
Marital status, and general status of American women, 165
  life style consequences of, 141–142
  and mental illness, 42, 141–143
  and outcome, 42
  and posthospital performance, 106–108, 162
  superior performance of married patients, 142n
Massachusetts Mental Health Center study, 49
Matching procedures, designation of normal neighbors, 71, 137
  and factor analysis, 155–156, 167
  marital status controlled, 149
  methodology affecting results, 158, 169
  selection of patients, 71
  See also Normal neighbors.
Maudsley group, London, 43
Mental health industry, 2–5
Mental hospitalization, attitudes toward, 28, 179–180, 179n
  data on treatment, 61
  diagnosis and, 50, 176
  efficacy of, 179
  elimination of long term, 182
  long term, 181
  patient census reversal, 179
  precipitating factors in, 73, 176
  prevention of, 50, 53–54
  significant other's attitudes and, 176
  trends in, 159
  ward organization, 38
Mental hospitals, admission and discharge rates, 22
  changes in, 20–21, 34
  current concerns about, 5
  deterioration, 19
  effectiveness, 58
  in England, France, and America, 18–19
  Federal Government expenditures, 3
  history of, 1, 17–20
  needs of, 180
  "open door" policies, 21
  patient populations of, 21
  practitioners in, 19
  staff attitudes, 21, 23
  state, 19–23
  tranquilizers used in, 23
Mental illness, attitudes toward, 28
  chronicity in, 166, 177
  definitions of, 5, 8, 175
  etiology of, 178
  as episodic disease, 166, 176–177
  multidimensionality of, 175, 178–179
  nosology. *See* Brain syndrome, Characterologic disorders, Diagnosis, Functional psychosis, Manic depressive psychosis, Psychoneurosis, *and* Schizophrenia.
  prevalence, 8
  psychiatrists' assessments of, 12, 66–67

Mental illness (*Cont.*)
　relatives' assessments of, 12–13, 170, 173
　as residual deviance, 172
　stigma of, 20, 144, 176
　and therapeutic community approach, 26
　treatment for varying degrees of, 178, 181
　See also Symptoms *and* Treatment.
Mental patients, addiction in, 74
　after-care services to, 75–76
　attitudes toward, 164, 175
　community needs of, 32, 181
　demographic uniqueness of, 164
　diagnostic categories, 73
　family and marital status, 164–165
　interpersonal relations of, 180
　nonhospitalized, 27
　nonstudy patients, 72–73
　in Ohio state hospitals, 22
　population trends, 3, 21
　self-perceptions of, 164
　and social mobility, 165
　and socioenvironmental factors, 178
　in state hospitals, 41
　as subjects, 12–13
Moral treatment, 18, 19

National Institute of Mental Health, 28
Neighbors. *See* Normal neighbors.
Normal neighbors, characteristics of, 140–143
　differences from patients, 141–143
　and factor analysis, 156
　refined analysis of, 150–154
　role expectations, 154–155, 162
　role performance of, 161, 167, 169, 175
　similarities to patients as deceptive, 169

Oakland, California, study, 45–46
Ohio, State of, 22, 62
　Department of Mental Hygiene, 62
　mental hospitals, 22
　mental patient populations in, 22
Outcome. *See* Posthospital outcome.
Out-patients, after-care services for, 181
　as alternative to hospitalization, 4, 25
　assessment of care for, 50
　nonpsychiatric services for, 76
　numbers of, 3
　psychiatric clinics for, 28

Patients. *See* Mental patients.
Palo Alto, California, study, 38–40
Performance, levels of, accommodation to low levels, 122–126, 171
　of community patients, 101–131, 170
　and disability, 177
　and expectations, 113–126, 147–148, 162, 171
　high performance and tolerance, 127–131, 161
　high performance of married patients, 108, 109n
　of male former patients, 44–45
　and marital status, 106–110, 141–143, 162
　of normal neighbors, 144–158, 161
　and posthospital setting, 40

SUBJECT INDEX

Performance, levels of (*Cont.*)
  psychiatric variables in, 161–162
  of returnees, 90–94, 98–99, 174–178
  symptoms and low performance, 170–171
  variables related to high levels, 163
 measures of, Cornell Medical Index, 140
  domestic performance, 56–57
  key dependent variables, 56–57
  Lorr Psychiatric Rating Scale, 66
  for normal neighbors, 139–140
  psychological functioning, 57
  reliability of, 68. *See also* Reliability.
  scoring of, 304–306
  social participation, 57
  total performance index, 57
Placebo, 52–54
Posthospital outcome, change in views about, 174
  criteria for evaluating, 40, 48, 134, 163
  and diagnosis, 41
  and family stress, 43
  longitudinal study of, 173
  need for research, 27
  prediction of, 82–84, 101–102, 105
  premises of research, 159
  previous research, 14, 38–39, 40–54
  social factors in, 41
  and tolerance of deviance, 44
Prevention of hospitalization, 53
  See also Mental hospitalization *and* Rehospitalization.
Psychiatric assessment, of community patients, 66–67, 166
  compared with interviews, 67
  compared with a sociological orientation, 66
  and diagnosis, 67
  of impairment at discharge, 75
  by psychiatrist and significant other, 67, 69–70
Psychiatric disorders, acute, 28, 176–178
Psychiatric social workers, 47, 64, 173
Psychiatrists, numbers of, 28
Psychological functioning, differences between patients and normal neighbors, 144, 154, 161, 163
  of married matched pairs, 150
  measure of, 57
  mild symptoms of normal neighbors, 144
  patient symptom areas, 68–69
  of returnees, 162
  significant other reports of, 67, 144
  and tolerance, 161
Psychoneurosis, 162
Psychotropic drugs, 20, 23

Race, 58, 76, 84–85, 162
Readmission. *See* Rehospitalization.
Rehospitalization, acute episodes in, 177
  avoidance of, 170
  causal factors in, 40, 47, 162, 174
  as dependent variable, 56
  florid symptoms in, 93, 96
  and illness history, 46
  and psychiatric variables, 40, 91–94, 177
  significant other's attitudes toward, 47, 94–96, 129

Rehospitalization (*Cont.*)
  social factors in, 82, 84–86, 174
  as societal rejection, 79
  and symptom severity, 176
  and tolerance, 87–88
  See also Returnees.
Rehospitalization rates, 4, 21, 46, 62, 80–82, 177–178
Reliability of measures, 68n, 69, 173, 185–187
Religion, 58, 76, 84–85, 162
Returnees, 70–71, 79–100
  compared to community patients, 99
  early and late, 96–99, 162–163, 176–177
  episodic illness of, 163, 176
  illness and performance of, 95–96, 99–100, 177
  needs of early, 181
  psychiatric characteristics, 82–84
  social characteristics, 97–98
  social class of, 97–98
  tolerance of, 87–88, 159
  See also Rehospitalization.
Role expectations. *See* Expectations.
Role performance. *See* Performance.
Role theory, discussion of, 113–114
  and married women, 168
  norms for evaluating performance, 48, 56
  sex roles, 11, 56
  sick role, 7, 9

Schizophrenia, 51–52
Schizophrenics, 67–69
Self-expectations, accommodations of, 172
  measure of, 59, 139, 307

of normal neighbors, 147–148, 152
  of patients, 114–118
Significant other reports, 148, 150, 167–168, 173
Social breakdown syndrome, 24–25
Social class, 46, 76, 112, 136, 162, 165
Social participation
  of married women, 152
  measures, 57, 139, 147, 305–306
  of normal neighbors, 147
  and patient attitudes, 162
  as role performance, 24
Socioeconomic status. *See* Social class.
Stockton rehospitalization study, 47–48
Study innovations, 7–14, 159–160
Study samples, 70–73, 137–138, 160
Study sources of data, 26, 61–62, 138–139
Symptoms, early effects of, 164
  of expatients, 166
  minimal or mild, 144, 167
  remission of, 166
  severe, as factor in readmission, 45, 148, 174
  severity of, 50
  See also Diagnosis.

Therapeutic community, 21, 24–26, 180
Tolerance of deviance, and accommodation, 171
  defined, 44, 126
  discussed, 6, 79, 110, 148
  of eccentricity, 176
  and expectations, 127, 130
  and marital status, 110
  measure of, 59, 139, 308
  of normal neighbors, 161–162

Tolerance of deviance (*Cont.*)
  in patient families, 172
  patterns of, 127–128
  and performance, 44, 127, 130–131, 170
  and psychological functioning, 162
  and readmission, 99, 176
  in refined analysis, 153–155
  of severe symptoms, 127–128
Total performance, change in, 68
  and drug therapy, 103
  and expectations of family, 87–89
  and expectations of husbands, 123
  and hospitalization, 58
  and Index of Status Characteristics, 76
  measures of, 57, 139, 305
  occupational performance, 11
  and outcome, 159
  and psychiatric diagnosis, 102–103
  of returnees, 163
  social factors in, 141–143, 162, 170
Treatment, definitions of, as community based, 159
  current dilemmas, 178
  failure of treatment, 177
  and hospitalization, 179
  and manpower use, 29
  and patient role, 9
  and success of drugs, 180
  and therapeutic community orientation, 180
 modes, controversy about, 179
  cost of, 3
  group therapy, 26
  moral treatment, 18, 19
  for out-patients, 49–50
  posthospital, 76
  pseudomedical, 19
  and psychiatric orientations, 36
  short term, 159
  surgical, 19
  See also Drugs (in treatment).
 outcome, 4, 5, 9, 42, 66, 182–183
  See also Posthospital outcome.
 programs, community based, 159, 164, 183
  intervention within, 182
  new framework, 28–29
  to reduce institutionalization, 25

Validity, 187–191
Veteran's Administration Hospital at Palo Alto, 38–39

Warner Index of Status Characteristics, 58, 112, 124
Women, 10, 11, 12–13

York Retreat, 19